The three autho... ...her
through their in... ...and
through a share... ...ing
Black women's struggle...

BEVERLEY BRYAN was born in Jamaica in 1949. She came to England at the age of ten. She has taught in primary and further education for fourteen years and is currently teaching adults in south London. She has been active in Black, community and women's politics since the late 1960s and was a founder-member of the Brixton Black Women's Group. She has two sons and lives in south London.

STELLA DADZIE was born in 1952. Her mother is English and her father Ghanaian. She studied and taught Modern Languages in a London comprehensive for six years as well as teaching in a centre for young offenders for two years. Following this, she spent four years teaching Black studies and coordinating courses for the unemployed and for Black women at a north London college. Stella Dadzie is now on secondment, studying for an M.A. in Afro-Caribbean/Afro-American studies. She is a founder member of OWAAD (Organisation of Women of Asian and African Descent). She has a son and lives in north London.

SUZANNE SCAFE was born in Jamaica in 1954. Having taught English in secondary schools in both London and Jamaica, she now teaches at and coordinates a Black supplementary school in Brixton. She has worked with the Committee of Women for Progress in Jamaica, and has been a member of the Brixton Black Women's Group for several years. She lives in south London.

The Heart of the Race uses history and analysis, as well as the compelling and courageous voices of many women, to describe Black women's struggle to create a new social order in this country, and to celebrate their culture.

I am weaving a song of waters
Shaken from firm, brown limbs
Or heads thrown back in irreverent mirth.
My song has the lush sweetness
Of moist, dark lips
Where hymns keep company
With old, forgotten banjo songs.
Abandon tells you
That I sing the heart of a race
While sadness whispers
That I am the cry of a soul ...

from 'Song' by Gwendolyn B. Bennett

The Heart of the Race

Black Women's Lives in Britain

Beverley Bryan, Stella Dadzie
and Suzanne Scafe

To Olive Morris and Sylvia Erike who were true
sisters in the struggle. May this book keep your
memory alive.

Published by VIRAGO PRESS Limited 1985
41 William IV Street, London WC2N 4DB

Reprinted 1986

British Library Cataloguing in Publication Data

The Heart of the race: black women's lives in
   Britain
   1. Women, Black—Great Britain—Social
   conditions
   I. Bryan, Beverley   II. Dadzie, Stella
   III. Scafe, Suzanne
   305.4'8896041   HQ1593

   ISBN 0-86068-361-3

Typeset in North Wales by
Derek Doyle & Associates, Mold, Clwyd
and printed in Great Britain by
Anchor Brendon, Tiptree, Essex

Contents

Acknowledgements

It has taken us four years to complete this book. During this time, many many women have given us their time, their help and their support either by allowing us to interview them and talking about their lives; or by helping to type, transcribe, discuss and criticise the text. Without the support of these sisters, and the help and encouragement we received from our families and good friends, this book could not have been written. Our thanks go to all of you. This is as much your achievement as it it ours.

Abena, Keleche Ade, Pat Agana, Ama, Louise Bernard, Gerlin Bean, Deborah Barke, Pat Bell, Louise Bennett, Kelly Burton, Marlene Bogle, Cynthia Brooks, Jean Brown, Carmen, Yvonne Collymore, Beulah Coombs, Denise of Abacush, Roslyn Donovan, Olive Edun, Nefertiti Gayle, Gerry, Pat Gordon, Blossom Gonzales, Haleem, Iyamide Hazeley, Margaret Henry, Olga Henry, Karen Holness, Vivienne Johnson, Kath, Mel Langley, Ingrid Lewis, Arlene Mason, Janet McKenley, Donna Moore, Sylvia Morris, Monica Morris, Doris Morris, Maria Mars, Jennifer Oliver, Sylvia Oliver, Pat Parkin, Dorothy Palmer, Carol Sherman, Sonia Small, Dawn Smith, Sona, Sharon Townsend, Lindiwe Tsele, Julie Walters, Val Turner, Monica White, Claudette Williams, Michelle Williams, Pauline Wilson, Jocelyn Woolfe, Valerie Wright.

The names of certain individuals, locations and institutions have had to be omitted or changed in some interviews in order to protect the identity of those concerned.

Introduction: The Ties that Bind

When we first came together to write this book, it was because we felt that it was high time we started to record *our* version of events, from where we stood as Black women in Britain in the 1980s. Over the past ten years, we had seen the appearance of volumes of material documenting our struggles as Black *people*, and of course we welcomed this for we had relied for too long on the version of our story put forward by white historians and sociologists. And we had seen the women's movement follow suit, documenting 'herstory' from every angle except our own. But, despite the efforts of Black men and white women to ensure that we were no longer 'hidden from history', there was still a gaping silence from Black women. Thanks to our sisters in the United States, this silence is at last beginning to be broken, and for the first time ever Black women have a voice. But that voice comes from America, and although it speaks directly *to* our experience in Britain, it does not speak directly of it.

Inspired by their respective experiences of racism and sexism, Black men and white women have often made well-intentioned attempts to analyse ours. They have tended,

1

however, to portray Black women in a somewhat romantic light, emphasising our 'innate capacity' to cope with brutality and deprivation, and perpetuating the myth that we are somehow better equipped than others for suffering. While the patient, long-suffering victim of triple oppression may have some heroic appeal, she does not convey our collective experience. That our race, our class and our sex have combined to determine the quality of our lives, both in the Caribbean and in Britain, is undisputed.

But what matters to us is the *way* Black women have challenged this triple state of bondage. Black women in Britain today are faced with few positive self-images and little knowledge of our true potential. If we are to gain anything from our history and from our lives in this country which can be of practical use to us today, we must take stock of our experiences, assess our responses – and learn from them. This will be done by listening to the voices of the mothers, sisters, grandmothers and aunts who established our presence here. And by listening to our own voices.

It is not easy to record history as it is still being made, particularly when so much of our story lies buried, so there is much which has yet to be said. We have touched on many issues in this book – the work that we Black women do, the education, welfare and health care we do (or do not) receive; the responses of women in our community to our experience of life in Britain; and the struggles we have waged to preserve our culture and sense of identity. Our aim has been to tell it as *we* know it, placing our story within its history at the heart of our race, and using our own voices and lives to document the day-to-day struggles of Afro-Caribbean women in Britain over the past forty years.

As a people, we have rarely been accorded recognition for the part we have played in shaping this land. If acknowledged at all, we are usually portrayed as the passive victims of an historical necessity which began on the 'dark continent' with the Slave Trade and eventually brought us to the inner-cities of the 'Mother Country'. Schoolteachers and television programmes do little to expand our knowledge of these circumstances. At a time when our presence is regarded as 'a problem', and our right to be here is questioned almost daily by politicians and the media, we find that we are less and less informed about the chain of events which made the presence of Black people here so inevitable. Yet the Black community did not arrive in Britain through some accident of history. Our links with this country, like the links of many other non-white peoples living here, stretch back over many hundreds of years. An understanding that the basis of these ties was – and remains – economic, is fundamental to any grasp of our lives in Britain today.

Chapters 1, 4 and 5 each begin with an history of Afro-Caribbean women's role as workers, fighters, organisers and preservers of culture. By interweaving our past with our present in this way we hope that the importance of the part played by our foremothers in determining our lives now, will become more alive, more immediate and above all more accessible.

We take up our story in Africa, six thousand years after the Ancient Egyptians first began to establish Africa's creativity and genius in the world, and shortly before the Europeans first set foot on African soil for the purpose of plunder. By this time, our African ancestors had established a variety of cultures and societies, using whatever different means of production were available to them. We were living as nomads, as hunters and gatherers, as members of settled farming communities and as residents of flourishing trading towns and cities. We were living in feudal societies, paying taxes to local chiefs and rulers; in slave societies, where power, class and privilege were already strictly established; and in communal societies, where resources and decision-making were shared, often on a matriarchal basis. Above all, we were living in societies which we ourselves had determined.

With the exception of Ancient Egypt, which is more often than not portrayed in books and films as a civilisation in which full-blooded, Black African people played no part, we rarely hear talk of the Africa which existed before the Europeans arrived. Yet African societies matched, and in some cases excelled those in Europe. There were the powerful

3

Amharic dynasties of Ethiopia; the wealthy empires of Benin, Congo, Mali, Ghana and Songhai, with their highly developed mining, military and trading skills; and the thriving seaports along the East African coastline, where Arab, Indian and Chinese merchants mingled and inter-married with the local populations. To cities such as Kilwa and Quelimane, goods ranging from cloths and spices to jewels and works of art were brought by caravan, crossing the continent regularly from west to east. And they carried religious, cultural and scientific ideas with them too, giving rise to a dynamic exchange of ideas and the rapid spread of Islam. The land of our ancestors was not a dark, unexplored continent as the history books are so keen to convince us. Flourishing commercial sectors, money-lenders and strong handicraft industries were all well-established features of Africa in the fifteenth century, which may or may not have given rise to modern capitalism, had European intervention not robbed us of our right to self-determination.

When Europeans first began their voyages of exploration five hundred years ago, they already knew the reputation of the continents they sought. Capitalism in Europe was in its infancy, and there was a growing need for raw materials and new trading routes and markets. This was the purpose behind the voyages which heralded our 'discovery' in the late fifteenth century. Why else did those school-book heroes like Vasco da Gama and Christopher Columbus set sail? History teachers would have us believe it was a thirst for adventure, but we have a different understanding. They were motivated, first and foremost, by the need to find new trade and resources to satisfy their newly-developing money economy.

So Europe's first contact with the land of our ancestors had one purpose – to extract as much as it could. And Europeans were in a position to take the offensive. They had already learnt about the potential of gunpowder from the Chinese, and internal wars had ensured that they had a highly-developed knowledge of guns and canons. Using force and other dubious forms of persuasion, they set about exchanging their second-hand clothing, household utensils and guns for what later proved to be among Africa's most

4

prized resources – gold, for much-needed coinage, minerals such as iron, and precious substances like ivory. But this exploitative relationship was only the beginning. Africa would pay an even greater price in years to come, in the form of her most precious resource of all – us, her people.

Plunder became the order of the day, and while European merchants were busy looting the African continent, other 'discoverers' were making their way to the 'New World'. Columbus, commissioned by the King of Spain to find an alternative route to the Indies (India) lost his way and landed instead in the Caribbean. He renamed the islands the 'West Indies' and claimed them for Spain. The Arawak and Carib Indians who populated these islands were attacked, enslaved and eventually all but wiped out by the Spanish and other marauding Europeans. That infamous instigator and architect of the Triangular Trade, John Hawkins, petitioned the Spanish King for access in 1565, but such diplomatic niceties were not usually Britain's style. In his wake came the mercenaries and pirates like Drake, who led frequent raiding parties against the Spanish. The French too sent ships to intimidate and steal whatever they could. Before long, the Caribbean became a battlefield where European nations fought each other for land – land which was never theirs to fight over in the first place. Then, as now, war was their way of carving up other people's world.

Eventually Spain lost its grip on this scattered territory. St Kitts, Barbados and finally Jamaica fell to the British, who sent troops in to seize control and quell any resistance from the indigenous peoples. Once the original population had been depleted by massacres, imported diseases and enslavement, it became clear that the West Indies' potential could never be fully realised without an adequate alternative supply of labour. Poor whites, mainly convicts and indentured servants brought from Europe, proved unsatisfactory, in terms of both expense and efficiency. The early colonists were left with fertile lands, the possibility of great and lasting profits, but no workers. They would have gone to the moon to find our labour, but Africa was not quite so far. The ties had been formed. The racist justifications for their

5

'civilising' missions were readily available. And so the trade in our lives began.

The horrors we faced during the Slave Trade are well documented in later chapters, but it is the economic basis of that trade which concerns us here. Guns, spirits and cotton goods were exchanged on the West African coast, at some considerable profit, for slaves. The one in seven of our ancestors who survived the 'Middle Passage' were forced to establish the plantations and to produce raw materials such as sugar, cotton and tobacco. Although we were dispersed throughout the Americas, the fruits of our labour were all ploughed back into Europe, together with huge profits resulting from the sale of endless shiploads of slaves. The cotton and sugar we produced provided employment in Europe's developing manufacturing and refining industries, whose surplus products were, in turn, shipped back to Africa to begin the whole cycle again. The overall benefits from this triangular venture were enormous, and eventually turned Britain and France into the strongest trading nations in the world. Most important of all, however, is the fact that it was the blood, sweat and tears of Black women and men which financed and serviced Europe's Industrial Revolution, a revolution which laid the basis for Europe's subsequent domination and monopoly of the world's resources.

The British version of these events, which most of us have been taught, grossly distorts this particular period of history for fear of revealing the extent to which our labour is bound up with this country's rise to power and glory. Yet none of Britain's achievements can be separated from the achievements of Black people. The sheer volume of goods we were made to produce provided the incentive for inventions and research into new and more efficient machinery. The profits from our labour made it possible for British patrons to reinvest in ships, factories and land. Competition with her rivals spurred Britain into establishing a monopoly over the Slave Trade on the high seas. Britain's debt to us goes back centuries. Yet the Industrial Revolution and its repercussions are to this day presented to us as the achievement of a few clever inventors and of the 'naturally superior' British ruling class.

In fact, it was the British ruling class which had the highest stakes in prolonging our enslavement. Members of the Royal Family, churchmen, Members of Parliament – they all had interests in the West Indies. But it was not simply a case of the privileged few acquiring wealth and massive profits. The ordinary British people were able to reap the rewards, too, from the plunder of Africa's people and the exploitation of our labour. The Slave Trade provided new industries and employment, new markets and investments and overall profits which can never be fully assessed. When, a century later, Black people began to enter Britain as immigrants, we came to a country we had already helped to build. Our labour provided the foundations upon which many financial institutions, seaports and industrial centres were built. A local writer said of Bristol at the time that 'there is not a brick in that city but what is cemented with the blood of slaves'. The same was true, to a greater or lesser extent, of Glasgow, Liverpool and Cardiff and of industrial cities like Birmingham and Manchester. Many of Britain's best-known high street banks and institutions emerged as a direct result of the trade in our lives – banks like Lloyds and Barclays, for example, whose proprietors had progressed from being tradesmen and merchants to plantation owners and bankers. The insuring of heads of slaves and slave ships against the hazards of the Middle Passage, and of plantations against fire, proved so lucrative to Lloyds of London that even after the abolition of slavery, and up to the present day, they have been able to maintain their position as the world's leading insurers.

The impact of the Slave Trade on Britain was not confined to the material. Our presence in eighteenth-century England was an accepted reality. Black women and men were sold openly at auctions; the busts of 'blackamoors', emblems of the trade, commonly adorned local townhalls. Black servants were common too, and our children were the inevitable appendages of slave captains and high-society women. Freed and runaway slaves were conspicuous among London's beggars and were known as 'St Giles Blackbirds'. Though in constant fear of recapture, we lived side by side with the white working class, intermarrying with them and taking part in the life of the community. Indeed, many Black communities today, such as those in Bristol, Liverpool and Cardiff, were established long before the post-war immigration of recent years. And even when isolated and dispersed, we still made our mark on Britain. Black people were speaking out against racism and participating in British life as writers, musicians, actors, soldiers, nurses and in any other profession which was not barred to us, over two hundred years ago. Mary Seacole, the Black Crimean nurse, and William Cuffey the Chartist, made as great a contribution to Britain's history as Florence Nightingale and Feargus O'Connor. This country's past is littered with the names and deeds of Black women and Black men, frequently anonymous and unsung, who have helped to shape it into what it is today. By no stretch of the imagination can we be described as new arrivals.

But for those Black pioneers who established our presence here all those years ago, life can have been only an endless struggle against racism. Not simply were they the targets of individual bigots who taunted and attacked them in the streets, they were also up against a whole barrage of racist myths and justifications, expressed through the institutions of the day, designed to exonerate those who profited most from our enslavement. The Church was among the leading exponents of the merits of slavery, easily accommodating its inhuman practices as all part of God's plan. The slave trader John Newton gave thanks in Liverpool's churches for the success of his voyages, even asking God's blessing to aid him on future African excursions. The attitude of the Church and its followers simply mirrored the ideas of a society whose whole economy was directly or indirectly linked with human exploitation. Christianity has rarely been able to rise above the economic imperatives of the day.

It was the Church's support and collusion with the system which became the politicians' ultimate justification for the inhumanity of the Africa Trade. But their ability to sanction such systematic cruelty on an entire race of people is only one of many examples of the racist hypocrisy which has continued to characterise British politics and attitudes over the years. Even today, the economic system, because it has the support of ideology and religion, is able to determine the beliefs and values of the entire society. The same myths which were used to justify our subservience as a people in the past have permeated every facet of British culture, and their legacy is alive and kicking. Today's stereotypes which portray us as being fit only for manual and menial labour, or as idle scroungers who do not wish to work, can be traced directly back to the insulting, and contradictory, views which prevailed about Black people throughout the eighteenth century. The undermining assumptions of today's teachers, the attitudes of social workers and journalists about our 'childlike dependence', the fears of politicians and police when we rebel — all have their roots in Britain's racist past, when the possibility of Black equality became the source of this society's most fundamental paranoia. This is why the philosophy, literature and science emanating from Europe continue to be saturated with notions of white supremacy. To admit otherwise would require a total re-assessment of Western thought, culture and economic practice.

It is usually suggested that Abolition was achieved as a result of a wave of humanitarianism, spearheaded by individuals such as William Wilberforce. Teaching in schools particularly perpetuates this version of events. But there were many factors which led to the breakdown of the system, and agitation by humanitarians was only one of them. European industrialisation, which made it cheaper to hire and fire 'free' workers at will than to own and maintain slaves for life, was undoubtedly a more important consideration for those with interests in slavery. The Napoleonic Wars, internal conflict amongst Europeans for more markets and trading posts, and arguments put forward by both Black and white Abolitionists, all contributed to the system's eventual demise. Central to the abolition of slavery, however, was the resistance which we, the slaves, put up. The successful slave revolution in St Dominique (now Haiti), led by Toussaint L'Ouverture, sent a shock-wave through Europe and did much to undermine the morale of planters on other islands in the West Indies. The revolution also destroyed once and for all the deliberately cultivated myth that we were docile and incapable of initiative. The House of Commons, on hearing the news of revolution in St Dominique, ruled that the importation of slaves from Africa should be immediately suspended, for fear that new slaves, still steeped in their culture, would be a potential revolutionary force. But there was little need for imported agitators. For us, insurrection was nothing new, and the events in St Dominique were simply a source of further hope and inspiration.

Our on-going sabotage and rebellion meant that slavery was becoming less and less profitable. The inevitable problems of policing us where we were in the majority posed a direct threat to the lives of plantation owners and their families. By the end of the eighteenth century the planters had begun to realise that their days as slave owners were numbered. It was the unprofitability of the system and the self-interest of those involved, rather than humanitarian motives, which forced Britain to concede to Abolition.

The Africa Trade was abolished by the British in 1808, following a futile attempt by politicians to persuade the British 'West Indians' to improve our conditions on the plantations. The act proclaiming our emancipation was passed over a quarter of a century later, in 1833, and took effect the following year. It made slavery 'utterly and forever abolished and declared unlawful throughout the British Colonies'. However, after two hundred years of reaping the rewards of selling and exploiting our labour, this could not be the end of it.

Colonialism took over where slavery left off, ensuring that our labour would continue to bolster and maintain the British economy for years to come. In Africa, where we were still reeling from the effects of nearly three hundred years of human plunder, we were faced with a new onslaught as Europeans turned their attention to plundering our material resources. Pioneers and missionaries began to pave the way for the invasion of the continent by soldiers, settlers and colonial administrators, whose purpose was to seize Africa for the white man by any means necessary. Despite fierce and prolonged resistance, the Bible, taxation and the Gatlin gun eventually won the day.

In the West Indies, meanwhile, little had changed. Despite Abolition, the islands continued to rely on a plantation economy, ensuring that we had no other sources of livelihood. Colonial governments, based thousands of miles away in Europe, did nothing to develop alternative industry. Then, as now, their interests in our islands were based solely on what they could extract and exploit.

As we began to embark on the long road from slavery to freedom, we found ourselves faced with a new system which was in almost all respects only a milder version of what had gone before. Many plantation owners never came to terms with the fact that slavery had been abolished, and continued to exploit and abuse our labour with the full support and collusion of the newly-installed colonial administrations. Our working and living conditions were virtually unaltered. But the Apprenticeship System, introduced as a stepping-stone to 'free' employment, had to be hastily abandoned because of our refusal to allow planters to continue to treat us like chattel. As ex-slaves, we were beginning to demand the right to live free from the tyrannies of the plantation system. We were asserting our right to our own land, culture and way of life. Those of us who could, scraped together the means to buy small plots of land. Those of us who couldn't, squatted on the back-lands of the plantation estates, growing enough food to meet our day-to-day needs and trading any surplus for other necessities. Even as we did so, the British government found ways of hindering our bid for self-reliance. In order to prevent us from acquiring land, they introduced huge land taxes and insisted that any prospective landowners buy a minimum number of acres. As a consequence, the majority of us had no choice but to continue to use the only bargaining tool we had ever had – our collective refusal to comply.

This reluctance to grant us land ownership continued, and the British Parliament, itself full of absentee landowners, was faced with the same problem which had first given rise to the Slave Trade. Here was an abundance of land, but no willing and 'docile' workforce to cultivate and exploit its resources. We were refusing to toil for the planters on their terms while there was even the remotest chance of working for ourselves. And it was this situation which led the House of Commons Select Committee on the West Indian Colonies to conclude, in 1842, that, 'one obvious and most desirable mode of endeavouring to compensate for this diminished supply of labour is to promote the immigration of a fresh labouring population, to such an extent as to create competition for employment'.

Once the arguments in favour of bringing a new labour force to the islands under contract had been accepted, the only problem was to find this new labour. The appalling conditions on the plantations proved far more difficult to justify when no racial arguments could be advanced in their defence. Indentured labourers from Portugal found life in Trinidad so miserable that they petitioned the governor to transport them home. To begin with, the British relied on their warships to intercept Spanish slaveships heading for the Spanish colonies of Brazil and Cuba, on the pretext that they were simply putting pressure on Spain to cease trading in slaves. In reality, however, they were capturing much-needed labour. The possibility of encouraging black workers to come from other West Indian islands was ruled out, since none of the colonial governments in Europe would have tolerated large-scale migration from their already under-populated islands. And so they were left with only one alternative – to encourage immigration from British colonies in other parts of the world, such as India and, to a lesser extent, China.

One of the major ironies of the period of Indian immigration to the West Indies was that for every Indian who came there to work, three West Indians left to seek work elsewhere. Britain had imported a new population of workers in the hope that they would reduce wages by competing with us, the freed slaves, for available work. However, the result was our large-scale migration. This fact, coupled with the desire of many indentured workers to return to India at the end of their contract, still left the British colonialists with a diminishing workforce. Despite their vehement opposition to the sale of land to ex-slaves, they were forced to give land to Indian indentured workers as an inducement to stay. Plots of land were frequently offered as an alternative to a return passage to India, enabling the recent immigrants to establish themselves as planters and traders, while those of us who were ex-slaves were forced to continue to look for work elsewhere. Needless to say, the divide-and-rule potential of such a situation was not lost on the British, who never missed an opportunity in the future to exploit the inevitable divisions which resulted.

Throughout the nineteenth century, greed and self-interest continued to be the main features of Britain's relationship with our islands. Political and economic power remained firmly in the hands of the British Parliament. Still no attempt was made to develop industry and resources beyond what was needed to line the planters' pockets and service the British economy. Many landowners ran their estates and companies from abroad and, with no thought of living on the islands themselves, they made no attempt to improve the quality of life for those of us who did.

The stranglehold of the plantation system continued into the twentieth century, with each island making its own contribution to the British economy, alongside the many other reluctant members of the British Empire. Jamaica produced sugar, Grenada cocoa, Monserrat and St Kitts grew cotton and Dominica, limes. In Jamaica, the sugar which was the lifeline of the people was frequently subject to the whims of European competition, particularly as sugar beet's use as an alternative to cane increased. Not until Britain itself began to feel the effect of this competition did the Norman Commission of 1897 turn its attention to how our islands could expand their resources and diversify their economies. Despite the opening of the Canadian market to West Indian sugar in 1912 and the boom in the economy brought about by the First World War, as labourers we saw little improvement in our standard of living. Our grandfathers who went off and fought for Britain in the 'Great War' returned home to conditions which had, if anything, deteriorated during their absence.

As the world-wide depression which characterised the 1920s and 1930s set in, the sugar industry throughout the West Indies declined even further. Those of us who lived in Jamaica, Barbados, Antigua, St Vincent, St Lucia, St Kitts, Grenada and Trinidad were all to feel the effects, since we all relied on sugar to a greater or lesser extent. Our wages remained at or below subsistence level, and on some islands they had hardly advanced beyond the daily shilling rate which had been introduced after Emancipation. We continued to live in dilapidated barracks around the plantations, or in rat-infested wooden huts within easy reach of the estates. These and many other relics of slavery still existed a hundred years after its abolition. It was because of these conditions that many of us drifted into the towns, which were ill-equipped to cope with an influx of hungry, unemployed workers. There we were faced with serious overcrowding, slum housing and insanitary conditions. Our general poverty meant that malnutrition was rife and left us prey to chronic sickness and disease. For some, the only answer to this intolerable existence was to emigrate, either to other islands where prospects were rumoured to be better, or to the American mainland, where we became agricultural and factory workers. For the majority, however, there was no choice but to stay and fight for better conditions at home.

Until the 1920s, no collective voice had emerged to speak the people's grievances. A strong workers' movement could not develop, mainly because of the punitive legislation which existed against it. Unions were liable to pay damages to employers, who were well organised and fully supported by the colonial governments. Moreover, the competition for jobs was enormous. Landless peasants, disaffected soldiers from the Great War and the underemployed jostled shoulder to shoulder for whatever work was available. Many of us worked long hours, to the point of exhaustion, to preserve what little we could. Naturally, employers took full advantage of the situation.

But our response was not long in coming. It took the form of massive political upheaval throughout the 1930s. By now most of us felt that, in spite of the legal restrictions, we had nothing left to lose. Dockers, sugar workers, shop girls, street cleaners, domestic workers and casual labourers took to the streets and demanded better conditions and living standards throughout the West Indies. The most striking feature of these revolts was that, despite the apparent lack of any organised or coordinated plan, on nearly every island we made our mark within the space of three years. From 1935, when the St Kitts' sugar workers went on strike, to the General Strike of 1938 in Jamaica, we lived with continual unrest. Later on, in England, this experience of militant action would serve us well.

But these events did more than re-affirm our tradition of militancy: they laid the basis for the emergence of new political parties, which pledged to fight for the rights of workers and the poor and unemployed. They were the beginnings of an organised working-class movement in the West Indies, and of allegiances which would later pave the way for our independence struggles in the fifties and sixties. Yet, when the Second World War began, many of us, both men and women alike, went off to make our contribution for European freedom. Some of us went as farm and factory workers to America, following the footsteps of those who had already gone before; others enlisted in the Armed Forces, rallying to Britain's call for her colonial subjects to come and fight the fascists; the rest of us stayed home, to suffer the shortages and near-starvation which were the consequence of war in Europe. As a result, the impetus for the new workers' movement in the West Indies could not be sustained, and the end of the war brought no new freedoms for those of us who had fought and died for the Mother Country.

It was this climate of grinding poverty and unemployment, coupled with our stubborn and centuries-old tradition of refusing to be crushed, which laid the basis for the emigration of thousands of West Indian women and men in the post-war years. Britain, having lost many of its industries, homes and workers during six years of war, needed a cheap and ready supply of labour. And we needed jobs. This was the economic magnet which lured so many of us to the Mother Country in the late forties and fifties. We responded readily to the persuasion and the propaganda, to the lure of 'streets paved with gold' and of 'jobs for all'. Little could we have known the realities which we would have to face, as we entered a society so steeped in its racist past. Little could we have known that our vision of hope, sustained through centuries of exploitation, would be so hard to realise when we set foot on British soil.

1

Labour Pains: Black Women and Work

The Black woman's experience of work in Britain mirrors our experience of work over the past five centuries. This has been one long tradition of back-breaking labour in the service of European capitalism. Because it was as slaves that Black women's full labour potential was first established, and as slaves that our response to exploitation was first tested out, it is here that we begin. It was because of our ability to work that Black women were first taken as slaves from Africa to the Caribbean, and it was that same labour power which brought us from the Caribbean to Britain four hundred years later.

From the beginning, no real distinction was made between Black male and Black female labour. We were expected to work just as hard and as long as the men when we were slaves, and this has never changed. Our role as slaves was to work as fieldhands on the plantations or as domestics, washerwomen, cooks, seamstresses and nannies in the slavemaster's house. In the eyes of the 'backra' (or overseer) we were equal to the men just as long as our strength matched theirs. But in our eyes, we were *more than equal* to the men, for having completed our work on the estate, it fell to us to tend to the children and perform domestic duties such as preparing food and cultivating any available plot of land for ground provisions. For Black women, therefore, the 'double day' was an established feature of our working lives long before we arrived in the Mother Country.

A working day consisted of anything up to twenty hours for the Black woman slave, regardless of climate, age or pregnancy. After slaving from sun-up to sun-down in the burning heat or the torrential rain, four or five hours were considered adequate for sleep and for the performance of all additional tasks. In some cases, the life-expectancy of slaves after being bought was no longer than a year, during which time the planter could expect to extract enough work not only to repay his initial investment but also to show a good profit. At the end of the season, the slaves, like the oxen, were often reduced to mere skeletons. Despite this laborious and debilitating routine, Black women acquired the reputation of being strong and proved a better investment for slaveowners, living on average four or five years longer than Black men. Even so, in a situation where labour was plentiful, it was considered more profitable to work slaves to death than to provide the basic human requirements which would have prolonged our working lives.

Conditions in the slaves' quarters were insanitary and overcrowded, and because of our additional domestic role, Black women bore the brunt of the squalor of the huts or barracks we lived in. There was little or no provision of bedding or furniture and clothing was limited to a bare minimum, usually no more than two sets a year. Food was severely rationed, and we frequently had to supplement the meagre diet with vegetables grown in our own time. For diseases such as malaria, dysentery and yaws we received no adequate medical attention. Slaves were expendable and easily replaced. We suffered permanent disabilities because of lack of rest after childbirth, prolapses due to carrying excessive weights, ruptured organs, rheumatism, malnutrition – all direct consequences of overwork and neglect.

For those who were born into slavery, the routine of forced labour and drudgery began at a very early age. By the age of four, young girls were performing such tasks as feeding the hogs and weeding. By nine or ten, they were put to work in the fields or given domestic duties in the masters' house. Whatever their age, women slaves who worked as domestic servants lived under the whims of the household, attending to every need and frequently satisfying sexual and sadistic urges as well. Rape and sexual abuse were a common experience for us, compounded by the sufferings associated with childbirth and motherhood under slavery. Many a Black woman knew the miseries of giving birth in the fields, or nursing babies in surrounding ditches, under the perpetual threat of the backra's whip. So while racism justified the evil which decreed that Black people would be enslaved and exploited, it was because we were women that our experience of slavery was harsher than that of our men. This is equally true of our experience of work in Britain.

Mother Country Calling: The Early Years

Black women knew about the realities of underpaid and undervalued employment long before we began to consider working for Britain. We had been fighting hard in the Caribbean to become trained as teachers and nurses, or to find the means to become self-sufficient:

> I grew up in a very poor but strict family in Georgetown, Guyana. Life was rather hard, generally, but even more so if you were a woman. Women were like second-class citizens. The only jobs available to them were of the domestic type, like cleaning or taking in somebody's washing, and the only decent jobs they could do were teaching and nursing. I was a nurse before I married. When I got married, I gave up nursing and did sewing for other people. Even jobs in stores were hard to get, because you had to be fair-skinned before they would take you on. If your skin was dark, you could only get a market-stall job. After about six months of sewing, I had 100 dollars, enough for a deposit on a general store which cost 300 dollars. Eventually I bought it.

19

For the majority of Afro-Caribbean women, however, particularly in the rural areas where we were concentrated, our struggles to sustain and improve our lives were limited. As agricultural workers or domestics, the money we earned was often the sole source of income for the entire extended family. By taking in washing and sewing, or by trading any surplus goods we extracted from the land, we supplemented our wages to sustain our children and, in many cases, our menfolk too. Even when married, we continued to be the breadwinner.

I got married in 1949, and had my first child in 1950. Before we got married, we built a house. My husband used to work hard in the fields but I had two jobs. I used to work in the home, as all women did, but I also used to work in the market, because the things he planted, I used to go and sell. I was a higgler. We raised a lot of cattle, and we had chickens too.

After Abolition, the few Black women who could escape from the land joined the growing numbers who fled to the towns, looking for waged work. We exchanged the oppression of the canefields for that of the cities' kitchens, an experience which prepared us well for the services we would render to European colonialism in subsequent years. A small but significant minority of urban-dwelling women later found work as secretaries and clerks in the sugar industries, or as independent seamstresses and traders. Others found work as domestic servants, continuing the roles we had performed under slavery, often for the same families. Others became shopgirls. Some of the hardest work performed by women was as labourers at the wharves, heaving fifty to seventy pound bags of coal and sand from the barges. In all cases, of course, our wages were lower than the men's.

So, although our labour was now 'free', we continued to suffer some of the worst exploitation, and this was true throughout the West Indies. Women domestic servants worked from six in the morning to nine at night, seven days a week, and relied on the goodwill of their employer for any sick leave, holidays or time off. Shopgirls often earned as little as £1 a month and faced equally long hours and poor working conditions. Where jobs were scarce and workers plentiful, dissent and unrest increased, culminating in the mass strikes and demonstrations of the thirties. Black women were visible among those who took to the streets and demanded a better deal. And when the war brought no new freedoms for us, we too joined the growing ranks of those who left the islands and headed for places like Canada and America, which held the promise of a better future. Meanwhile, for those of us who stayed behind, the fight for a better life at home continued.

As Black women arriving in Britain from the Caribbean after the Second World War we were well prepared for the hard work we came here to do: our lives had been shaped and moulded by the inescapable need to find or create the work which would maintain us.

> Most women who were poor worked in the fields or as domestics in Jamaica. If not, you were out of a job. You had to have a certain amount of education, because for somebody who didn't go to the best of schools, there wasn't a lot of opportunity. There were a lot of people who were passing exams but not getting jobs. I found work sewing raffia for the tourist trade. We were all young girls between sixteen and eighteen, earning about four shillings a week.

The need to travel in search of work had been a long-accepted reality for us: from the countryside to the town; from one island to another; to Cuba, Canada and the USA, motivated always by the desire to improve material conditions for ourselves and our families, and to escape the treadmill of poverty.

> People kept talking about coming to England. One man who had gone there came back and told us how much better it was, job-wise. There was a lot of excitement about emigrating for this reason. Plus it was nothing new to us. I had family who had gone to Costa Rica and to Cuba to work for a while. Even my brother went to America as a

farm worker during the war. I was keen to go to England to get the money to build a decent life. I asked my husband if he would go. He wasn't too keen, but I knew that I was ready to leave without him. Anyway I wanted to get away from having all those children.

I didn't actually think I would stay here so long without going back even for a visit, but I haven't been back since I came to this country twenty years ago. I don't think anyone came here with the intention of staying for good. If people came as a family unit, they came to make some money and go back home. With people like myself, you came with the intention of working here for about two years, and if you liked the place you would probably stay here for five, getting any amount of money you could actually manage to save and go back home.

England was seen as the Promised Land simply because prospects in the Caribbean were so limited.

I came here independently, because everybody was saying 'come to England'. The impression we got was that you could get a lot of money working here, and it wouldn't take long to accumulate it. They were saying that there were better opportunities and jobs, and everyone was signing up to go and work in England. I wasn't recruited. I didn't need to be. I think the Queen came over and was broadcast on the radio, saying that we should come over and work to build up the Mother Country. Of course, that was the way Britain was seen in those days, and a lot of us really did believe that the streets were paved with gold.

It was with this history of migratory labour and high expectations that we left home. We left children, family and friends behind. And when we arrived, we had little choice but to take whatever work we could find:

I remember getting up every morning to go to the Labour Exchange to see if there were any jobs. I was actually looking for nursing work, but they wouldn't have me. Someone had told me that they would take me on as an auxiliary nurse and that later on I could train. But when I got to the hospital, the woman there offered me a cleaning job.

One of the many racist myths about Black workers is that we came to Britain and stole white workers' jobs from under their noses. However, the reality was very different. The entrenched racism of employers and workers alike meant that, although jobs were available, we had to search hard for them:

When I first started working here, jobs were scarce. You had to spend a lot of time looking before you found anything. There was a girl living in the same house as me, and she wasn't working either. We used to walk and walk, wearing out the shoe-leather looking for a job. After some days, we went to King's Cross, and she got a job in one of the hospitals. That left me to tramp the streets on my own. Of course I kept on looking. Eventually I took the train to Bermondsey in east London, and I got a sewing job there, doing trimmings.

Another popular notion is that because we came from backgrounds of relative poverty, our new lives in Britain must have been qualitatively better than anything we had known before. The power of the myth of a better life caused us to leave even when we had the skills, jobs or social status for a good life at home. But Britain was not the land of milk and honey we had been led to imagine, and the jobs we secured rarely afforded us the opportunities we had hoped for.

At home in Trinidad my husband had a good job and our life was okay. He was working on the oil rigs, and his wages were quite high. When we were about to come here, his sister did tell us that conditions weren't all that good, but we thought she was fooling us and we decided to take a chance. When we got here, we were very disappointed. I mean, some people came to this country because they had no work and needed to find a job in order to survive. But my situation was different, because my husband was working and we had been able to pay for everything we needed. All we wanted was a decent education for the children. I didn't even have to work when we were at home, but once I got here I had to find a job. It was hard, especially when you would go for a job and they would always say it had gone. Eventually I found a cleaning job in a hospital, which I have had for twenty-two years. If you come to a different country and go back with nothing, it's hard. You can't go back and start all over again. All those stories you heard about people coming here and saving a lot of money weren't true.

As the promise of a better life in England, Canada or America continued to attract many skilled workers and professionals, a 'brain-drain' resulted throughout the Caribbean:

If our government was smart, it would have let us go for a period of about five years so that we could get the money to come back and build up our own country. Instead they were willing for us to leave in our thousands, to go to some unknown place. Although they didn't want the skilled workers to go, they couldn't really stop them, and they didn't do anything to encourage them to stay. I think the country suffered because of that, because so many people who were skilled and trained did leave to go abroad at that time, thinking they'd make a better living somewhere else.

But within a few weeks of arrival, most of us found Britain a bitter disappointment.

When I left home, I told my sister, 'You just wait and see. I'm going to get a lovely house in England.' That was because of the pictures we saw on the postcards people sent, and the way they made it sound in the recruitment adverts and broadcasts. When I came here, it was terrible. I came in May but it was still cold for me. I got a job about two weeks after I arrived. I never really thought about coming here to stay or to go back, because I didn't come on my own. I came here to join my husband, because he was here before me.

Although some Black women came to Britain to join husbands who had come on ahead of them, many more came independently as recruits, or simply to seek employment. A survey conducted in 1961 showed not only that the number of Black women who emigrated was equal to the number of men, but that nearly three-quarters of the women were single. With no formal government efforts to assist those who came to settle, we relied on friends and relatives for support and accommodation, and on our own resources to help us through the early traumas of adapting to a new and unfamiliar environment:

I didn't come to this country to join my family, I came to join my friend. I didn't like it when I came at first, leaving home and coming to a different country, where there was a different atmosphere. I missed my family terribly. It was such a strange way of life to me, and I had to learn all over again. Shopping was different, getting on the bus, going places on my own ... This was 1960. I found things really difficult at first, because at home I always had my mother to help me out, but here I had to stand on my own two feet.

Black women were faced with no other prospect than to fill the jobs which the indigenous workforce were no longer willing to do, in the servicing, semi-skilled and unskilled sectors. Service work was little more than institutionalised housework, as night and daytime cleaners, canteen workers, laundry workers and chambermaids – an extension of the work we had done under colonialism in the Caribbean. The alternative to this was factory work in small, ununionised sweatshops, where conditions were poor and negotiated conditions non-existent. On the assembly line we worked side by side with other immigrants from Asia, Ireland and southern Europe, producing the food, clothes, shoes and light, household goods which were so essential to Britain's post-war economic boom.

I've had a lot of jobs since I've been in this country. My first job when I arrived in 1958 was as a finisher, doing hems, buttons and so on. I didn't like the work because it

25

was tedious, but I stayed there for three months. I was getting £5.2/6 a week; 2/6d was my train fare for the week, and they kept 1/3d for tax and insurance. I was promised a raise after three months, and when I didn't get it I went to the woman to explain why I needed it. Anyway, on the Friday my wages were a few pennies short. The next week I was sent for and sacked. They didn't give a reason. My next job was as a chambermaid at the United University Club in Trafalgar Square. It wasn't a bad job, but it was part-time. I worked from 8 a.m. to 1 p.m. The residents were openly prejudiced and I was scared because I didn't know what they would do. I used to go out looking for another job every afternoon after I finished work. I went to the Labour Exchange, and got a job at the Eccleston Hotel in Victoria, serving tea and coffee and sometimes dinner. I stayed there for about a year. I got on well with the other workers. I think this was because we were all foreigners. The chef was Polish, and the other girls were Irish. I lost the job because I was pregnant. They didn't have maternity benefits in those days, so I just got my week's wages when I left. When I'd had the baby, I went to see if I could get my job back, but it had been filled. Then a woman I knew took me to the BOAC Catering Department for a job. I only stayed there for about two weeks, though, because the manageress wanted me to work Saturday nights, and I couldn't because of my family. So she sacked me. Next I worked at a laundry in Nine Elms, sorting out the good and bad clothes. They didn't pay you any holiday pay there, they would just close the firm down during the holidays and send you away without any pay. This was one of the reasons I left. The other reason was because I was ashamed to tell them I was expecting my sixth child. Straight after than, I got a job in Bermondsey in a factory which made tins. I was soldering them. I stayed there until it was time to have the baby, then I left.

These poor working conditions were compounded by the racism we experienced at the hands of both bosses and workers. British workers felt threatened by our presence and were unable to shake off years of racist and sexist conditioning. Even though our arrival usually ensured their own promotion to less tedious and better paid sections of the industry, the fact that we were there at all was openly resented. The Race Relations Act of 1966, far from outlawing such attitudes, merely entrenched them. The act outlawed individual acts of incitement to racial hatred in places of public resort, but left racism virtually unchallenged in every other area of our lives, such as housing, employment, etc. The unions believed that their role was to protect the rights of the indigenous British workforce, rather than to take up and defend the rights and working conditions of Black workers:

At the new firm, they had to employ Black workers or they would get taken to court, so they employed two of us. The other workers gave us a hard time. They called us all sorts of names and even went on strike and brought in the union. The union told them there was nothing they could do, when the firm paid the bonus we would get as much as them. In the canteen,when we sat at a table together, we knew full well that no one would sit at the table with us. Some would even prefer to stand up to eat their meal. After working there for a while, I applied for a job in Woolworth in Waterloo in person, and I was turned down. I went home and applied in writing, and I was accepted. When I turned up for work, she was shocked. She asked me where I came from, and I said 'Ceylon', although I knew nothing about Ceylon at that time, and I doubt whether she did, either.

The blatant racism of employers only added to our sense of alienation, and in the absence of any union protection, many of us had no choice but to accept daily harassment as a fact of life.

My first employers were South Africans. The father was okay, but when he left the son took over. After that things got really bad, because he didn't like Black people and was trying to get rid of all the Black workers. There were three of us, two others and me. I left anyway, because I was pregnant, but the others had to leave because he was making life unbearable for them.

Many Black women did, however, make an individual stand against the racialist assumptions and intimidation which were the common practice of our bosses:

I remember an incident when I came back a minute late from lunch-break. The manageress told me to come back on time in future, and it got on my nerves so much that I had to say something. I got a written warning. I needed the money, so I put up with it. Another time, there was some money missing from the till, and I was sent upstairs to be interrogated by the manager. It wasn't me, and I stood firm so they couldn't put it on me. I was brought up not to steal, and I wouldn't. Anyway, I would have been finished work-wise if I'd been a thief – can you imagine having a label like that *and* being Black?

In every job we did, there were difficulties like these. The tedium and exhaustion were augmented daily by such petty institutionalised racism. However, as women we also bore the responsibility of caring for the home and family. After working all day, we had to return home and face yet more drudgery: cooking, cleaning, washing, shopping and tending to the needs of husbands and children. Indeed, it was our children who were the most decisive factor in limiting the kinds of work we could do outside the home. Most Black women who came to Britain in the fifties and early sixties were young women who had just begun or were about to begin families. The children we left behind with aunts and grandmothers were young, too, and had to be supported. When we joined men, or were joined by them, there were more children. Contraceptives were neither free, safe nor easily available, making frequent pregnancy almost unavoidable for the majority of us. Those of our children who were born here had to be cared for, but we were no longer able to rely on other women in our families for childcare, and childminding arrangements therefore posed a major problem for us. Local councils had no understanding of our needs and offered little or no assistance, particularly to those of us who were married to or living with a man:

When you had children in those days, it was very difficult to go out to work, in fact, because you had to take the children to a childminder. I worked full-time in an engineering firm. Once I sent my children to an Englishwoman who did minding, but sometimes when I collected the baby in the evening, he'd be soaking wet. The nappy had been left on all day. I had to leave the child between 7.30 and 5.30 every day. That meant I didn't spend much time with him at all. I had to wake him at 6 a.m. and he went to bed at 8 p.m. I did try to get him into a council nursery, but they told me I couldn't have a place because I was married. I was very upset. They said it was my husband's responsibility, yet I was the one who was feeling it. I can remember when all three children were talking to me at once, each one trying to get my attention. They needed me, but although I was listening to them, my mind was on rushing off to work.

In the early 1960s, the State was still busy trying to encourage (white) women to stay home and embrace domestication and consumerism. It wasn't prepared to offer any childcare support to Black women who had to work. In such a climate, we were compelled to develop other strategies. Those with their own homes, bought as a means of escaping the often desperate conditions in rented accommodation, or because racist conditions of eligibility denied us access to council homes, were able to take in children, particularly Black women who had a young family themselves. Others had to rely on fostering arrangements. Coming from a culture which has always encouraged trust between women in sharing childcare, we were sometimes too ready to place our children with a foster mother. But this arrangement could not compare with the care of our mothers and grandmothers at home. Often it meant lengthy separation from our children, and traumatic effects on the children themselves:

I left my three older children with my sister in Trinidad, and brought the baby with me to England. For the first year I was here, I fostered him out. I had to advertise for someone to look after him, and eventually I found an English family in Kent. He was a fat baby when I took him there, but when I went to visit him, he was so skinny ... If the woman offered him something to eat and he didn't want it, she would just leave him in the cot all day, without bothering to take him out or feed him again. In the end, he became a bit withdrawn. After a year, I took him back home with me. By then he was two years old, and I was worried by his lack of speech. I took him to various doctors, but they said there was nothing wrong with him, and after about a month he started to speak. It must have been the shock of me leaving him that caused it. The day I left him, he cried and cried, and I think he must have grieved from the day we left him until we came and took him back home with us again.

Because it was women's work, childminding was, and still is, grossly undervalued, and the women who did it (both Black and white) went unrecognised and unsupported. Frequently castigated for not giving the children the stimulation they needed, nevertheless childminders were given none of the training or resources which would have made this possible. So for the most part, particularly where Black women were concerned, childminding was not undertaken in any professional capacity, but simply as an alternative means of making a living.

Homework provided then, and still does today, another means of overcoming the lack of nursery provision, and the need to supplement a meagre wage. This involved either sewing or light assembly work, and was highly favoured by employers. It enabled them to pay the lowest wages, and to offload overhead costs, such as heating, lighting, electricity, machinery and rent, onto the workers themselves. Homeworkers were classified as 'self-employed', which freed the firm from paying National Insurance contributions and fringe benefits such as sick pay or holiday pay. Being self-employed increased our vulnerability, and employers took full advantage of the opportunity to make direct cost savings. Taken on as additional labour during production peaks, homeworkers would be laid off during 'troughs', with the firm free of any liability to pay redundancy money, and immune to accusations of unfair dismissal. This practice was particularly favoured in the seasonal trades such as finishing or toy-making, which employed large numbers of Black women, as they do today. Then, as now, homework was one of the most feudal and exploitative forms of employment, and it is no coincidence that it has remained almost synonymous with cheap, Black, female labour.

For the majority of Black women, however, it has been night and shift work which have enabled us to carry out our responsibilities as mothers and breadwinners. Inadequate sleep, exhaustion and ill-health were the price we have had to pay if we wanted to spend time with our children and feed them too – even when we weren't struggling to do it alone:

> After my son was born in 1964, I gave up full-time work and went back to working part-time in the evenings. When my husband got home from work, he would look after the children while I went to work. When they were a bit older, I took up shift-work. I started at 9 a.m. and finished at 3.30 p.m., then I went back again at 5 p.m. and worked through until 8 p.m. I found it a great strain, but at the time I wasn't thinking of myself. After some really bad experiences with childminders, I figured it was better to look after my own children. Then at least the children can grow up close to you and you know they are well looked after.

The overriding need to work to support ourselves and our children also meant that in the early years Black women had to rely on relationships at work and in our immediate communities if we were to avoid social isolation. In the Black communities of Toxteth, St Paul's and Cardiff, which were longer-established, this did not present itself as such a problem; but in most other areas, racial tensions and the pressures of a hard, long working routine made loneliness and isolation a reality for us, particularly in the fifties:

> I had no social life outside of work. After the children came, I took them to church and two of them were in the choir. The only other social life was at weddings or christenings. The receptions would be mostly at people's homes. At Christmas time, there was nowhere to go unless someone invited you to their house. We didn't get invited to white parties, though, unless it was the firm's do. It was because of this that we started to hold house parties.

This largely isolated existence, coupled with the effects of the 1962 Commonwealth Immigration Act, gave impetus to our growing need to have our children join us here. This act, aimed at the Black Commonwealth only, was designed to reduce the total inflow of non-white immigrants by prioritising different categories of workers according to skill and desirability. A survey carried out in 1965 showed that 85 per cent of Caribbean women were still sending money to support families back home. But as the economic boom came to an end, marking the beginning of the economic crisis which would continue into the eighties, the material conditions we faced became more difficult. The economic necessity of supporting two families proved increasingly hard to sustain, and we were faced with the choice of returning home with our ambitions largely unfulfilled, or sending for our children to join us here. While many chose the former option, the majority of us chose the latter, often because there was no other alternative available to us:

> When I saw what little I had left after paying the bills, I realised that I would have to be here longer than I had intended. After buying food and paying the rent, there just wasn't enough left over to save to go back. So I decided to send for the children and to get a house.

Sending for our children in the Caribbean, however, was an added financial burden on our limited resources:

> Out of my wages of £6 a week, I used to send £3 a week back home. My weekly rent was £1.15 and the rest of my

money, plus my husband's £6, went towards everything else, such as fares, food, bringing up the baby, raising the deposit on a house and saving for the fares to bring the three children over.

Until 1962, we had had the right to live and work in Britain with no restriction on our rights of entry. With the new Immigration Act came controls which were to have lasting implications for our families. Applications had to be made, and credentials checked out, and many of us faced permanent separation from our children as the British government became less and less prepared to honour our right to bring them to join us here. Meanwhile, our children were growing up. Those in their mid-teens were particularly affected by the new laws, for they were regarded not as children, but as aspiring workers whom the British government no longer wanted. Those who did gain entry underwent the traumatic adjustment to the last few years of schooling here, or of having to enter the job market directly on arrival when schools declined to admit them on the grounds of their age. The foundations were laid for the perpetuation of our role in this society: the children for whom we had worked so hard and sacrificed so much prepared to step into our shoes. It would ultimately fall to them to alter and re-chart the route we had taken in pursuit of a living wage and a better life.

Tooth and Nail: Fighting Back on the Shop Floor

The experience of Black women workers in this country could be seen as a long catalogue of hardships suffered in menial, low-grade jobs. However, it is our responses to these hardships which lend optimism to our story. Despite our relegation to the lowest grades, and our bitter struggles outside the workplace to support our families, we have always been able to find the energy and the will to resist. From the late 1960s onwards, Black women began collectively to oppose the exploitation we confronted in our places of work. Since then, we have openly defied employers who have sought to deny us our basic rights as workers. We have been labelled 'trouble-makers' in our struggles for a better deal. But we have shown that Black women are not prepared to accept poor wages, bad conditions, racism and sexist discrimination in our workplace without a fight

I started with ————— in February 1970 and when I went there the boss was a very pompous, cocky man. He used to treat the workers like dogs, servants and footstools. When he came in in the morning, he would walk past you and not say, 'Good morning' to anyone. All the white people were frightened of him. They would just creep when they saw him come in; some of the Black workers did, too. I swore that I would not creep. No way would I pray to this man, because he was human just like me. Sometimes when the girls used to go out for lunch, if they were two minutes late back he would sack them. I didn't like it. I always said to myself that if they did not get a union in that place, I didn't think I would stay there because I couldn't put up with this man's ways. Everyone would be working hard and he'd come up behind them and they would tremble. I couldn't take that.

One day in August when I was going to lunch, I met some people at the gate. This man was giving out cards for people to join the union. He said he wanted to bring the union in there. I was very glad, so I took one of the cards, filled it in and sent it to the office. It came back a couple of weeks later and they sent me some more to take on to the shop floor for others to join. I urged them to sign up and they filled the cards in and got a union. Once we had a certain number of members, the union would be allowed to come into the factory, and the boss wouldn't be able to stop them. They would also be able to hold meetings. The boss didn't want to know, he was furious. But he couldn't sack me. In fact, he couldn't sack any of us, because we were now union members. He said that ————— had their own union and that if he'd known the workers wanted to join a union, he'd have got them in. When our union official came to hold the first meeting, he wasn't allowed on to the premises. So he took us to a pub near Clapham, and we held our meetings there. We had to put up a real fight to be able to hold our meetings on the shop floor.

The boss went to where the union had an office, and told them that another union was on their patch. He didn't want any outside union, he wanted the firm's union. Yet all this time, the firm's union had been based at their other branch and they didn't bring it to Battersea because there were a lot of Blacks working in the Battersea factory and they were cheating the Black workers all the time. When the workers got a pay rise at the other branch, the people in the Clapham factory didn't get to know about it. We were working on radios and televisions, and the boss told us that if we didn't join the AEUW, the firm's union, we would not be working on the radar, which was what we were changing over to. Many people were afraid and went over to the AEUW, but a lot of them stayed with us. I then became a shop steward to keep the people together, and a young man become the convenor. The boss was furious when he found out that our union had caught on so well. He had to be more polite. It worked out that most of the white workers joined the AEUW and the Black workers stayed with mine. I carried on in the union there for a long time.

Some bosses do not respect their workers, whatever colour they are. But if you find they are picking on you, especially if you are Black, you should complain to your shop steward who must then take the matter up with the boss, because the union is meant to represent your interests. One example of this I can recall was when we had a member with several young babies, who kept coming to work late. She was warned once, and I went to the boss and told him he shouldn't warn her because he should take into consideration the fact that she had young children. I told him he should make some allowance for her to come to work a bit later because she had to get the children up and take them to the nursery and then come to work. In the end, he saw my point of view and left the woman alone when she got in a few minutes late.

In 1971, agency night-cleaners employed to clean large office blocks came out on strike for the first time ever and West Indian women were in the forefront of that long and bitter struggle for more money, better working conditions and the right to belong to a union. Similarly, the strikes at Mansfield Hosiery, Imperial Typewriters, Grunwick and Chix were spearheaded by Asian women and supported by many other Black women. It is no coincidence that we have stood side by side on the picket lines, for we are united by a common experience of racism and sexism on the shopfloor. In particular, the strike at Grunwick not only demonstrated the militancy of Black women workers, but also exposed the racism that permeates the trade union movement. By depicting the objective of that struggle solely as one of union recognition, the trade union movement allowed the real issues as they affected the mainly Black, mainly female workforce to be ignored. If we learnt anything from Grunwick, it was the already familiar lesson that we cannot rely solely on the law or the unions to win our battles for us.

For many of us, this is a predictable conclusion. Our experience of the unions in this country has not always been a positive one, and despite the Race Relations Act and Equal Opportunities policies, real support by our unions has been rare, particularly when we have complained of racial abuse or sexual discrimination on the shopfloor. Getting the unions to support our struggles has been a whole struggle in itself, and many of us have had little choice but to take on our employers as individuals.

Because I argued with them a lot, the management never liked me. There were a lot of Black assistants at the shop, but they didn't stay long. That was their way of fighting back. With me, now, I had to stick it out a bit longer. At the time, I was six months pregnant and they were still picking on me. I was carrying some boxes, which were really heavy one time, and I asked this girl to help me but she said she was busy; so I didn't pick them up again. The manager came and told me I had to. I told him they were too heavy for me, and he accused me of not doing my job properly. I was sent to the personnel officer and given a final warning and sacked on the spot. Of course it was unfair. It was racial and sexual discrimination. I took them to the Tribunal and won my case for unfair dismissal. I got about £1000 and they settled out of court because they already had a bad name for the way they treated their Black employees ... After I left, things began to change. Some of my friends even got through to management. I like to think it was down to me.

In recent years, our response has been to come together as Black workers within the unions to discuss and work out a strategy for dealing with racism in our unions. The establishment of the Black Trade Unionist Solidarity Movement took this initiative one step further in 1983, by recognising the contribution of Black women workers and ensuring that BTUSM would 'be run in a non-sexist and collective spirit', setting up a coordinating committee made of Black women and men in equal numbers. Caucuses have also been formed within individual unions such as NALGO. These have taken on the racism of employers and unions alike, raising the issues which affect Black workers with an unyielding militancy.

The fight to improve our working conditions has been won not only on the shop floor. Black women have had to campaign vigorously for childcare, for example, which is of paramount importance to all women who work. By concentrating our efforts within local parents' groups and within our community, we have succeeded in setting up nurseries for our children which would never have existed without our determination. Thus, one of our most important contributions has been to make the vital links between workers', women's and community struggles, pointing the way to other workers in this country. Where no adequate local authority provision has existed the advances we have made in establishing nurseries and creches in our communities have been mainly through our own efforts. Only recently in the wake of the 1981 Uprisings, the Scarman Report, and various metropolitan councils' efforts to heighten public awareness of our position as Black women, have we succeeded in securing any meaningful support from outside. We have applied for grants, premises and paid workers, making it possible for us to establish a range of childcare services, from mobile creches to after-school playgroups. These have helped to fill the void left by inadequate local authority provision, albeit only on a temporary and annually renewable basis.

Today, as the recession of the past two decades deepens and mass unemployment becomes an accepted reality, the significance of our experience and contribution as Black women workers is becoming more and more apparent.

Working the Wards: Black Women in the NHS

Our experiences within the National Health Service are crucial for they both highlight and sum up our role in this economy as Black women workers, underpinning the foundations of the Welfare State. Our concentration in the least prestigious areas of the service – a service which has consistently failed to cater for our own health needs when we have become patients – emphasises how racism has excluded us from the benefits of a society which relies so heavily on our labour. Now, as we are eased out of these jobs with the increasing privatisation of health care, the expendability of our labour is exposed for all to see.

Our first contact with the NHS was in the fifties, either through direct recruitment or with the aid of subsidies from our home governments. The expanding British economy was particularly short of labour in areas such as transport and health, and the nursing profession, with its low wages and unsocial hours, held little prestige among British women. In the Caribbean, however, it was (and remains) a highly-rated profession, respected enough to attract Black women already in work to give up their jobs, and come to Britain to train as nurses. Higher earning power, better educational opportunities and the experience of a new way of life were the carrots offered to us.

Black women entered the NHS prepared, as in other areas,

to work hard to improve conditions for ourselves and our families back home. Gaining entry to the service was not easy; nor was the work we were required to do.

I came to Britain because it was a way of getting out of Guyana. The job opportunities there were poor and there was no hope of me getting a decent job at home. It was a bad time for getting into England, because there was a law in 1963 which said that you had to have a job to come to. My only alternative was to come through the hospital. I had this friend who was trying herself, and she gave me a couple of hospitals to try. They all turned me down. However, my friend was successful eventually; she got into a hospital in Hornchurch. So she sent me the address and I applied there too. They wrote and said I had to go through the Ministry. I had to fill in an application form and attend an interview. I also had to sit a maths test, which I failed the first time, but I took it a second time and passed. After that, I was on my way. I paid my own fare and left Guyana. There were other recruits on the same flight, and we were met at the airport and taken to the hospital. The very next day, I started working on the wards as an auxiliary. I was going to study to become a State Enrolled Nurse [SEN] but my course hadn't started yet. At first I was very depressed, because I was homesick. It helped to have my friend there, plus there were other Black women, mostly from Barbados. They were recruits, the same as us, but they were subsidised by their government.

The work at the hospital was hard. It was a geriatric hospital and some of the patients were very old and senile. They would easily get confused and report you for some trivial thing. Even knowing their mental state, the sister would come and tell you off. The Black nurses were given all the roughest jobs, like cleaning out the sluice. As for the other workers, some were nice and others were just plain ignorant. For example, one of the girls cut her finger on the ward, and this white woman found it really amazing that her blood was red. I suppose they thought Black people had black blood, or something.

As time went by, things got a bit better. But you could see no chances of promotion or advancement. I had to think of the future. I had left my daughter in Guyana with my mother. It was really rough, living in a nurses' home, paying for board and lodgings and trying to save money for her. I used to send £6 a month for her, and tried to live off the rest.

The deliberate policy of recruiting Black women as State Enrolled rather than State Registered Nurses effectively limited our career prospects and our chances of returning home. Many of us entered the hospitals on the mistaken assumption that we would receive SRN training. Others were told that only an unspecified period of time spent as an auxiliary would qualify them for proper training.

On the plane over, I got chatting to a woman who I found out was a nurse over here. I told her about the hospital I was going to, and she asked me whether I was going to be a pupil nurse or a student nurse. Well, I hadn't registered any difference at the time. Then she explained that SEN pupils were lower than SRN students and that Trinidad didn't even recognise the SEN qualification. She told me I could change when I got here, since I'd passed the General Nursing Council exam at home. I wasn't worried then, but she did drum it in that I should tell them I wanted to change as soon as I got here.

When I got to the hospital, it was too late so I had to leave it till the next morning. That same night I met some nurses, one student and one pupil. I said to them that I was going to be a student, even though my letter stated that I was a pupil. One of them said, 'How are you going to manage that, then?' and I said, 'Well, I used to be a teacher'. I was really quite naive and they both looked up to the heavens as if to say, 'Yes, she'll soon be brought down to size!' The next day, before I could see the matron, I had to be fitted for a uniform. Of course, the lady in the sewing room started measuring me up for an SEN uniform. She handed me this old, patched up uniform, and I thought, 'Have I come from Trinidad for this?' I told her no, I would be getting the starched, green uniform and she said, 'But all the coloured girls are pupils'. That really got me going. I went to the Matron and demanded to change. They were taken aback, but there was nothing they could do about it because I'd passed the test. I didn't realise then that they thought that if you were Black, you were stupid. You learn quickly though.

Over the past thirty years the NHS has got – and is getting still – a huge captive, low-waged Black women's labour force. Stories abound of Black SENs who were unable to go on and train as SRNs because of the poor references they were given by their seniors. Those Black women who succeeded in overcoming the obstacles and gaining SRN training often found that they were simply extending their period of cheap labour by a further two years. The highly regulated power structures within the NHS served to isolate overseas nurses and to intensify our experiences of racism, at both at a personal and institutional level.

If I had to return to the NHS I would continue to work nights: you have freedom from a lot of things. You can control your work and your workload and you're not subjected to so many racist remarks, particularly when you're working with the public. You're not dealing with that sort of onslaught of racist abuse when you work nights. There are aspects of racism which Health administrations won't deal with and Black nurses in particular have difficultly taking up, because it goes unrecognised. But Black nurses need to recognise this and to do something about it collectively. I know I was accused of giving preferential treatment to a Black patient once, because there was a Black woman on the ward and her hair needed doing and when I asked her about it she said there was no one to come in and do it for her. I agreed to do it, but the only time I had was during my break, so I did it then. And I was told off. So I told the sister that it was my break and I'd do what I liked with it, it was my business how I chose to spend my own time. But you need a lot of strength and confidence to do that. If you're in a position where you're on a visa or a work permit, this is more difficult. I know a lot of Black student nurses who were afraid to answer back because they wanted their visas renewed. If you have offended the ward sister with some utterly trivial piece of answering back, it will reach the Nursing Officer before you know it, and through her the Director of Nursing Education. This can mean that you get labelled as a troublemaker, so that when you finish, you won't get a job. The other trap is that you only have to get reported for something three times and you can be transferred to another ward.

The rigidly hierarchichal structures in hospitals were bound to create such anxieties, particularly in women who managed to become Nursing Officers. Even in the lower ranks of health workers, there are few opportunities for promotion, and for Black women who became ward sisters, there was considerable pressure to conform.

Nobody expects Black people to get this kind of job, or to be able to manage it if you do. To survive as a Black sister, you either succumb to that and operate as a white person, joining in with their criticisms and so on and giving the Black nurses a hard time, or you try to make a stand. It's difficult, because nurses lead a politically sheltered life, meaning they're not encouraged to think or in any sense analyse. When I first became a sister, I did have a hard time. I upset some of the domestics who thought I was snobbish and they were really uncooperative. If you have a ward where this happens, life can be hell. I was getting a lot of pressure from white people, too. The other white sister kept overriding me, but I tried not to make a scene. She was more experienced and had been there longer than me. That was only the half of it, though. I was Black, and it was difficult for her to swallow the fact that I'd been promoted. Even after all these years, some of them still find it hard to work with me.

Those of us who could not tolerate the hierarchy or who,

because of family commitments, could not adhere to the rigid timetabling, became agency nurses. This freed us from the tyranny of those working over us, and also gave us greater flexibility in our working hours. However, it also meant giving up all benefits, like holiday pay, sickness benefit, promotion prospects and job security.

A lot of hospitals, especially the teaching ones, have trouble getting staff for night duty. Although their students can provide a certain amount of cover, as they have to do it, they find it difficult to recruit trained nurses. I know quite a lot of Black women who work during the days *and* at night. They leave the kids with a babysitter or their husbands, but if they're not working again the next day, they're there with them. If you have a family, you have difficulty nursing in any case, and as an agency nurse it's much worse, starting at 7 p.m. and finishing at 5 a.m. When do you sleep? You can't build a relationship with your patients because you are always going from one ward to another, and you can't have a relationship with your family because you are always tired.

Despite the obvious disadvantages, agency nurses have often been blamed for the sorry state of the NHS; we are accused of not caring enough to fit our lives around its dictates.

For many Black women who joined the NHS with the intention of becoming nurses, this was to remain an elusive goal. Relegated to the hospitals' kitchens and laundries, or trudging the wards as tea-ladies, cleaners and orderlies, we were to have first-hand experience of the damning assumptions which define our role here. The patients saw it as fitting that we should be doing Britain's dirty work and often treated us with contempt.

Just imagine: some patient says to you that he wouldn't do the work we do for £100 a week. Then just as you clean, they mess it up again and then say to you, 'You're here, you clean it up, that's your job'.

Such attitudes are also widespread among white nurses,

who often regard us as the second cousins of the nursing profession, there to relieve them of the more unpleasant tasks.

During my first year here, I really blotted my copy-book. I was just training, there to watch what they were doing, and one of the patients shit on the floor. When I told them what had happened, nobody moved. They wanted *me* to clean it up!

Because of the pressure on us to conform, minor incidents often become major matters of discipline:

Sometimes things get blown up out of all proportion. There was a Sister who was continually watching our every move. One night she decided we couldn't play music in our room. It was our block, our space, and only eight o'clock in the evening. My friend had just got a new record from Jamaica through the post, so we were all listening to it as we rushed around trying to get ready for our once-a-week rave. Sister came in when my friend was in the bathroom and just turned the music down. And we were grown women! My friend came out of the bathroom and turned it up again. Then Sister came back and turned it down again. This went on a few times. Finally my friend came into the room when she was doing it, and told her to get out. What does she do now, when white authority is threatened? Of course she calls for the night superintendent. There were quite a few of us and so we went off to the dance, and didn't give him any help in deciding who to harass.
    The next day, we were wondering what would happen to us – if we'd be reported. I was really shocked when I was called downstairs to be hauled over the coals by Matron. It seemed that the night superintendent couldn't tell us apart, and when Matron started abusing me, I started shouting as well, explaining very loudly what had actually happened and what her mistake was. The noise attracted the attention of the Chief Administrator, who had to agree with me that Matron should have checked her

facts first. She was mortified, but it would not have happened if she hadn't been so blinkered.

In the structure and distribution of hospital work, Black women are concentrated at the base of a pyramid. This is reflected in the kind of work we do, in shifts and nursing rotas, in the hours we work and in the contemptuously low wages we receive.

The NHS reminds me very much of a colony in the way it's run. Generally, the relationship between Black nurses and ancillaries is good, because we're all in the same boat really. In terms of off-duty time, we all know that Sister can give out whatever she thinks fit. In terms of work on the ward, the SENs and the auxiliaries do most of it. Take the Wednesday morning shift, from 7.30 a.m. to 4.30 p.m. you'll find that the workforce on that shift is as follows – one white, three Black nurses, one student and one pupil nurse. The white sister will act as manager, organising the work for her Black nursing staff, and then spend the morning sitting in the office.

It is no exaggeration to assert that without our contribution the NHS would not have survived, even in its present beseiged and truncated form. Moreover, it was through our labour in the hospitals that many white workers and patients were first forced to question their own prejudices and assumptions about us. This process laid the foundations of later allegiances between Black and white workers which the drastic cuts and redundancies in the service in the eighties have demanded. Our struggle as workers in the NHS has enabled us to influence those areas of work where, formerly, unquestioning acquiescence had been the rule. We have been able to redefine the meaning of workers' action, and to throw a new light on concepts of women's work.

It's a kind of indoctrination, a nurse's training. Women who do nursing are supposed to be single or devoted spinsters. They are taught that to be a good nurse involves a lot of self-sacrifice, working long hours, caring, always being there, just like mother! It completely contradicts the notion that you have some rights as a worker. Even with the union, your rights as an individual are literally swept away from under your feet. Any nurse who comes in and starts anything is labelled an activist, just because you're fighting for your rights.

The popular notion of Health Service workers as 'carers' who tolerate every indignity in the interest of their patients was shattered in 1972 when ancillary workers, consisting largely of Black women, came out on strike.

My first experience of strike action was in 1972. We didn't stay out very long. We wanted more money. At that time, we worked in the hospital, scrubbing and cleaning. You came to work at 7 a.m. and went home at mid-day, then back again at 2 p.m. and left at 7 p.m. At the end of the week, you had £10 in your hand.

It was a wonderful experience, striking. We marched and we shouted. From 1972 up to today, we have had to fight for everything we have won. Now we no longer work the split shift, but we work harder than before, because after 1974 they introduced the bonus system. Where there were four of us to a ward before, there are now only two.

Through this 1972 initiative we demonstrated that hospitals were not exempt from organised action. Since then, nurses too have taken action. Increasingly aware of the attacks on their jobs and working conditions, they are not prepared to accept the steady erosion of health services and their own jobs which we are witnessing today. The arguments of Black nurses, who have always been the first to feel the effects of cutbacks, now seem almost prophetic. The combined effects of racism, discrimination against women workers and the steady loss of health services for working-class people generally have been more apparent to us than to any other group of hospital workers, because we have experienced them simultaneously, on all three levels, for some time.

Over the past twenty years, since the 1967 Salmon Report, they've been attempting to change nursing from a skill to a profession. To make it easier, for example, for men to become nurses. By introducing managerial structures into the hospital hierarchy, men can now come in easier. And as soon as men began to come in, the number of Black women went down! Managerially they organise hospitals like factories now. And for all the same reasons that exist outside the NHS, men get into those managerial posts – they don't have to leave to have babies, they're supposed to have better managerial ability, etc., etc. Plus, because of racism, any Black person entering the managerial level is seen to be lowering the profession, particularly in the large teaching hospitals where there's a recognised career structure. Also, they don't train us. We tend to be the part-timers and now they are even getting rid of part-time workers because of the cuts. And to get around the problem of making part-timers redundant, they tell you either to become full-time or leave. Or sometimes they use more subtle means, like the rota. Nowadays you don't have the ward sister doing the duty rota, it's all done on a computer which can't take account of people's individual needs and domestic responsibilities because a computer can't deal with the human element. But the cuts have thrown up a lot of things – the demolition or shedding of Black staff and also the closure of hospitals in Black areas, because those are already the most run-down hospitals. For example, where I worked two years ago, it would have taken about three million pounds to bring that hospital up to standard, because it had been run down so much. You'd be doing the injections or preparing medications and the lights would all go – and once when this happened, there was no one around to replace the lights!

The combined effect of attacks such as these on the nursing profession and the health service culminated in the bitter health workers' struggle of 1982/83 in which nurses joined with other health workers in a long and determined campaign. Although low pay and the demand for a decent wage was a major issue, the strike action also centred around other important concerns for health service workers, such as cutbacks in the service, hospital closures and the increasing privatisation of ancillary support like laundry and catering. These cuts have seriously affected all Black women's jobs in hospitals, particularly the jobs of Black nurses:

If you're asked to lift a patient and you don't feel you can do it without damaging your back – and this often happens – you can refuse to do it and call a porter, and tell the Sister, 'Look, I'm not going to lift this patient because I'll damage my back.' In that way nurses can fight back, but to mobilise nurses is very difficult, and this kind of reaction is an exception. A lot of auxiliary nurses are practical nurses, bedside nurses, and they can't get out of it without giving themselves a record. They've got all the arguments to contend with about, 'Look, you're meant to be a nurse and your role is to care and to put the patients' needs before your own.' The 1983 Ethical Code of nursing makes it clear that we are meant to do whatever a patient desires for their comfort – empty bins, serve meals, do porters' duties, domestic and ancillary work, you name it ... So they've dealt with the cuts by enshrining these kinds of non-nursing duties into the code. And the important thing about this code is that if you are Black, you can be reported or struck off and told you're not a nurse anymore for refusing to carry it out. All of this is well-calculated, especially in the light of the anti-unionism that's pushed on to nurses. What it means is that they can actually get rid of trouble-makers more easily. That's how they are going to use it. And you can't call upon your union for support if you're refusing to do something like empty bins when it's written into the Ethical Code. As it is, we don't get enough support from the union. But these days, people are becoming more and more aware of what's happening to us, and we're looking for support from other areas.

There has been widespread public support for our actions, with many examples of secondary strike action. This prompted the government to declare such actions illegal, thereby challenging the whole basis upon which workers' solidarity in this country is founded. Consequently, the health workers' actions revealed a new level of consciousness and mutual support among Black and white workers and the public in general. The effects of this new consciousness and militancy have been far-reaching. Attempts by the Tories to outlaw strike action in the 'essential' services were a direct response to the growing determination of the health workers when faced with insultingly low wage offers and drastic cut-backs in the service.

In the hospital where I work we are in a very, very bad situation. In 1978, the Area Health Authority came to the hospital and notified us about the closure. From then they have been putting on the aggro. But a lot of people didn't take it seriously. In 1980, the Health Authority brought in a terrible lot of people to supervise us. Under them, we are worse than prisoners. I have never seen anything like the way they treat us. They've had their orders to hammer us down, and the patients as well. It was chaos. They started to close down the wards. We formed an occupation committee, and gave out leaflets to the public. And we told them, anything happens to us, we'll occupy.

They sent me to a ward with twenty-seven patients, to do three people's work. As I'm the shop steward and the health and safety rep, I decided to follow union policy. I did my own work and no more. I have worked at the hospital nineteen years. This Sector Administrator, who was brought in three months ago, and the superintendent who was only there about eleven months, they came into the kitchen where I was warming up some milk for a patient. And they pushed me and poked me and ordered me to do the rest of the work. But I refused. My blood pressure went sky high. I had to go off sick for weeks.

They want me out because I'm militant, but I'm not budging. I am fighting for my rights and for our National Health Service, and I'm not going to let the management step on me. These people have no qualifications to organise the hospital. They're only put there to terrorise people and harass us. So I've decided I shall be militant.

When I came back to work, they called me to a

disciplinary hearing. My union official wanted me to sit down in there but I refused to sit down with management. I said, 'I'm going to ask the members in to get you to drop this hearing.' I got up from their court and went and called the other members in. And all the members came in and occupied that office. It was *wonderful*. I think it was marvellous. We brought in our machine to make leaflets, to carry on the occupation campaign from the office. The management were scared, they didn't know what to do. Then we occupied a hospital ward they were closing, and they took us to court.

I didn't go to court. I went on a demonstration instead.

The contribution of Black women during this continuing series of actions cannot be overlooked, even by the media for whom traditionally we have been invisible. Our firm and obvious presence on the picket lines is a testimony to the many years we have struggled, without due recognition, to establish and preserve our dignity as workers in the Health Service. These struggles have both pitched the level and paved the way for the on-going public opposition to health service cutbacks and closures in recent years.

Black Women and the Recession

With unemployment at around four million and rising workers everywhere are now feeling the pinch as never before. The Tory government's attempt to streamline and trim the economy has made unemployment and redundancy inevitable. Many thousands of workers have lost their jobs, and the miners' long campaign of 1984/85 has proved conclusively that all workers, Black and white, male and female, risk being discarded if they are not prepared to fight to defend their right to work. Black women have always been exposed to policies of 'last hired, first fired', so this experience is no new one for us. Nevertheless, the present crisis in the capitalist economy has had a direct bearing on our chances – and those of our children – of finding work.

The decline of Britain's heavy industries, so strong in the

post-war period, has particularly affected our job prospects. We have suffered heavy job losses as a result of the decline in the support services on which the steel, iron, heavy engineering and shipbuilding industries relied. The food, clothing, textile and light engineering industries, all areas in which Black women have traditionally maintained a major presence, have been hit by closures and mass redundacies. In a climate where most of these goods can be manufactured and assembled more cheaply through the super-exploitation of Third World labour (particularly women's), they are deemed no longer profitable.

For Black women, the current emphasis on making industry more competitive and productive through increased mechanisation, means that our labour in particular is not wanted anymore. No longer at war or in the throes of an economic boom, the moment has never been more opportune to present the Black female workforce as superfluous to Britain's labour requirements.

The explosion of the new technology and micro-electronics industries has compunded these moves to make Black women redundant. Clerical work, which for years closed its doors to Black women, has only recently become more accessible to us. Now, with the advent of word processors, computer systems and other labour-saving features of the electronic office, Black women are once again being excluded from jobs as typists, telephonists and post-room workers. In this climate, the onus on us to accept whatever employment and conditions we can get, has never been greater. And the need for us to step up our demands for better access to vocational and in-service training has never been greater, either.

> I work from 5 p.m. to 10 p.m. every evening. I took this job eight years ago because the hours suited me. I would be with the kids all day and go to work when my husband got home. Now they're at school, I'm still there to meet them, so in that way the job is good. But what satisfaction is there as a punch-card operator? The job doesn't offer me any scope for promotion, and getting the training is

impossible. There's no way they're going to send someone like me, a part-time worker and a Black woman at that, for in-service training. So, although I'm lucky to have a job when so many people are unemployed, I still wish I could go to college to improve my prospects.

Probably the most significant and ominous feature of the 1980s recession has been the government's initiative to organise the young labour force into a readily exploitable pool of cheap labour, under the guise of the Youth Opportunities Programme (YOP) which became the Youth Training Scheme (YTS). YOP was formulated as a hasty response to youth rebellion, which came to a head in the summer of 1981. Young people, both Black and white, rose up in anger across the country at their treatment by police, politicians and society. Their uprising posed the severest challenge and the most explosive youth response to the system we have ever witnessed. It was the direct threat of their potential to bring about radical social changes which forced the government to seek out ways of containing and regimenting working-class youth.

Today, young Black women are visible in disproportionate numbers on inner-city YTS schemes which offer a dubious twelve-month 'training and work experience programme' to the no-longer-employable ranks of school-leavers.

With over half of all young people leaving school condemned to long-term social redundancy, it is estimated that the unemployment rate among sixteen to nineteen-year-old Black girls is already three times higher than the national average. For them, YTS has become little more than disguised conscription, removing young people from the labour market into compulsory 'traineeship' where unemployment benefits are dependent on YTS participation. Each generation of school leavers is given the 'opportunity' to acquire one or more dubious skills in a hierarchical structure of training categories. Inevitably, it is young Black women with no qualifications who fill the lower category training placements, while 'Category A' training (involving work experience on employers' premises) is reserved for those who

have 'succeeded' in the education system by acquiring O
levels or high grade CSEs.

I had gone to the Careers Office explaining to them that I
was interested in working with children but I didn't know
what to do. The careers officer told me about a job and
made it sound really important, not telling me it was
YOPs. I had heard about YOPs and the things they did,
but when I started the Care Assistant course, I started it
not knowing it was YOPs. I got £25 per week, but I
thought that was because I was training. When I got to the
place of work, everything seemed dull. I was expecting to
be taught about working with children and to come away
at the end of it with a certificate or something to prove it.
By the end of the induction course, I realised it was a
YOPs course, but at the time I thought it was better to
continue with it, because I was able to go to college for two
days a week. We all thought we were going to get a job at
the end of it. It seemed to me they just used us to do the
work no one else wanted to do. I spoke to my mother
about it, but she wanted me to carry on because I was
getting some money. We all needed the money to help our
parents, because we had to give them something towards
our keep. There were some girls who were only interested
in the money, not what we were being taught. My friend
who was on the course with me didn't want to do the
YOPs at all. She was determined to do the NNEB [Nursery
Nurse Education Board] when she left school. That's the
only thing you look for, nursery nursing or office work.
But if you have ambition, the course destroys you, because
at the end of it you find yourself having gone through a
whole year doing nothing and achieving nothing. I think
they should abolish the YOPs and send people to college
to do a proper, recognised course because when you tell
anyone you're on a YOPs course, they're not impressed at
all. I knew the YOPs wasn't worth anything when I saw
there were hardly any white people on it. If there had been
white girls on it, I would have seen it as something
worthwhile. When I looked at the students on the NNEB

course at college and saw there were only two Black girls on it, I was disgusted. I went to the YOPs conference and there were a lot of people there who felt the same way as I did – that they had been forced into it under false pretences. Being on a YOPs course is more embarrasing than signing on the dole.

This creaming-off process serves to validate the notion that youth unemployment can be explained in terms of the personal failings of young people themselves. It also gives employers and local councils access to an ever-growing pool of cheap, young, unskilled labour, for a 'wage' of between £15 and £25 a week. Described in all-too-familiar apartheid terms as 'separate but equal' to the workforce, young Black women are fully aware of the thinly disguised nature of their own exploitation.

It's like being at school. We don't have any say in what we do on the scheme. If you come in a few minutes late, they just send you home and dock you a day's wages. That saves them the trouble of having to teach you, plus it saves the government a day's money. Last week I was sick, and we're meant to get paid if we phone in, but they docked me two days' pay. I got £15 out of my £25, which is what I normally give my mum each week for my keep. So I was left with nothing to live on for the rest of that week. No fares, nothing. Everything is done under threat – 'If you don't do it, you can go home and we'll dock you your wages.'

When I left school two years ago, I went to college and passed my BEC General. So when I saw the publicity and it said you'd get work experience, I thought I'd actually get to work in an office and that it would improve my chances of getting a job. But all that is misleading, the work experience we do is a rip-off. We even had to find our own placement. We walked along the High Road looking for places which might be likely to take us on. Then we typed the letters asking them if they'd take us on as YTS trainees. I mean, it's just like slaving, isn't it? They say, 'Yeah, I could do with a bit of extra help', but they're not paying, so they would say that. I went for an interview with an estate agents and the bloke told me I wouldn't be doing any typing or clerical duties. I was meant to sit there all day making phone calls to the clients about their houses – and that was meant to be clerical work experience! So I just said 'no way'. There used to be a lot of Black girls but they just left eventually. They got fed up. It's just slave labour for £26 a week.

They expect you to act like adults but they treat you like kids. First of all, if you're coming straight from school these days they tell you you've got to join a YTS scheme, or you won't get paid. That means that most of the trainees are there because they have to be – it's like school, there's no difference. They shouldn't force you to do YTS, and if they expect you to gain work experience they should pay you the going rate for the job. I mean, a lot of us just end up making the tea and sweeping the floor and doing all the shit work that's going for £26 a week. And you see some of the other people who work there sitting around with their feet up saying, 'Do this, do that,' and telling you you shouldn't come in late or take two minutes longer on your tea break because you're meant to be learning what it's like to be a real worker. But at the end of it, there's no real work to go to, so it's all a big con. As far as I'm concerned, it's just their way of keeping us off the streets and fooling people into thinking that they are doing something positive about youth unemployment.

With unemployment rising almost as fast as the youth disaffection which it has helped to create, the future of young Black women coming off YTS appears bleak. Prepared at best for a short career of 'temporary sequential employment', they can look forward to a partial, erratic and increasingly de-skilled working life as cashiers and shelf-fillers in large supermarket chains or as low-grade, low-paid workers in the surviving industries. Relatively few can hope to gain access to certified vocational training courses in Further Education, such as nursery nursing, hairdressing, engineering or computing courses. Young

Black applicants who have the relevant qualifications are frequently turned down in favour of their white counterparts. Even nursing has become barred to all but a few of us, with the new requirement of several O levels for entry to SEN training.

But despite the apparently bleak prospects of training and employment, today's generation of young Black women are refusing to admit defeat. Many of them are rising up through the ranks of the unemployed to create their own job opportunities in the form of cooperatives and other forms of self-reliant work, proving their creativity and initiative as workers despite the odds which are stacked against them. Some have teamed up and formed catering, childcare, hairdressing and toy-making co-ops; others have fought to gain training in less traditional areas such as car mechanics and carpentry. A small but significant number have succeeded in qualifying in areas such as teaching and youth work, and others are working as computer operators and technicians. Whatever area they are working in, they are proof that their mothers' struggles over the past forty years have not been in vain. That obstinate refusal to bow down to the requirements of the economic system has left behind a rich tradition of militancy and dogged determination upon which today's young Black women can draw. The experiences of their working mothers and grandmothers have never been more relevant, not only for those who have overcome the odds but also for those who have never been granted the right to work. Our struggles within the workplace have confirmed that we are able to take on the system and win – even when we appear to be in a position of relative powerlessness. Young Black women, many of whom have no experience of paid employment themselves, have learnt this lesson from their mothers, aunts, grandmothers and older sisters. Consequently, they show no hesitation in challenging the State's right to discard them, even when the fact of their unemployment is the only tool they have to fight back with.

Black women came to this country because we wanted to work. We have made a lasting contribution to the British

56

economy and we have paid for it with our blood, our sweat and our tears. We worked hard and long so that our children would be assured of a better future, and we fought many a battle against racism and exploitation, to ensure that they would be spared a similar fate. Whatever the future holds and whatever the implications of the technological revolution, we have made it clear that we will settle for nothing less.

2
Learning to Resist: Black Women and Education

Black women cannot afford to look at our experience of Britain's education system merely from our perspective as women: this would be to over-simplify the realities we face in the classroom. For Black schoolgirls sexism has, it is true, played an insidious role in our lives. It has influenced our already limited career choices and has scarred our already tarnished self-image. But it is *racism* which has determined the schools we can attend and the quality of the education we receive in them. Consequently, this has been the most significant influence on our experience of school and society.

Like our relationship with the police or our treatment by the judicial system, education has been a crucial issue for the Black community, for it has highlighted the true nature of our relationship with the State. The education system's success can be measured directly in terms of Black children's failure within it. By institutionalising the prejudices and the undermining assumptions we face in our everyday lives, the schools have kept our children at the very bottom of the ladder of employability and laid the blame on us. The schools' ability to churn out cheap, unskilled factory fodder or 'multi-skilled' YTS trainees may have served the economic needs of this society; but it has not met the aspirations of a community which has always equated education with liberation from poverty.

For Black women, therefore, challenging the education system has been part of a wider struggle to defend the rights and interests of the Black community as a whole. For this reason, education struggles have been central to our political development. Caring for children has always been seen as 'women's work', and since we bear and rear the children, overseeing the institutionalised care provided by the schools – an extention of child-rearing – has also been seen as our responsibility. Many a Black mother has had to confront, challenge and counteract the second-class, no-hope provision we have been offered, either alone or with the support of friends and the wider community. Our response has often been direct and stormy as we reacted to the individual and institutionalised racism of teachers and to the racist assumptions of an inward-looking, Eurocentric curriculum.

So it is our consciousness as Black people, rather than as feminists, which has led us to take collective action against the education authorities. For us to campaign for non-sexist text-books or careers guidance, when the racism in those areas has already pre-determined what our daughters could do; or to demand their right to do motor mechanics or play football, when our sons could aspire to nothing else, would be a denial of reality. Nevertheless, the campaigns we have taken up as mothers, teachers and schoolgirls have been given added strength and direction by the experience we have brought to them as women.

Education has always been a burning issue for Black women. Viewed, in the aftermath of slavery, as virtually the only means for us and our children to escape the burden of poverty and exploitation, it was regarded in the Caribbean as a kind of liberation. Our families made enormous sacrifices to send us to school, even though they could often offer us only the most basic education.

59

There were women from the churches who set up schools and taught you. They were like Victorian schools, where things were beaten into you. I remember being frightened of the atmosphere, because it was one of awe of learning, that had to be taken seriously. I happened to read quite early and so the teacher used to give my grandmother magazines for me to read at home – even though I wasn't really interested in them. There was a real lack of material for kids at home. I don't remember having any books that you could say all the class got. We had exercise books, our multiplication tables, just the very basics. Anything else we got was from the teacher's mouth. My grandmother did a lot to keep up that atmosphere at home. She used to give my brother and I some very long recitations to learn – long poems, about four or five pages long. Attending school early helped us. It helped many of us to get a scholarship, and this was the most important thing – entry to a good secondary school. Otherwise our parents would have to pay, which was an impossible task. So the emphasis was on getting as much as we could from those early years. Even so, it was difficult getting primary education in Jamaica, because it wasn't universal at the time. It was hard. You had to be on the list for a long time. I remember my father having to try a number of schools in our area for me … there was a lot of anxiety about our education. Our parents never gave up, though. Whenever they could afford it, they used to arrange for us to have evening classes from the same teachers who taught us during the day. This was going on right up to the time we came to England.

Even when we left the Caribbean, this desire for an education remained with us. On arrival here, however, it was not seen as an issue of immediate concern because permanent settlement in Britain was not something we contemplated. Expecting an early return home to rear and educate our children, we made no demands on the British education system, for whom the isolated Black child posed no real challenge or threat.

Our hopes of a swift return, however, were not to be realised. Thus we resigned ourselves to the inevitability of a long stay and began to send for our children. The British education system made no effort to prepare for their arrival. Regarded as a temporary though unavoidable ill born of economic necessity, their growing presence in the schools in the early sixties was viewed with distateful complacency. Black children were nothing more than a short-term phenomenon, which would eventually disappear of its own accord. From the outset, the educationalists with their colonialist superiority regarded Black children as a privileged minority, who should be grateful for any education they got.

Consequently, the first Black schoolchildren to step into Britain's inner-city classrooms suffered traumas which were largely ignored. Yet for young children who had been uprooted to join mothers they could often barely remember and entire new families of brothers and sisters, the pressures were enormous – quite apart from the need to adapt to a whole new process of schooling.

> I'd been separated from my parents for six years and came here when I was ten with my two younger sisters. I was glad, in a way, to be coming here, because I had always associated my family in England with the nice things we didn't have, like food parcels with fresh soap and minty toothpaste inside! It was different when I arrived, though, especially in a family with four new additions, all under five. As the oldest, I had to do a lot of babyminding and nappy-changing. Added to this, I had what was seen as a funny way of talking – real Jamaican country! My uncle, who had acquired this thin layer of gentility and refinement since he'd come here, was sometimes heard to murmur: 'But mercy! Is 'ow de pickney chat so bad?' Of course, I was just speaking in my own natural way at home, but it carried into school, where sometimes they didn't seem to understand me at all.

What the educationalists flippantly dismissed as 'culture shock' was often a far more profound and traumatic experience. In most cases, schools were situated in the worst areas of the inner-cities – the only places where housing was available to us – presenting us with a seedy, depressing landscape and a totally unfamiliar environment. This physical hostility was compounded by a barrage of verbal, physical and psychological attacks on our sense of place and identity.

At the beginning of my first playtime at school, one of the more friendly white girls led me into the playground, where all the others crowded around me. Two boys started to call me 'Blackie' and 'golliwog'. This made me very upset. I remember taking my beret off my head and holding it up to my face and saying, 'Look, I'm not Black, this is!' When I told the teacher, she just said, 'Take no notice.' This sounded useless to me. How could I not take any notice? It was so hurtful. And it was the same with my parents, they just told me to ignore it too. I felt really depressed, especially since the name-calling grew steadily worse. Then they started to mock my accent, saying things like, 'What are you saying, golliwog?' and 'Speak English please.' School became a nightmare for me. They poked and pulled at me. 'Is your hair knitted then?' 'Do you live in trees?' When it got too much I ran home, but my parents seemed unable to understand what a torture school had become. 'Just do your work and don't pay anybody any mind' – but I couldn't.

Teachers and pupils alike displayed open curiosity, as they struggled to reconcile the images from a lifetime of racist conditioning with the reality they now saw in front of them.

I remember being constantly asked by the teachers and the children where I came from, what was it like, did I live in a house or a tree, did we wear clothes, did we speak English? You begin to feel so different, you feel uncomfortable, and because you are so young you don't know how to deal with it. The way I dealt with it was I decided I wasn't going to fight it. I gave in to whatever they said. Every day at school, we had to write a diary of what we did at home. I wrote that in Jamaica we lived in trees and ran around with whatever they told us we wore, and I even drew pictures. I think it got to the stage where I wasn't sure what was true anymore, the pictures they were showing me or the memories I had in my head.

This assault on our sense of identity, which we were rarely prepared for, made us vulnerable and isolated, as we struggled to find the language and gestures which could convey our response. It also singled out many Black parents as 'troublemakers', when they went into the schools and articulated this response on our behalf.

I remember my early schooldays as being a very unhappy time. People were watching you all the time, and if you did anything it wasn't because you were you, but because you were Black. There was a time when this teacher pulled me up in front of the class and said I was dirty and that she was going to make sure that my neck was cleaned – and she proceeded to do it, with Vim. My father is usually a quiet man, but he went up there with a machete.

When teachers not only failed to challenge the playground taunting, but frequently compounded racialist attitudes through their own ignorance, we were compelled, in many cases, to defend ourselves physically.

My memories of school are of being really laughed at and everyone calling me a golliwog. In my first three years, I was the only Black girl at school, and consequently I had fights with every single girl and some of the boys too, because of their racial taunting. It wasn't until I went to that school that I realised I was Black, as such. All my friends were white. I even wore bows in my hair, like they did. It wasn't until an Australian teacher called me a blackie that I realised. It was a terrible moment.

This cruel rejection of our children was something which Black mothers had to respond to. In some cases, hardened by similar daily experiences in the workplace, our response was clearly inadequate. What appeared to the children as a failure to understand the experience was often the bewildered or angry reaction of someone who found her own experiences of racism difficult to articulate. Nevertheless, many of us did find ways of supporting and reassuring our children, as they learnt to cope with the mental bruises.

> When I sent my daughter to school, I can remember her coming home one day and asking me why God had made her Black. That really hurt me. I asked her if she didn't like being Black, and she said no, she didn't, because she was the only Black child in her school. I told her God chose to make some of us Black and some of us white, and there's no difference between us. But still she didn't want me to plait her hair, I had to put it in a pony-tail all the time, otherwise she would cry, because all the other kids had their hair flowing down ... That made me aware that there was a lot of prejudice in the schools that was affecting the kids deeply.

The hurtful ignorance and implacable hostility of other children was probably the most common experience of the first generation of Black children to enter British schools. It is no surprise that we were viewed as oddities, given the colonialist diet on which our peers were still being fed. Our hair, habits, language and customs were seen as the manifestations of savagery, confirmation of our uncivilised past. Even to young children, and at a time when televisions were not a common feature of every working-class home, we represented the foreign hoardes which had been tamed and disciplined under flag and empire. Indeed, it was the attitude of the teachers which did the most lasting damage. They were to interpret Black children's disorientation and bewilderment as a sign of stupidity. Their concepts of us as simple-minded, happy folk, lacking in sophistication or sensitivity, became readily accepted definitions. Theories about us, put forward by Jensen in America and endorsed by Eysenck here in the late sixties, gave such views a spurious credibility by popularising the idea that race and intelligence are linked in some inherent way. The effect of this process was inevitable. Those of us who had lived in those 'foreign' places either built our own defences or leant to reject the lessons and teachers that presented our lives in such a derogatory way.

I didn't do Geography after the Third Form, but when I realised that the countries the teacher was talking about in that far-off, abstract way, were actually countries which Black people came from, Africa, the Caribbean etc., I realised that teachers didn't always speak the truth. It was so inaccurate, so biased, such a negative way of showing how we were meant to live, that I began to feel angry. But we didn't have a community, as such, in those days. There wasn't any way for our parents to get together to express their dissatisfaction. I just became more and more disheartened and frustrated with what was being presented to us at school.

Because of such reactions, we came to be labelled 'dull' and 'disruptive'. However, what appeared to teachers to be disinterest or unresponsiveness, was often our only way of responding as children to the negative school environment we had to enter daily. Those of us who had come to England with a joy for learning and a deep-seated respect for the value of education, often found our enthusiasm dampened by the arrogant, insidious assumptions of the school curriculum. In lessons and textbooks we were either ridiculed or ignored. Rarely, if ever, were we acknowledged in a positive way, on equal terms.

I had always liked reading, and could have really enjoyed literature at school. I suppose I liked the strange and different world I found in books, especially the ones about life as it was supposed to have been like in Britain. This couldn't last though, because reading often became a nasty, personal experience. You would be getting deep into a story and suddenly it would hit you – a reference to Black people as savages or something. It was so offensive. And so wounding. Sometimes you would sit in class and wait, all tensed up, for the next derogatory remark to come tripping off the teacher's tongue. Oh yes, it was a 'black' day today, or some kid had 'blackened' the school's reputation. It was there clearly, in Black and white, the school's ideology. The curriculum and the culture relies on those racist views.

Rigged scientific theories about race and intelligence combined with the cultural introversion of the school curriculum to ensure that those of us who went through school here in the sixties found it a negative and wounding experience. From the earliest Janet and John readers onwards, we found ourselves either conspicuous by our absence or depicted as a kind of joke humanity, to be ridiculed or pitied but never to be regarded as equals. Right across the curriculum and at every level, the schools' textbooks confirmed that Black people had no valid contribution to make to the society, other than to service its more menial requirements. Children were presented with a world view in which blackness represented everything that was ugly, uncivilised and underdeveloped, and our teachers made little effort to present us or our white classmates with an alternative view. Having been raised on the same basic diet of colonial bigotry themselves, they simply helped to make such negative stereotypes and misconceptions about us more credible. According to them, we 'could not speak English' and needed 'special' classes where our 'broken' version of the language could be drilled out of us. We were quiet *and* volatile. Best of all, we were good at sports – physical, non-thinking activities – an ability which was to be encouraged so that our increasing 'aggression' could be chanelled into more productive areas.

In the first form, they found out that I was good at sport. They had the Triple A's Award Scheme and I beat everyone. I became district champion for that year. Then they decided that I could win all the medals for them. But one day, during some special Sports event, I was talking to my friend and missed the race when they were calling me on to the track. It was horrible for me, after that. Because I'd missed the race, my teacher wouldn't have me back in his classes! I decided then and there that I'd had enough of running, but they never stopped trying to coax me back.

66

All I wanted to do was to become an air hostess, but the teachers said I wouldn't be able to do that because I wasn't clever enough. This hadn't seemed to bother them when I was missing classes to train, though. One teacher told me I would never amount to anything and would be better off cleaning the streets ... so I ended up leaving school without doing any exams. There was no one in school to give me any help and explain things to me, except when it was to do with sport.

Inevitably, the low expectations of teachers affected our performance in school. Our generally poor results in intelligence tests like the 11+ exam seemed to confirm their views. Throughout the sixties, this test was the greatest arbiter in our future, designed to select and grade the future workforce. Because of its class and cultural bias, we were bound to fail, as were the majority of working-class children. The consequence for us was relegation to the secondary moderns and later to the lowest streams of the comprehensives. The education authorities disregarded the fact that bad schools with poor resources and indifferent teachers had existed in the inner-cities long before our arrival and our presence became associated with the lowest educational standards. For most of us coming through that system, we were well on the road to ESN (educationally sub-normal) labels or dismal job prospects.

There were no chances or options offered to me. I would have liked to have stayed on at school, but I left in the fifth year. As far as I can remember, I only saw a Careers Officer once, a few weeks before leaving school. She didn't encourage us or offer any help in getting a decent job. I was fairly good at needlework, and because of this, dressmaking was the only line they were prepared to push me into. They never asked me if I wanted to do anything else. I didn't really want to just leave school and go and do piece-work in a factory, but that was it. Out. It's only when it was too late that I began to realise what had happened.

The undermining attitudes of careers officers were designed to make us believe in the myth that we had nothing to offer British society. Nevertheless, we had learnt from our mothers' experiences and knew our own value. So we rejected the careers which had been mapped out for us by the schools, determined not to follow our mothers' footsteps to the hospitals and the factories.

They never encouraged you or asked you what you would like to do when you leave school. I had always been made to feel that because I was Black, I was stupid and not good enough for much. You got that impression from TV as well – that we were just maids, butlers, servants in fact. My Careers Officer tried to send me to a factory interview. It was the best they felt they could do for someone with no 'O' levels. But I didn't turn up for the interview. Although I wasn't qualified, I didn't want a factory job.

In spite of all the obstacles, some of us managed to slip through the net. We struggled out of those low streams, from 1c to 2b to 3a. We stayed on in the sixth, despite pressures from all around to leave at sixteen and enter the job market. Our parents, anxious that we should escape the menial, low-paid work they had been forced to accept, urged us to seize any educational opportunity which came our way. Our aspirations were usually dismissed as over-ambitiousness by careers officers, who could hardly hide their scepticism when confronted with talk of 'A' levels, college or university for any Black pupils. But our earlier experiences of school in the Caribbean undoubtedly influenced our ability to survive in the classroom.

Having had a substantial part of my education back home, I felt grounded in my culture and quite confident about my abilities. I would not allow myself to be swayed by suggestions that we were inferior. Our parents had striven too hard for us in the Caribbean to instil pride and self-respect into us. The church also helped. Not just religious education, although that was there as well, but the teachers who came out of the church. They were often women – very strict but also very sure of themselves. With the family, they fostered an atmosphere of learning, of having certain goals and objectives to fulfil.

This atmosphere of learning – competitive, selective and frequently exclusive at secondary level to those who could afford it – had conditioned our tenacity. In the Caribbean, colonialism had left us with a school system which was designed to allow a small proportion of us to succeed. This was necessary after Independence in order to keep the State machinery running. Scholarships and university places, though few and far between, or a job in the civil or diplomatic service were carrots worth fighting for, and often presented the only opportunity for upward mobility. Shared books, over-zealous discipline and frustrated ambitions were considered the inevitable rules of the competition which we entered at an early age.

Once in England, many of us fought for credibility, adopting the same stubborn determination to make it through the education system, despite the odds. When we found our ambitions frustrated, not through lack of money or too fierce competition this time, but by the teachers and schools themselves, we signed up for evening classes and Further Education courses. Night cleaning, auxiliary nursing and factory work often financed the education which the schools had failed or refused to give us.

I used to get up at five in the morning and take the first bus into the West End to do cleaning in those big office blocks. There was a group of regulars who all used to travel on the same bus every morning. I got to know a lot about them because we all used to chat to pass the time. They were nearly all Black, with a couple of exceptions, either factory workers or cleaners like me. Some of them used to go straight from four hours cleaning to their full-time jobs. One woman worked in a canteen from ten till four and then she used to go home and look after the kids and her husband. So I used to think of myself as being really lucky, you know, because all I had to do was support myself through college.

The Black women of this generation who were able to acquire the skills and qualifications they had set out to gain, did so despite the discrimination and institutionalised racism we encountered in every area of our lives. Where we succeeded, we were projected as examples of the neutrality of the system, as token Blacks who had proven the exception to the rule. Although a few did succumb later to the perks which relative success can bring, many Black women, recognising how the system had been organised, went back into the schools as teachers, to wage an often solitary battle against the kind of racism which had made our own struggles necessary.

Many of the women teachers who did go back into the schools were to become involved in the Black education struggles of the seventies, inspired by the Black Power movement with its call for social justice and militant resistance by Black communities when under attack. This movement began in the States in the sixties, and its influence spread rapidly to Black communities everywhere. Alongside parents and other Black activists, we began to challenge some of the assumptions about Black children and to take up the battles to defend their rights in school.

It was our community's growing readiness to mobilise in support of our children which ensured that our anger or bewilderment as parents could be channelled into a collective response. Probably the most important early initiative was the ESN campaign, which was spearheaded by Black parents and teachers. Earlier bussing policies, designed to 'dilute' large concentrations of Black low achievement, had been successfully opposed in some areas. The response of the authorities was quietly to transfer large numbers of Black children into schools for the 'educationally sub-normal', under the guise of providing 'special' education for them. The by now familiar arguments about 'low IQ', 'broken English' and 'hyperactive behaviour' were once again put forward to justify the disproportionate number of Black children who were being classified ESN, some directly on arrival from the West Indies. The whole community, galvanised by Bernard Coard's exposé of 'How the West

Indian Child is Made Educationally Sub-Normal in the British Education System' began to challenge these arguments. Foremost among those who opposed ESN schooling were Black mothers.

At first I didn't realise what was going on because I really thought they were sending her to a 'special' school. The school sent me a letter telling me they were going to transfer her and that she'd get more attention, they never really spelt out what kind of school it was. But when I went up and visited, the penny dropped. As soon as I saw that most of the other kids there were Black, I knew something was going on. There was a lot of kids there who had nothing wrong with them, and as far as I was concerned my daughter was one of them. I mean, how can you reach ten years of age and still be learning your alphabet? I didn't know what to do, I was so angry. The only thing I could think of at the time was to give her as much extra help with her writing and sums at home as I could. But I went along to this meeting one Sunday and there were a lot of people there with kids in ESN schools who felt the same way. That's how they came to set up the Saturday school, because everyone was saying if the schools wouldn't educate our children, we should do it ourselves. My daughter really got a lot out of those sessions, because it wasn't just about reading and writing. They taught the kids about Black history and showed them that they had nothing to be ashamed of because Black people are as good as anyone else. It took me three years to get her back into the ordinary school, and I really had to fight to get them to accept her back. In the end, she left school with two CSEs because they said she'd missed too much to do any other exams. But after that she went to college, and passed five O levels.

It was our recognition of the need to challenge racist assumptions about the intelligence of our children which gave rise to Saturday and Supplementary Schools up and down the country.

We were concerned about the education our children were getting. The teachers expected nothing from them. We formed a group because we wanted to see how we could get a better deal for our children in the school system, and how we could make sure that all of us parents knew our basic rights. Some of the parents hadn't been in the country for long, so we had to make sure they understood what was happening to the Black children over here. We started running a school on Saturdays – it was too much to do it evenings as well – and we all worked as volunteers, contributing whatever time we could. I worked in the school for over a year, and what it did for me was to make me more aware, more conscious. The children did well in the school, and this tended to encourage other parents to come along. A lot of Black parents turned up to our meetings. We got all kinds of people to come along and talk to us – educational welfare officers, councillors, even the Social Security official. So we didn't just concentrate on the children's education, we organised meetings to educate Black parents as well. But the school was the main thing.

Embracing the message of self-reliant community responses to the community's needs, enthusiastic Black volunteers were recruited, many of whom were women, whose task was to teach Black history alongside maths and English. There were many acknowledged successes, as Black children who had been classified ESN went on to take 'O' and 'A' levels. Such activities raised a high level of awareness and debate within our communities and were largely responsible for the militancy which characterised the behaviour of many Black schoolchildren in the seventies.

By the mid-seventies increasing numbers of Black mothers had begun to demonstrate a readiness to defend the rights of our children, both in the form of individual confrontations with the authorities and within organised campaigns. The response of the State was to round on us. Sociologists blamed our inadequate 'broken' homes and the fact that we went out to work, instead of providing the secure environment and stimulation necessary for proper intellectual development. They overlooked our history, and the fact that we *had* to work to support our children. They disregarded how seriously we had always regarded the education of our children. They undermined the deep sense of responsibility which we felt towards our children, who were battling daily to retain a sense of identity and purpose with the system.

> They [the schools] were pretending to do so much for people's children, and in the end they were doing nothing. They mucked up my kids and other people's children too, with their false pretences. They gave those children nothing to aim for for the future. But like many West Indians, I thought the teachers knew best, because that is how it was at home.

As working Black mothers, we were spending large portions of our income on childminding arrangements, in order to work to support our children both here and in the Caribbean. We were being forced, regardless of our skills, into part-time and night work, because of the State's inadequate day-care provision. The work we were able to do, our standard of living and the very quality of our lives here were largely determined by our responsibilities to our children. Nevertheless, the educationalists, sociologists and psychologists pounced on theories about irresponsible, inadequate Black parents, for they provided such an easy scapegoat for what was, in reality, the failure of the schools.

But by the mid seventies a new generation of Black schoolgirls were coming through the system, who were very different to those who had entered school in the sixties from the Caribbean. A variety of factors had helped to form and mould this new breed. Most had been born or brought up here, and knew no other home. We were not so inclined to regard the schools through the less critical eyes of some of our parents or older brothers and sisters. More importantly, we were able to draw on the legacy of the Black Power era. For most of us, cultural pride was no longer a matter for discussion. We had been raised in an era when blackness had become a source of strength, and militant Black response a source of general inspiration. For young Black women, the visible signs of this new mood were apparent in the exchange of straightened hair for Afros, and the donning of 'Free Angela Davis' badges and Black berets. Many schools were antagonistic towards this outward show of Black consciousness and attempted, unsuccessfully, to repress it. As the influence of Black nationalism grew, so did the militancy of our response. In State schools, where we were in sufficient number, we took up the demand for Black Studies. Unfortunately, where we succeeded in getting it included in the curriculum, we soon learnt that this new dimension of knowledge was not sufficient in itself to counteract all the other negative forces which prevailed. Taught alongside the geography lesson, which depicted the 'developing' Third World as being totally dependent upon western generosity, and alongside the history lesson which concentrated on glorious white conquest, the value of Black Studies alone was always debatable. When the Black community realised that it was being used by some schools as a convenient means of social control, enabling 'non-examinable' Black pupils to be pacified and controlled, while white pupils got on with their 'O' levels and CSEs, the demand for Black Studies in schools became less audible.

> The teachers have their stereotyped views. They think that if they give you one lesson a week of Reggae, that's enough. That's meant to prove they're not racist. But it doesn't. They're the ones who need Black Studies, not us. It's for them to change their attitudes towards Black people, because I think people are racist in this country but they don't even know it because it's built into their culture and they don't even realise it.

The lessons we learnt from our experiences ensured that we were now prepared to question the attitudes and practices of our teachers in a far more pointed way. Our increased consciousness enabled us to articulate and expose the basis of their thinking and the logical outcome of their assumptions. Above all, we gained the confidence to resist them.

One time we were in the buffet and something or other happened which resulted in everyone of us who was Black having to go and see the Head. My friend Donna wasn't there when it happened, so she went mad when they said she had to go too. She wanted an apology, but they wouldn't apologise. Instead of trying to remember who was there, they just called all the Black girls and never even asked who was there and who wasn't.

Teachers, like others in the society, could not resist the influence of an hysterical media, obsessed with ideas about Black criminality. 'Mugging' had by now come to be seen as an exclusively Black crime, and the notion that our presence on the streets and in the schools was a threat to the British way of life was aired daily in TV and newspaper reports. When a rule was broken or a crime committed in the school playground, we were always the first to be accused:

Once some dinner money was stolen and it was said that a Black girl had taken it. There were no questions asked. We were furious. How could they just blame us? All of us Black girls got together and decided to stage a protest. Instead of going to classes, we staged a boycott. We went to the library and stayed there all day, instead of going to classes. After one day, the Head had to do something. Then the dinner lady admitted that she couldn't be sure that it had been a Black girl, and they apologised to us.

We had found the language with which to take on the racism of the school system, and the schools' inevitable response was one of paranoia. Teachers expressed this frequently, by dispersing us if we stood chatting in groups in the playground, because more than one of us was seen as a 'threat'. But increasingly we stood up to them, using the only forms of resistance available to us:

When I went to my last school, I noticed straight away that if they saw a group of Blacks together, they thought it spelt trouble. Typical. Black people together can start a riot. We were type-cast as the troublemakers. They used to get the male teachers to disperse us when we stood together in the corridors, chatting or eating our sweets. Sometimes we even got searched! One time, I was suspended in the fourth year for 'attempting to lead a rebellion'. Me and this white girl were trying to quieten the class down because we had a supply teacher for that lesson and they were all misbehaving. The Head came in and got the wrong end of the stick. The white girl wasn't suspended, though, and the reason they gave my mother was that I was already on report. But the white girl had been truanting for months.

Incidents such as these were, and still are, occurring daily. Trivial though they sometimes were, they proved that Black pupils had begun to question the whole basis of a system which encouraged racist practices, and which actively discouraged us from achieving our full potential. Increasingly, we came to view school as a pointless, punitive exercise. Reacting to a daily experience which was more about behavioural control than expansion of the mind, we quickly learnt school's only relevant lesson: that factory, health and service workers don't need 'O' levels.

Non-cooperation, disinterest, truancy, strikes and demonstrations were the ongoing response of many Black pupils throughout the seventies to an education which was increasingly seen as irrelevant. While our actions were not always a collective act of conscious resistance, they were nevertheless an expression of our growing disaffection with what the schools – and the society – had to offer us. However hard we studied, the most we could aspire to were a few CSEs, which even at Grade 1 came nowhere near the value of an 'O' level, as everybody knew. Countless Black pupils were shunted into CSE and non-exam classes, because our behaviour or attitudes were considered inappropriate for an 'O' level class. The fact that this behaviour was symptomatic of a deep-rooted dissatisfaction with the education system was neither acknowledged or investigated. Sport continued to be the only subject we were encouraged to excel in. But we knew that while we dissipated our 'aggression' on the track or in the gym, or languished in rows outside the headteacher's office, many of our less rebellious white classmates were able to pursue their exam classes in relative peace.

The response of the authorities to growing pupil unrest was to continue to lay the blame on us, the children, and our parents rather than admit to the possibility that the schools could be at fault. In individual terms, this resulted in arbitrary and often long-term suspensions, to which many a Black mother reacted with bewilderment, anger or bitterness.

When my daughter was twelve or thirteen, she got into a fight at school. I was at work when I received a phone call from the school saying that she had hit the teacher, then run out of the school and gone home. I couldn't believe it. But I went home and there she was. I thought I'd give her a good hiding after I'd got to the root of it. But to my surprise, the teachers didn't want to hear her side of the story. They weren't at all sympathetic and suspended her for the rest of the term, even though it seemed to me she'd been provoked. That really hurt me. I apologised to them and wanted to apologise to the teacher concerned, but they wouldn't allow me to see her. In the end, all I could do was cooperate as best I could. They said they weren't sure they would have her back the next term because they couldn't handle her. I didn't even know she had any behaviour problems, but the next thing I knew they referred her for psychiatric treatment and to another school in the area. At the centre where they interviewed her, they seemed to think that because we were a one-parent family, there would be problems at home. But she didn't have any, as far as I knew. They simply said she was a bully, and expelled her. That's how I got involved in the United Black Women's Action Group, because I didn't know who to turn to for help.

It was the Black community's angry response to the disproportionately high number of Black children who were suspended, which was responsible for the decision of some local education authorities, in the late seventies, to introduce disruptive units into their schools. These units enabled local education authorities both to hide embarrassing suspension figures from public scrutiny – containing 'the problem' within the education system – and to maintain their liberal facade. They were able to express concern about the recruitment of white schoolchildren to organisations of the extreme right, such as the National Front, and to shed public tears about the low level of Black achievement in schools, while doing little to confront their own malpractice. Black mothers played a leading role in the campaign against the 'Sin Bins' and were successful, in some areas, in getting the authorities to reverse their policy of segregating those of us whom they could not educate.

After going along to the first Black women's conference in 1979, where education dominated the discussion, our group decided to hold a public meeting on what was happening to our kids locally in the schools. At that meeting, everyone was talking about how many Black kids were getting suspended or leaving school without any qualifications, and so we set up the Haringey Black Pressure Group on Education to see if we could take up some of these isues with the education office. Quite a few of the women in our group were involved, plus some local parents, teachers and youths. One of the first campaigns we set up was against the 'Sin Bins'. Haringey had decided, without any consultation with the parents, that they were going to set up disruptive units in all the schools, and from the documents we saw, it looked as if the pilot units were going to be in the schools where the Black kids are concentrated, in Wood Green and Tottenham. We knew they would cater mainly for Black kids, whatever school they were in, because our kids were the ones who they were throwing out all the time, for all kinds of petty reasons. One of the schools had circulated a kind of blueprint to all their teachers about this unit they were planning, and we managed to get hold of a copy. It was incredible. In one bit, it talked about how to identify a disruptive pupil, and actually listed things like nail-biting and desk-drumming as the signs to look for! Anyway, we went to the school and handed out leaflets to the children to take home to their parents. They got really alarmed by that. They called the police on us and there was even talk of suing us for libel, because of what we'd said in the handout. But in the end we got them to change their minds.

In those areas where relegation to the educational dumping grounds was not challenged, disruptive units and special schools have taken over where ESN schools left off. The same low-level remedial work, social and life skills training and dubious behaviour modification programmes ensure that they provide no meaningful preparation for life, other than for the worst jobs and the dole queues. For Black schoolgirls in such units, the experience has often been little more than an exercise in containment and control.

They put me in the disruptive unit when I was in the third year. It was a place called 'the Centre'. We didn't do any work. The teacher said I was to come to the Centre instead of the classes I didn't get on with. I was given a file with my name on it and had to write 'My Personal File' on it. Then she told me to write down anything personal in it. She used to take me into a room once a week and ask me if my parents were beating me, those sorts of questions. I never answered them, because I knew that whatever I said would get twisted around. Most of the time in the unit you played a game called Sorry Lawrence. I thought it was great, at the time. They didn't help any of the children who got behind in their work, though. They treated us as if we were mentally handicapped. There were some ESN people there, too. They let you get away with everything. I used to go in there and she used to say, 'Take your coat off', and I'd say, 'No, it's too chilly'. I gave her hell for two weeks.

The more liberal response to this kind of widespread disaffection was to call for the multi-cultural curriculum to be introduced into schools. For the first time, the grievances which we had been voicing for years began to gain some credibility. A small but significant number of teachers joined forces in organisations like NAME (National Association for Multi-Racial Education) to present a critical analysis of teaching materials and practices in multi-racial schools. However, their emphasis on cultural differences, rather than on the real issue of racism, diffused their initiative. Patties and steel-bands may have lent the school Open Day a multi-cultural atmosphere, but they presented no serious challenge to the numbers of Black pupils relegated to non-exam classes in the fourth year. Multi-culturalism enabled many schools to appear to be responding to our needs, while in reality it simply served as another form of subtle social control. How many dub poems, for example, were really introduced into the classroom as a serious exercise in widening critical faculties; how many more as an easy answer to boredom and disobedience? The concerns of a few teachers ultimately made it possible for the liberalism and defeatism of many others to masquerade as care and concern.

> There is a kind of racism which you have to be really sensible to realise. For example, you would think that teachers were being really nice to you if they told you they didn't mind whether you came back to the lesson after break. But they didn't mind and they didn't come and check on you because they didn't care. As far as they were concerned, they didn't expect anything of you because you were Black, so it was easier on them if you stayed away from their class.

There can be few more subtle ways of ensuring failure than to surrender all responsibility for guidance. Through this action, teachers effectively allowed almost an entire generation to leave school illiterate, innumerate and with few of the skills necessary for critical thought.

Today, public tears about Black under-achievement and lipservice to the multi-cultural ethic ring very hollow in our ears. The drastic effects of cuts in education spending, school closures and staff redundancies have hit our community particularly hard, and no amount of ethnic advisors and record-keeping can begin to counter them. As Black mothers, we have been directly affected by huge increases in the price of school meals, the scrapping of school dinners and free school milk, and the withdrawal of subsidised travel to school. As pupils, we have found ourselves in schools with even fewer resources. Too few teachers and textbooks and overcrowded classrooms are nothing new to us, of course. But as the education cuts take their toll, an already inadequate provision is declining even further. These cuts have coincided, quite predictably, with a steady rise in unemployment and their effects can be seen clearly as each successive generation of Black schoolleavers joins the end of the growing dole queues.

For many Black girls leaving school with minimal qualifications, the current prospects appear limited. In areas of high youth unemployment, the only immediate option is the Youth Training Scheme. The racist hierarchy and the narrow sexist bias of such schemes have simply compounded the attitudes which already exist in the schools and careers offices. Low level clerical work, catering and childcare command a lead as the most common YTS courses on offer to Black girls, and often the opportunity to attend college on day release is the only redeeming feature of an otherwise unrewarding year. However, thirty-six days on a Welfare Assistants' course cannot hope to compete with an NNEB, and Black trainees know this. The Black schoolgirls who leave school to enter such exploitative non-unionised training schemes frequently find that at the end of the year their long-term employment prospects are no better. Half-learnt skills and maybe a few weeks of work experience cannot make up for the failure of the schools to give us the education and training we need, if we are to compete in a racist, sexist and rapidly shrinking job-market.

Thus, in just over twenty years the British education system has succeeded only in entrenching our position at the bottom of the ladder of employability. And with mass unemployment threatening to become a permanent feature of society, we have once again been compelled to rely on our own resources as we struggle to break out of the poverty

81

trap. Given the failure of the schools to prepare us for skilled employment, night classes and adult education courses have become one of the few remaining escape routes. But a few hours of study a week, fitted around our children and domestic responsibilities, can make this a painfully slow process – particularly if we are hampered by a lack of basic literacy and numeracy skills:

I went back into education because I felt it was high time I got some qualifications. I was almost illiterate when I left school, and I resented the way society was treating me. Even before people realised I couldn't read, they were ready to walk all over me. At first I was very frightened. I had no confidence. I thought it was going to be like school, going through the same kind of miseries I had been through all my school life. But after about six months, I began to feel better because it was a different experience altogether. At school, no one bothered about me. I wasn't even put into a remedial class, they just left me sitting there at the back of the classroom and I couldn't follow most of what was going on. That's why I started truanting, I just couldn't cope with it. The little I learnt to read, I learnt by accident. Since I've been back to college though, I feel good within myself. I've learnt a lot and I enjoy what I'm learning. I'm taking a couple of 'O' levels at the end of the year, and even though I'm not over-confident about passing them, I still feel good about doing them, because there was a time not so long ago, when I'd never have thought myself capable of studying. I suppose in a way I'm starting all over again, from the beginning. I'm only twenty-two, so I've got the time.

Returning to study has not been easy, but the large number of Black women of all ages who have chosen to do so attests to the fact that we are still refusing to be deterred by our lack of qualifications, the demands of our families and other pressures. Taking advantage of recent policies of 'positive discrimination' in favour of ethnic minorities and women, some of us have been able to seize opportunities which never existed before to improve our qualifications or secure a profession. But the vast majority of us have had to achieve this without the aid of such dubious policies, making our way through the system with dogged determination and fighting for our credibility on the way.

I went back to college because I wasn't qualified to do anything. I was fed up with the factory jobs and I wanted something better. The other Black women on the course had come for the same reasons – to widen their opportunities by gaining some qualifications. All of us had high expectations.

In many ways, these needs weren't met. I don't think they made it clear that we couldn't just come in and do a year and end up qualified to work as secretaries or hairdressers or whatever. But this is what we'd expected. Plus we all had problems of our own. We weren't used to studying. I, for one, had really bad housing problems at the time. There were a mountain of problems, really. Anyway, after eighteen months I felt as if I still wasn't qualified for anything, so I applied to do the NNEB course. I hadn't come to college originally intending to do Nursery Nursing, but it seemed like a good qualification, and I'd already got the experience of bringing up my own children.

Well, now I'm on this course, and I still have some real doubts about it. They sap a lot of your self-confidence. A lot of the time, I don't know what I'm doing there. You feel as if you're on the front line all the time. You're always expected to be on your best behaviour, and you have to be on your guard all the time. On the college-based part of the course, you're continuously assessed, which puts you under a lot of pressure. And you have to remember to be polite to the staff and show the right attitude. Play the game, in other words. They mustn't be made to feel uneasy. None of this is ever said, but you know that these are the rules.

On placement, now, it's even worse. There are a load of crankly old self-opinionated biddies with half-dead ideas. They feel threatened by the students, and even more so by the Black ones. They try to belittle you, it's like a war, a power-struggle. I know these are terrible things to say about a course which is meant to build up your confidence, but that's what it's like. Anyway, I'm going to try not to fail, even though I know the nurseries only take in a few Black students who qualify. The NNEB is a white course, although a lot of young Black girls want to do it. Because of that, it looks bad if you're Black and you're having problems. But when they say things like, 'Your English is letting you down', you know what they're getting at. If you're saying something and the teacher keeps on saying, 'Pardon? pardon?', as though you're talking double Dutch, that's bound to sap your confidence, isn't it?

The course isn't all bad, though. It's given me some really positive help as a parent, whether or not I qualify. I know now how these people think, and I also know *what* they think. Once I went to my youngest daughter's school, when she'd just started, and asked how she was settling in. The teacher looked at me really sharply, as thought she hadn't expected me to ask something like that. Another time, I asked the PE teacher about my son's hand–eye co-ordination, because the teacher had made a complaint. You could see him wondering how this Black woman could know about hand–eye co-ordination. Black parents are supposed to be ignorant in their eyes. But I'm not. So I can watch what they're doing to my children in school and work out how to correct it myself.

So learning how to take the system on as my kids go through it has been one of the most positive benefits from doing this course. Even so, I haven't done as well as I should have, and I know it. Courses like this aren't designed for people who have kids or who aren't straight out of school. And they're not really aimed at Black people. So where we are concerned it's a case of either fit in or drop out.

Return to Study and 'Access' courses have gone some way to confront the kinds of difficulties we have faced over the years on traditional courses, by offering us a route into further and higher education which by-passes the more formal stages of progression. Nevertheless, we have had to struggle just as hard to meet the required standards, and the notion that 'positive discrimination' makes things easier for us is a fallacy. Because of the general failure of colleges and adult education to prioritise the needs of women with childcare or domestic responsibilities, equal opportunities policies have fallen far short of their potential to give Black women a meaningful opening into training or employment. Quite apart from the adjustments necessary on returning to study after several years, the attitude of white teachers, like their training, has not changed. And childcare still remains our most impeding obstacle, particularly if we are bringing up our children alone:

> The reason I decided to do the General Education course was because I couldn't stand it being stuck at home anymore. I haven't worked since I had my children and my mind was vegetating. The only time I spoke to anyone, apart from my immediate family and friends, was in Tescos and the only writing I ever did was the shopping list. I was getting so depressed living from hand to mouth on social security.
>
> The course I did had a creche which meant I could leave my children there when I went to classes. None of us who were on that course would have been able to go to college if there hadn't been childcare provided. Out of fifteen of us on the course, twelve of us were Black women and every one of us was there because we wanted to improve our chances of getting a job. When I started, I thought there were things I would never be able to do, like maths, and my idea was to concentrate on the typing and my English. But after about a term, I began to feel a lot more confident about my own abilities, and that made me see the other subjects differently. I realised I didn't have to stop at RSA Typing because there are other things in life that I can do, if I put my mind to it. I suppose this was because I woke up to the fact that it wasn't just me who

was in that boat. All the women on that course were struggling to bring up their kids and to make a life for themselves, and I figured we couldn't all be failures. There has to be something wrong with the system, because all of us were facing the same kind of problems.

I wouldn't say that going back to college was easy for any of us, particularly for those of us who were single parents. Every time the kids got sick, you had to miss classes. Once I had to wait in for the Council to come and do some repairs and I missed about two weeks of college because they kept saying they were coming and then not showing up. And the most difficult thing of all was the studying – I mean, the only time I ever got to do any reading or homework was at about ten o'clock at night, after the kids were in bed, and it wasn't as if I could just sit down and write an essay just like that, because I hadn't done anything like that for years. It took ages before I got the hang of how to organise myself and my work so that I could stay on top of it. But now I know what I am capable of, and I don't think I could ever go back to the kind of life I was leading before. For a start, I could never really be bored again now that I've started reading and taking an interest in what's going on in the world.

The most difficult thing of all is finding a way of carrying on with my studies. They make a lot of fuss about equal opportunities for women, but you try finding a college with a nursery – they are really few and far between. Plus, there's the problem of the money. They don't exactly hand out the grants these days, and you can't get social security if you're doing a full-time course. But even so, now that I've seen a way of getting out of that rut, I'm determined to do it. Even if it takes me the next ten years, I'm going to train, I'm going to qualify and I'm going to do something with my life that's worthwhile.

It is because of our own efforts and our determination to overcome the odds against us that we are no longer such an isolated rarity in professions such as teaching, but we still have a long way to go before we are properly represented in the schools. Despite the recent spate of 'ethnic' posts, products of the new growth industry in ethnic minority welfare, we are still vested with none of the power to make the changes and formulate the radical policies which are needed, if our presence is to have any impact. We are frequently given responsibility for the behaviour and monitoring of Black pupils in 'problem' schools, where attempts are made by the all-white management to exploit our knowledge of our own community to its detriment. For those Black teachers who do push for meaningful and lasting changes, the likelihood is that we will be labelled 'subversive' by our employers and the white parents, who see us as a threat to the status quo. And those who don't, risk permanent isolation from their own Black community, who regard them as having 'sold out'. Given such a choice, Black women have tended to go into the schools prepared to do battle with the system, demonstrating that our desire for economic success or status will always come second to our concern for the collective welfare of our children and our community.

Probably the most hopeful and lasting result of our struggle to gain access to further education – and one which augurs well for the future – has been the opportunity we have had to re-examine critically our experience of school. Taking part in the education process again, as mature women, has enabled us to gain a far better understanding of the impact our schooling has made on our lives, and its likely impact on our children. Courses which have offered us access to the professions or training in non-traditional vocations such as plumbing and carpentry have had a liberating influence on what many of us felt we could do and achieve. And whatever the level or the eventual goals of such courses, they have highlighted for us the individual and collective intervention which is possible in areas such as education.

It's only since I've been at college that I've realised what it was all about at school. I didn't know before, but now I do. It makes me feel as if I could go right back to the beginning and start all over again ... I never made the connection between learning and having a good job; you get married and have a family. You get this idea from school and from society, even though for most Black girls work always comes into it, whether or not you're married. I think it's outdated to think that way, and I fought it all along. I always felt as if I didn't have the brains because I thought women were stupid before. Now I'm beginning to think very differently.

The opportunities for developing this new awareness are clearly influenced by the kinds of courses available to us and how accessible they are. Our already limited access to further education is placed under constant threat by government economic policies, and since significant numbers of skilled and qualified Black women are hardly desirable in a climate of mass unemployment, such courses are particularly vulnerable. However, the very fact that Black women are still fighting, despite the obstacles and the sacrifices involved, to gain a valid education bears witness to the crucial importance education continues to play in our lives. Our struggles, after years of second-class schooling, confirm that we have not given up and that no amount of racism and discrimination can deter us, now that we've come this far. This refusal to give in and accept the confines of our race, class and sex has been the single most important factor of our survival in Britain.

3

The Uncaring Arm of the State: Black Women, Health and the Welfare Services

When Black women began arriving in Britain after the Second World War to provide the newly-established National Health Service with much-needed labour, we came into a service which regarded us not as potential clients but as workers. Our role was to become the nurses, cleaners and cooks who would supply and maintain the service for others. From the very beginning, the NHS had one purpose – to replenish this country's labour supply with fit, white, male workers. Six years of war and devastation had led to a renewed popular demand for 'homes fit for heroes', and this demand could not be ignored, particularly by a Labour government keen to establish itself as the champion of the working classes. The creation of the NHS enabled the needs of capitalism to be reconciled, albeit temporarily, with the demands of the people, and the import of Black women's labour was the convenient short-term means by which this goal would be achieved.

Since we were never identified as potential consumers of the service, our health needs did not enter the debate about the kind of health provision the country would establish. The NHS was geared, first and foremost, to meeting the needs of the white man as economic producer and – to a lesser extent – those of the white woman, as re-producer. These priorities have remained enshrined within the NHS ever since. They are reflected in every facet of the service, from the allocation of its resources to the structure of its workforce. As such, our treatment within the NHS is probably the most clear and damning indictment of our social and economic value to Britain.

When we approach the Health Service, as clients, we are confronted with a set-up which is both directed and controlled by white, middle-class men. This means that we can expect to face a barrage of assumptions about our race, class and sex by a profession which has no interest in the maintenance of our good health, and little genuine insight into the factors in our lives which cause us to fall ill. Yet because we are women, the Heath Service is central to our lives. We cannot avoid using it. It is us who bear the brunt of the responsibility for our own and our families' health, and we have little choice but to deal with whatever alienation and abuse we happen to encounter. With sick children, elderly relatives, and the general needs of the entire family falling squarely on our shoulders – quite apart from our many specific health needs as women – it is little wonder that we frequent the hospitals, clinics and doctors' surgeries in such disproportionate numbers. Because we are working-class women, we have no access to the growing number of private or natural alternatives, so favoured by those with the financial resources to go elsewhere. But above all, because we are *Black* women, whether we seek treatment within or outside the NHS, we invariably find ourselves dealing with a profession which is fundamentally patriarchal and racist.

It is in this context that any assessment of our health in Britain has to be placed. Race, class and sex have combined to ensure that not only can we expect to fall ill more often, but in our quest for treatment, we can expect to suffer physical, cultural and social alienation with nearly every encounter. Moreover, now that the technological revolution and world recession have made capitalism's need for fit, white male workers less and less pressing, neither the NHS nor our labour are needed anymore. Black women's health is therefore at the very bottom of an ever-diminishing list of national health priorities.

Hard Labour: How Employment and Unemployment affect our Health

Good health is not merely the absence of illness and disease; it is a state of complete physical, mental and social well-being. Whether we are healthy, therefore, is determined almost exclusively by our working conditions, the standard of our housing, our access to health and welfare services and the treatment we receive from them.

Black women have for years tolerated the lowest-paid jobs and the least satisfactory working conditions. Profits have always come before the health of employees, but there is no denying that we Black women have to deal with a disproportionately high share of health hazards at work. Even within the health industry, we face short-term risks and long-term dangers to our physical and mental well-being as a direct consequence of the work that we do there:

I've worked nights on the wards for years and it really does put a strain on you, there's no question about it. You get a lot of nurses and auxiliaries who suffer from the stress-related illnesses – hypertension, heart trouble, kidney problems, high blood pressure – you name it, they all come from those broken sleep patterns from working the night shift. You can't just go home and go to sleep during the day if you've got kids. When you come in from work, you've got to get them ready for school, do the shopping, do the housework, do the washing, and by the time you've finished it's three o'clock and time to collect them from school again, so you just don't get any rest. Sometimes you'll go seven nights and days with no more than about five hours of unbroken sleep. And with me, I live in flats where everyone else is up and about during the day, so most of the time it's too noisy anyway. What happens is you just adjust in time to getting less sleep than

91

everyone else, but over the years, that takes its toll. I used to know one woman who worked four nights a week as an agency nurse, and on her nights off, she worked days! I suppose she needed the money, like everyone else, but it really put years on her. Another thing you get among nurses is a lot of back troubles. What happens is you often find that there's only two of us on duty for the night, so if a patient has to be moved or lifted, we just have to manage it between us. If you're on a medical ward or they've put you on geriatric, sometimes you'll get a patient of about fifteen stone – or maybe someone who's senile and has thrown themselves out of the bed. And when one of you has gone on her break, and this happens, what do you do in a situation like that? Oh, you can refuse to do it, but it's more than your job is worth. As far as they're concerned, once you're a nurse you're meant to put the patient first, and if that means damaging yourself in the process, it doesn't matter, you just get on with it.

Outside the NHS, the situation is no better. The effects of long hours, shift work and the frequent need to hold down more than one job in order to support ourselves and our families are made worse by the particular risks associated with the kinds of jobs we do. As homeworkers, machinists and workers in garment and light-engineering factories, we suffer from impaired eyesight or cataracts as a result of having to perform close eye-work for years on end. In non-unionised factories and sweatshops, where Health and Safety Regulations are often non-existent, we regularly find ourselves exposed to dangerous substances and required to heave heavy equipment. Because we have had to accept jobs with poor conditions of service, we often have to work through periods of sickness or pregnancy, for fear of finding ourselves jobless. Today, many of the ailments which are increasingly prevalent among older Black women such as strokes, arthritis and rheumatism can be traced directly to the stressful, hazardous working conditions we have faced throughout our lives.

The very first job I had was at a factory, far away from the

92

place I was living. The wages was about £6 a week, and I worked from eight in the morning to six at night, six days a week. There were quite a few Black women working there and they gave us the worst jobs to do. The factory made rubber goods, and I had to put my hands into hot and cold water all day, feeding the machine with the rubber. The product came out at the other end. That was when I began to get terrible pains in my arms. I only stayed there for six months, because I was pregnant at the time, and I had to leave to have the baby. It was getting too much for me, because the factory wasn't very near to the station, and I had to run to catch the train. After I'd had the baby, I got a job in another factory – a jam factory. I suppose I was naive, but I was quite shocked to see that the women were expected to lift heavy boxes and other equipment, just like the men. I used to get home at night feeling exhausted, and I didn't know what to do with myself, my arms used to ache so much.

Conditions such as these have all had their effect on working Black women, particularly since we do a 'double day', combining the demands of our jobs with the demands of running a home and raising a family. This means high levels of stress and anxiety in our working *and* our domestic lives; we are constantly under pressure. In health terms, the result is that we are more likely to suffer from heart attacks, strokes and hypertension than any other group in this society.

So despite our years of hard labour for Britain, as we approach old age, we cannot expect to reap many of the rewards. The number of elderly Black women is growing daily, and although we tend to live longer than men, our chances of escaping the consequences of a lifetime of stress and hard work are slim. Our problems are often compounded by the fact that we may not have worked here long enough to qualify for a full state pension, meaning that our income is likely to be less than that of the poorest white pensioner. Even our chances of being pensioned off are greater than for most. In the present climate of factory and hospital closures,

Black women are the first to be made redundant, and if this happens in our forties or fifties, the likelihood of us finding alternative work is very remote, particularly when the physical consequences of a lifetime of hard work are beginning to take their toll:

I worked as a cleaner on the wards for over twenty years, but that didn't stop them making me redundant when they had to make staff cuts. I did try to find another cleaning job, but with my health as it is, I couldn't find no one to employ me, not even for a couple of hours a day. I went to the DHSS and told them I was unemployed and they gave me a pension book, even though strictly-speaking I'm not of retirement age yet.

When they told me I was not entitled to the full pension, because I haven't worked for thirty years I couldn't believe it. I came to this country when I was still a young woman, and I've worked all my life – just to be told I'm not entitled to a full pension. When they asked me if I had any savings I told them how much I had put aside and they said I would have to use my savings up before I could apply for any assistance. That money I had was from working and saving all my life, and I was hoping to use it to go home for a visit. I've not been back in twenty-five years. A lot of my friends is going back now, though. There's nothing for you here, once you're too old to work. I'd probably go, too, if I could get the drugs I need but I've heard too many people talking about how hard it is to get drugs in Jamaica. It doesn't matter whether you've got diabetes or blood pressure or what it is, you just have to manage without them. Even so, a lot of people who is my age is talking about going home to live out their old age.

In a situation where the possibility of redundancy and permanent joblessness is higher for Black women than for any other group, the effects of social redundancy are not confined to the elderly. Today, growing numbers of young Black women are also effectively denied the opportunity of ever working. We therefore find ourselves trapped within a cycle of poverty, at the mercy of the State and increasingly, it is the State which decides where, how and on how much we live. Despite the prevailing stereotypes so favoured by smug Tory politicians which imply that we have an easy life on the dole, the physical and mental effects of the stresses and frustrations of a life on welfare are for us, only too real.

Perhaps the single most important influence on our health and sanity, particularly for those of us who are unemployed, is the kind of housing we have access to. The cumulated effects of twenty-five years of racist housing policies have ensured that growing numbers of Black women are imprisoned on the upper floors of dilapidated tower blocks in every inner-city, with little hope of escape. If our white neighbours harass us, or if our men abuse us, we often have no choice but to leave, exposing ourselves and our children to the traumas of homelessness.

I had been living on this particular estate for eight years, but I really needed a transfer. First of all, the place was too small and in addition to that, things were getting really bad with the man I was living with. So I had to get out. After I'd had my daughter in 1976, I decided to try to get a transfer. To this day, I doubt that my transfer papers have reached the Town Hall. By this time, the domestic situation I was in had become unbearable, and I was forced to leave. I walked out with a bag for me and some clothes for the kids, and the same night I went down to the Town Hall and explained the situation I was in to them. I was in tears. The put us in a bed and breakfast the same night.

The bed and breakfast was pretty bad. The facilities were inadequate, it was dirty, and there was no privacy. People were coming in and out all the time, because the place was really for people in transit. They didn't serve breakfast until eight o'clock – and then *only* at eight o'clock – which was really difficult for me, because I had to be at work by eight. Because of the journey, my children had to leave well before breakfast time, so it cost me a lot of money in food and fares. They didn't have cooked food for ages.

95

My case dragged on for months. During the whole of this time, I was in that bed and breakfast. They made me a few offers of accommodation, but all of them were uninhabitable. The first two, I remember, were just lousy. The front doors were broken, the gas heaters had been pulled out and just thrown on the floor, the inside doors weren't on their hinges, there was rubbish all over the passageway, and all the wiring had been pulled out to prevent squatters from using the place. Anyway, I turned them down and stuck it out. I knew what kind of home I wanted for my kids, and I knew that it existed.

They can't leave you on the streets, but they sure make you go through hell to get a decent place. You have to go through all the miseries of being in bed and breakfast, so by the time they make you an offer you'll be so fed up you'll take anything. I was determined not to let this happen to me, but you have to be strong. People who have been in a situation like mine, who have been on the council list for nearly a decade, are entitled to better treatment.

In all, it took me two years to get a suitable place to live. I never thought I'd be able to put up with such dreadful conditions for so long, but at least I always believed there'd be an end to it. If the council had won, I'd have been stuck in those conditions for the rest of my life.

If we are bringing up young children alone or lack the resources to move, the effect of poor housing conditions on our health is often drastic. The mental hospitals and coroners' courts receive more than their fair share of Black women, driven there by the despair and isolation of life in bed and breakfast hostels for the homeless or in the high-rise ghetto of the tower block estate. Even if we manage to retain our sanity in the face of such odds, we are still exposed to all the dangers, known and unknown, of substandard council accommodation: exposure to damp, overcrowded, insanitary conditions and the ever-present risk of fire and domestic accidents. Inadequate State benefits include no provision for repairs and renovation of our homes, nor do they take account of the exorbitant cost of staying warm. In the winter, as the cold sets in we resort to buying cheap paraffin heaters, because we cannot afford the heating bills, increasing the risk of house fires and of illnesses such as bronchitis. The high cost of house repairs and the councils' reluctance to carry them out means that dangerous fixtures don't get fixed, increasing the danger of accidents to ourselves and our children, as this story illustrates in *The Voice* (25.2.84):

Council tell slashed boy's mum – 'It could happen again'

A twelve-year-old Black boy was recovering in hospital in Solihull last week, after his face was slashed by flying glass falling from a tower block window which had just been repaired.

Kenneth Gregory was playing with his friend, Stephen Hutton outside their Oriel House tower block in Chelmsley Wood when the pane collapsed from the kitchen window of Stephen's parents' seventh-floor flat.

He was rushed to Wordsley Hospital in Stourbridge where he had a four hour operation at the plastic surgery unit.

His mother, Petra Grant said, 'He is in good spirits but he wants to come home. He is a very brave lad. I'm so proud of him.'

Stephen's mother, Mrs Betty Hutton said she had been complaining to Solihull Council for about five years. She said, 'Stephen fainted when the accident happened and he is now having nightmares. I am frightened to death about the window.'

Although Solihull council housing officials have launched an urgent investigation into the accident, they warned that the same thing could happen again.

Mr Barry Hosker, Director of Housing said, 'Stronger window frames are being fitted in those places where a danger had been identified but I am not sure whether they would be strong enough.'

The possibility of racist attack, which is ever-present, only adds to our sense of anxiety and alienation, particularly since the police will rarely admit to any racial motive and frequently fail to come to our assistance, if called. It is only recently, in response to their exposure by Watchdog groups and Independent Police Committees that the police have even begun to acknowledge that we, too, are the victims of crime. We have always been regarded by them as the perpetrators. Only elderly white ladies, it seems, get mugged, burgled or attacked; but these two reports in *The Voice* (25.2.84 and 31.3.84) tell a different story:

THUGS SMASH MUM'S HOME

A young mother was called home to find her flat totally ransacked by a gang of mindless thugs.

They smashed down the front door, sprayed the walls with racist slogans, slashed her furniture and clothes and poured bleach all over the carpet.

The victim, Patricia Lawrence, 21, of Westone Mansions, Uphey Lane, Barking was at work in a London bank and her two-year-old son Keith was with a baby minder when the attack took place.

She returned home after neighbours who saw the attack called the police.

Still suffering from shock, Ms Lawrence said, 'It is horrible, it's like a madman went through the house. I can't think about it. I don't know why anyone should do this to me.'

Ms Lawrence has lived in fear of the vicious gang who have made her life hell. She had been receiving threatening letters and horrifying phone calls since she moved into the flat.

The worried Patricia explained, 'I have had threatening letters, weird phone calls and a fortnight ago a tape of a baby crying was played over the phone, I am terrified.'

Det Con Tom Rayner of Barking CID said, 'This was an unprovoked racial attack.'

Barking housing department have since rehoused Ms Lawrence and her son.

Mum victimised by racist vandals
Recent racist attacks on a young mother living on the Mayville Estate in Stoke Newington, London, have brought widespread condemnation and support from angry neighbours and local police.

The unnamed woman, who lives in Campion House on the estate with her seven year-old daughter, has been subjected to abusive phone calls and excreta through her letter box.

'She is a very nice woman,' said Myrtle Keen, chairwoman of the tenants association. 'This has made us very angry. We have always been very proud of relationships on this estate, so we can't make this out. We think it's a very serious case.'

Councillor Talal Karim, chairman of Islington Councils race relations committee, said:

'We deplore these attacks. Racism must be stamped out. The council and the police are working very closely together.'

Police Chief Inspector Bryan Lunn, who co-ordinated police observation on the woman's flat, told The Voice 'We would very much like to catch those responsible – though we haven't found them yet. It's horrible to be victimised for any reason, particularly when it appears to be racial, as in this case.'

'However, I understand the lady in question has now been rehoused,' he added. 'My colleagues and I wish her the best of luck.'

The list of physical and pscyhological assaults on our health is endless. When translated into Black women's terms, racism, unemployment and the wilful neglect of various State agencies do not amount simply to 'social deprivation'. The term is inadequate: they have been killing us out there.

A survey carried out by Brent Council in 1973 found that twenty-two Black babies per one thousand of the population were dying in the first week of life. That was over ten years ago, when the full effects of the recession had not yet been felt. Nowadays, the figure is undoubtedly higher, and although the tendency is to translate such statistics in a racist way, placing the cause of such deaths with the 'irresponsibility' of Black mothers, in reality they are the result of social and economic factors which are mostly outside our control. The kind of work we can or cannot do, the housing we have, the amount of rest we can get and the quality of food we can eat all have a decisive effect on our babies' chances at birth. And where the majority of Black women are concerned, we simply *do not have* access to the funds and information which would assure us of healthier lifestyles and more nutritious diets.

This increasingly high level of poverty among Black women does not merely reduce our chances of staying healthy. It also means that we do not have the luxury of choice in the kind of health care we do receive. There are a whole range of private alternative medical disciplines – many of which came directly from *our* cultures, such as naturopathy and herbalism – which remain largely unrecognised and unsubsidised by the NHS, and therefore inaccessible to us. Consequently we are obliged to rely on a Health Service which is committed primarily to the treatment and cure of symptoms rather than the prevention of illness through good, preventive health care and practice. With the erosion of the NHS and the attendant growth of privatised medicine, Black women will have even less access to the diminishing health services which do exist, however inadequate they may be. Increasing privatisation means that white, professional men and their families will soon be the only ones with sufficient resources to pay the high cost of staying healthy.

Body Politics: Health Perspectives for Black Women

As Black women, our experiences as patients are not only determined by our economic status. As women, we have inherited a long medical tradition of male neglect. Historically, the control and manipulation of women's bodies by an all-male medical profession has meant that we have been consistently denied access to essential knowledge about ourselves. We have been fed myths, distortions and lies, so much so that the majority of women today still adhere to male-defined concepts of our physical, sexual and emotional identities. As sex objects, as long-suffering bearers of children, or as menstrual beings, many women, Black and white, continue to accept roles which white men have chosen for us. Where our health is concerned, this has meant a consistent failure by male doctors to prioritise the health issues which most concern us. It is for this reason that we still allow ourselves to be wired up, legs akimbo, pumped with harmful drugs, peered into and subjected to inductions and interference we never asked for, when giving birth. It's for this reason that our gynaecological and other needs as women have been consistently ignored or trivialised. And it's for this reason that we've allowed ourselves to be permanently damaged in the interests of 'family planning', the main purpose of which is to preserve at all costs the sexual enjoyment of men, regardless of the actual or potential effects on our health.

In Family Planning clinics, doctors rarely spend time with us to explain the various contraceptives available. The pill is often presented to us as the best method simply because it is easiest to prescribe.

I was first prescribed the pill after I'd had my baby. I was breastfeeding, though, and they made me feel sick so I stopped taking them. The doctor at the hospital advised me to go along to the Family Planning clinic. There I was given another type of pill, but these brought me up in lumps and rashes. I went back to the clinic and told them, and they gave me yet another brand. This one gave me migraines and it got so bad that I could hardly open my eyes with the pain I was in. So I went back again, and got my fourth packet. This time, whenever I had a period I felt as if my stomach was going to burst. My stomach swelled up and I was in excruciating pain. Eventually I went to the doctor about it, and he phoned an ambulance and sent me to the hospital for an examination. But they weren't too concerned about me in casualty even though I was crying,

101

I was in so much pain. They left me on a trolley in the corridor for hours, and when I couldn't take it any longer I got up and discharged myself. This meant I had to go back to the clinic. They suggesting fitting an IUD. That was fine – no irregular periods, no pain – but it kept slipping so they had to take it out. It got stuck in the neck of my womb, and they spent half an hour at the clinic trying to get it out. At this point I felt that I'd had enough and I told them I wasn't prepared to try any more of their contraceptives. The woman started trying to patronise me and I left there very upset. I went home worrying about what I would use and I really started fretting, because the baby was still young and I didn't want another one so soon. Then my friend introduced me to one of the low oestrogen pills, and I went back to the clinic and asked if I could try it out. I really had to put up a fight to get them to prescribe it for me. You know why? Because it was a low dosage pill and they didn't think I was responsible enough to take it regularly at the same time every day.

Because we are considered a 'high promiscuity risk', Black and white working-class women are often encouraged to accept contraceptives involving less 'risk' – but the reduced risk of pregnancy is invariably considered more important than the increased risk to our health. And so we are prescribed coils, which can infect our fallopian tubes and cause sterility; or Depo Provera which can have dangerous, long-term side-effects. When a Black woman enters a doctor's surgery, there is another dimension to this experience, particularly if the doctor is a white, middle-class man, as he usually is. In addition to the alienation arising out of our different sex and class we also have to face false assumptions about our lives and a host of communication barriers determined by race and culture. All these factors combine to make us feel even more vulnerable and exposed and even less confident to question doctors' prescriptions or make demands about what is best for us. And our vulnerability is compounded by the fact that doctors frequently ask their most important questions when we are lying flat on our backs on the couch in the surgery when there is little dignity left to salvage, and little hope of challenging, on the spot, any of their sexist and racist assumptions about us.

Our abuse at the hands of the Family Planning service is intensified even further by the many popular racist myths and stereotypes which abound about Black women's sexuality, enshrined within medical science. Black women's ability to reproduce has come to be viewed as a moral flaw, to be frowned upon and controlled – so much so that doctors frequently take it upon themselves to exercise control over our fertility in the interests of (white) society. The consequences of this are evident in the numerous cases of Black women who receive unwanted sterilisations or terminations, or the damaging long-term contraceptive DP (Depo Provera), all in the interests of controlling the numbers of 'unwanted' Black babies. The fact that we may not view our unplanned children in this way within our own culture is of no consequence in a society where we are expected to conform to indigenous attitudes. Many paternal and apparently sympathetic doctors have persuaded Black women to accept an abortion or contraceptive she did not really want, out of a concern to control our fertility. And such attitudes are reflected not only through our experiences here in Britain, but in our countries of origin, where myths about the need for population control are used as an excuse for the unleashing of mass sterilisation and birth control programmes on Black and Third World women, often as part of the West's 'aid' package:

> If you're talking about Black women and fertility controls, you have to look first at the whole myth about the Third World being overpopulated. Even if you look at the land occupancy of our countries, you can see that this is a myth. Take Zimbabwe, for example – the population there is about seven million, which is roughly the size of the population of London alone, yet up until a few years ago they had mobile units going around the country every three months, pumping the women with Depo Provera

and often not telling them what the injection was for or what the side effects could be. And that was before Independence, when they were still trying to encourage whites to emigrate there. Now, how else are we to interpret this kind of policy? It's true that they use all these arguments about how there is too many of us to feed and how we breed too much, but the fact of the matter is that the world has more than enough food to feed every man, woman and child. It's the way those resources are distributed which is the root of the problem.

And in a context where your children are your wealth and the only guarantee that you'll be looked after in your old age, you're talking about genocide. There's no other word for it. So you have to take that into account when looking at what happens to us here in Britain. You only have to talk to Black women – the number of us who suffer the consequences of bad birth techniques, for example, where the afterbirth is left in and becomes infected; or the number of us who get sterilised against our wishes, because some doctor persuades us to have it done when we go into hospital for something completely different. Or the number of young Black girls who are persuaded to have an abortion that they don't want and their mothers don't want them to have either. I'm not saying that every case is like this, of course these things happen sometimes for sound medical reasons.

But seeing and talking to a lot of Black women, as I do in my job, I've found there are far too many cases where there aren't any justifiable medical grounds. If you just looked at things and didn't check what is happening to Black women everywhere else in the world, you'd probably put it down to the production-line techniques in the hospitals we go to. Or you'd say, well, that's just because we tend to go to the run-down hospitals where there's no resources and not enough staff. But it's not as simple as that. If they don't take any care, that neglect is deliberate. There are a lot of doctors who don't even bother to make a secret of the fact that they go along with the idea that we are sapping this country's resources, and see it as their professional duty to keep our numbers down. They say things like, 'Well, you've already got two children, so why do you need to have any more? You might as well get your tubes tied when you come in for that D & C.' It's only when you hear Black women talking and realise how many of us this is happening to that you see things in perspective. And you begin to realise that it's not just about bad resources or neglect. It's about racism. They don't want us here anymore and they don't need our kids to work for them, so it's easier just to quietly kill us off.

It's for reasons such as these that, when the Women's Liberation Movement took up the issue of 'Abortion on Demand' in the early seventies, Black women had to point out that we have *always* been given abortions more readily than white women and are indeed often encouraged to have terminations we didn't ask for. It's for this reason, too, that when the women's movement demanded 'free, safe, and available contraception for all women', we had to remind them that for Black women this often means being used as guinea-pigs in mass birth control programmes, or as objects of 'research' when new forms of birth control need to be tested. And when the same women talked about 'A Woman's Right to Choose', we responded that for Black women, this must also mean having the right to choose to *have* our children, planned or unplanned. For us, the politics of women's health have always had that added racist dimension – a dimension which has been overlooked far too often by the white, middle-class women who constitute the majority in the women's movement.

The campaign which served to highlight this racist dimension better than any other was the campaign against Depo Provera, launched through the combined efforts of Black and white women in the late seventies. It exposed beyond all doubt the racism which underlies the control and distribution of drugs both in Britain and elsewhere in the world. As a long-term, injectable contraceptive, DP has none of the risks of unwanted pregnancy that are associated with the Pill. Effectively, this relieves any woman who is given the drug of the responsibility for controlling her own fertility. At face value, most women would probably welcome such a 'reliable' form of contraception, were it not for the dangerous and erratic side-effects suffered by so many of those who have been given 'the jab'. Cancer of the breast and the cervix, long-term infertility, irregular or absent menstrual bleeding and massive weight gain have been evident in many women who have received the drug. And some of these side-effects were evident over two decades ago, when its multi-national manufacturers, Upjohn, were testing the drug on monkeys and beagle dogs. However, this was not enough to prevent DP being distributed widely among Black women in Britain, the US and particularly in Third World countries. And it is no coincidence that among the first women to be given the drug on trial were women in Jamaica – at a time when neither the United States nor Britain had approved its use on women in their own countries. Despite a prolonged campaign in Britain to have DP banned, its continued use here was recently sanctioned by the British Medical Safety Council, meaning that many more Black and working-class women will be exposed to its dangers in the future.

The Depo Provera campaign highlighted only one of many examples of the way in which the medical profession has actively colluded, over the years, in the racism that is part and parcel of the general health provision we receive here. But there are other more subtle examples, hidden behind a veneer of benign paternalism. Doctors readily prescribe expensive drugs and medical technology with no regard for the potential or actual side-effects on us. They frequently succumb to the advertising bombardment of multi-national drug companies, choosing to ignore the fact that the main interest of such companies is to make huge profits from the marketing of their products. And even when doctors do acknowledge that a particular drug may be harmful, it is cold comfort for us, knowing as we do that it is often as a result of

106

tests which have been conducted on Black women. Our social and economic vulnerability make us the obvious guinea-pigs – particularly for tests in fertility control.

This does not mean, of course, that we meekly accept the treatment we receive at the hands of the NHS. We frequently reject the 'conventional' treatment of our ailments and illnesses, and there is evidence of a growing mistrust among Black women of the doctors' all too hasty offer of a prescription, particularly if we know that the drugs we are being given are likely to be detrimental, rather than beneficial, to our health. But when we do question the value of anti-biotics, steroids, contraceptives or tranquillizers, doctors still respond as if it is not our business to know about our own bodies. The medical jargon which so many of them favour, and the general failure of doctors to answer our questions about the treatments they prescribe, are symptoms of a deliberate policy to keep us ignorant, dependent and gullible. Control over our bodies and of information about our bodies is also a form of control over our lives.

Responding from within Our Community

It is hardly surprising that Black women have, over the years, played such a vital part in exposing, denouncing, organising and campaigning around health issues. We have never been able to rely on doctors, Community Health Councils and health workers to do it for us, and have therefore been faced with no other choice but to rely on our own resources. It is precisely because Black women spend so much time running backwards and forwards to the hospitals, often travelling miles to specialist health clinics or staying up night after night with our sick children, that we have played such a dominant role in the health campaigns of the Black community. It could not be otherwise. And although, more often than not, our resistance has taken the form of individual battles with GPs, health workers or hospital consultants, in which we are vested with no power and little

107

influence, we have also found collective ways of fighting the entrenched racism within the NHS.

The best though by no means the only example of our collective response is the part we have played in the Sickle Cell campaign, where Black women have taken the initiative not only to inform our own communities about the facts of Sickle Cell, but also to raise funds and resources to sponsor the urgently needed research. Frequently unidentified or disregarded, those of our children and family who suffer from Sickle Cell Anaemia have for years had to put up with unnecessary agony because of the failure of doctors to recognise the symptoms of a 'crisis'. As a minority group, our specific health problems are of little interest to the multi-nationals, which allow profits rather than people to determine the drugs and medical technology they will invest in. Even a disease of such magnitude, which affects large numbers of Black people around the world and about one in ten Black people in Britain, has never been considered important enough to warrant adequate or serious investigation; and this, despite the fact that research into Sickle Cell was taken up in the United States well over twenty years ago. In the States, as in Britain, Sickle Cell Anaemia was virtually ignored by the medical profession until the Black community began to draw attention to it and to make its historical causes more widely known. There, the Black Power movement highlighted the racist context into which all diseases emanating from Africa – the 'white man's grave' – are placed. It became a priority for Black communities everywhere to understand the genetic origins of Sickle Cell, which lie in our blood's former defence mechanisms against malaria. These health education initiatives, along with genetic counselling and more research were all taken up here by OSCAR (Organisation for Sickle Cell Anaemia Research) in 1975. But unlike in the US, only a small percentage of the medical profession responded with interest, and today there are still only a handful of hospitals with the resources to detect and treat Sickle Cell Anaemia effectively. Consequently, much of the research funding continues to come from the Black community, thanks to the combined efforts of Sickle Cell sufferers and Black women, who have organised extensively around Sickle Cell, both within OSCAR and in Black women's and community groups up and down the country. As a result of the heightened community awareness which years of public meetings, slide shows and fund-raising events have brought about, some Community Health Councils have at last responded by setting up Sickle Cell Advice Centres. But perhaps the most important outcome of our response has been the generally heightened awareness among British doctors and health workers, who are now at least prepared to concede that Sickle Cell exists.

But there have also been wider and more worrying consequences, arising from our responses within the community to the health care we receive. The availability of State funding and the growth of the ethnic industry have brought forth a small but growing number of Black health advisors, many of whom are women. They have now assumed, as their paid work, the task of highlighting and researching Black health issues – a task which has always, in the past, fallen to Black women in the wider community. Although they have by no means replaced our grassroots initiatives, they have nevertheless come to be regarded as the spokespersons and experts on Black health issues, often supplying the medical profession with researched information and one-off training sessions. Although the role of such experts remains potentially progressive, the dangers of ghettoising Black health concerns within the NHS cannot be ignored.

Despite the appointment of Black health advisors whose role is to bridge the cultural gap between white medical professionals and their Black clients, the fundamental problem of racism remains largely unchallenged, particularly where training priorities and accountability for malpractice are concerned. With the current erosion of the NHS, moreover, no amount of Black health expertise will be able to disguise the very real effects of hospital closures and staff cuts on our own and our community's health. For Black women, who are on the frontline when it comes to health service attacks, the implications are very clear. Either we continue to fight tooth and nail for the preservation and improvement of the Health Service we have worked so hard to build; or we risk being ousted from our already unenviable position at the very bottom of the NHS agenda.

Our fight, however, cannot be confined to campaigns against cuts and hospital closures. Nor can we content ourselves with demands for a better understanding of our specific health needs. The State's increasing reliance on 'ethnic' diagnoses, coupled with the recent increase in the use of computerised health records, has raised for us another equally urgent area of concern. We are today witnessing a growing erosion of our individual right to confidentiality, not only where our health records are concerned but also in the wider context of the welfare and social security data which is kept on us. In seeking health or welfare benefits, we are required to supply detailed information about our personal lives to a variety of agencies – information which is computerised and therefore inaccessible to us. But it *is* accessible to doctors, social workers, DHSS officials, the police, the Home Office and a host of others, often at the touch of a button. Legislation designed to protect the NHS from 'abuse' by foreigners means that hospitals now record our medical history *and* our immigration status, alongside our race, our sex and our social status. In the light of our experiences of racism in the field of health it is little wonder that Black women regard the State's surveillance of our lives through the combined Health and Social Services with growing distrust. Increasingly alienated from potentially beneficial provisions, we have been among the first to question the overall power of the Welfare State to record, control and intervene in our lives.

Under Pressure: Black Women and the Welfare State

There is no single area of our lives which better exposes our experience of institutionalised racism than our relationship with the various welfare services. Here we deal regularly with people who are vested with the power to control, disrupt and intervene in our lives on behalf of the State. Any Black

110

woman who has ever spent a day at the DHSS office trying to claim benefit or who has had a child taken into care quickly learns that once contact with the welfare agencies is made, her life is no longer her own.

Despite this reality, our relationship with the Welfare State is presented as parasitic. We are described by the media as 'scroungers' and depicted as having a child-like dependence upon a benevolent caring (white) society. Social workers are seen as the twentieth-century missionaries who come into our communities to challenge ignorance and poverty. This image does not, however, expose the extent to which social and economic factors outside our control have forced us into this cycle of dependency on the State; nor does it convey the true nature of our contribution to this society. Black women's labour has propped up this country, not only over the past four decades but for centuries. Far from draining its resources, we have been the producers of its wealth.

For Black women, the benign face of capitalism hides a thinly-disguised form of social control. As the State's response to the economic, social and psychological pressures of our class, the social and welfare services represent varying degrees of State interference in our lives. Although they are ostensibly there to intervene in our lives to give aid and assistance in our own best interests, they are actually designed to protect capitalist society from the less desirable consequences of its own excesses. With poverty, unemployment, social deprivation and disaffection at crisis point in Britain, the provision of welfare is designed to make us believe in the myth that we are living in a society which is fundamentally humane.

The logic behind the Welfare State is that certain identifiable categories of individuals are less able to 'cope' than others and that particular groups are more prone towards deviant or anti-social behaviour. The fault invariably lies with the individual, whose 'case' is then taken on by one of a range of welfare agencies. If we rebel at school, there is the child psychologist; if we have trouble coping when we become mothers, it is the health visitor and the social worker; if the pressure gets too much and we crack under the strain, there is the State psychiatrist; if we have trouble making ends meet, it's the DHSS official; and if we resort to shop-lifting or some other form of petty economic crime, then it's the probation or prison officer. The list is seemingly endless. It represents a whole range of usually white, invariably middle-class professionals whose very jobs depend on perpetuating the miseries they are designed to alleviate.

Black women's relationships with social workers have been fraught with the antagonisms which result from this contradiction. Whether we are single parents, homeless young women or the parents of children in care, we are constantly confronted with racist, classist or culturally-biased judgements about our lives. The social background of most social workers and the training they receive give them no real understanding of our different family structures, cultural values and codes of behaviour. It is so much easier for them to rely on loose assumptions and loaded stereotypes of us than to try seriously to address the root cause of our problems. These assumptions become the justification for everything from secret files and surveillance to direct intervention of the most destructive kind.

When a Black mother confides to a seemingly sympathetic social worker that her daughter is in the habit of staying out late against her wishes she cannot afford to assume it will be taken as an innocent remark. She may find herself the subject of an investigation or discover that her daughter has been placed under a Supervision Order. Prevailing stereotypes of Black women as 'immoral' or 'promiscuous' render social workers hyper-sensitive to the possibility of moral danger, particularly among young Black women who show signs of being sexually active.

Similarly, when a Black woman is beaten or abused by the man she lives with, she may well approach a social worker in preference to calling the police, in the belief that their role is genuinely to assist. She may lack alternative accommodation, or may be hampered from leaving by several young children. But instead of helping her to resolve her situation practically

112

through an offer of alternative housing, the likelihood is that the social worker will interpret it as one of potential danger to the children involved, placing the children under a Care Order and the parents on a list of potential or actual child-abusers. Because of racism, domestic situations involving Black women lend themselves easily to such glib assumptions about our 'volatile' temperaments. Case notes which pretend to summarise our lives, are full of adjectives like 'violent', 'aggressive', or 'lacking in parental skills'. Culturally loaded against us, such jargon bears no real relationship to the lives and terms of reference of Black people. Nevertheless, such descriptions are usually at the root of social workers' judgements that we are inadequate, immature or strict disciplinarians. And it can be on the basis of such judgements that our children are removed from our homes and taken into care, either under the guise of offering short-term assistance, or by brute force. Once there, the onus is on us to prove and improve ourselves, in the hope that we may eventually get them back:

The thing with being in care is that if you have children while you're there, your children automatically go into care. I wasn't aware of this until it happened to me. I lived with a foster mother when I was fourteen, until I was fifteen. I became pregnant while I was at school and had my daughter. She automatically went into care and they took her away from me and put her with foster parents. I had to fight to get her back. They had the money, they were wealthy, they had a big house in Henley-on-Thames, and they said I couldn't see her, although legally I had the right to. I took them to court. I even got married to strengthen my case. Eventually we got her back. Then they gave me a decrepit old flat in Vassall Road – the houses were only fit to be condemned and they stuck us in there, in a place with nails sticking out of the floor. It was a basement and it was freezing cold. It was just terrible. Even the inspector who came to see the place said we shouldn't be put there, but they *did* put us there. And here was my child coming from this very upper-class background. It was supposed to be just a temporary measure because they were hoping to take the child back from me. The plans the social workers made with the foster parents was that I was so young I would never be able to cope with a toddler who was used to a completely different lifestyle.

But when they said I couldn't cope as a mother and that I would have to give her back, I decided no way, I would fight this. They started to say I was ill-treating the child. They took her away and took me to court. I went to court about two or three times. Then I became pregnant with my second child, and when I had to go to court the next time, I said to myself I can't take anymore, this is ridiculous. I went to the courtroom with a knife in my bag. I walked in, and when the magistrate was reading out all these allegations, I said, 'This is rubbish,' and he told me to shut up. And I told him not to tell me to shut up, this is my child you're talking about. This developed into a big row, and I thought, 'Right, that's it,' and I started to go for him. The court ushers tried to hold me down. I couldn't get to him, so I tore up all the papers on his desk. I just went crazy. They called the police for me. A few weeks later, they sent us a letter saying the child was still a ward of court, which was part of the plan, but they were getting her back for me. I think they realised I wasn't going to stop fighting them, so they gave in.

Fostering her the way they did, they could have given her to a Black family and it would have made things a lot easier for her coming back to me. I had nothing compared to what the family she went to were offering her. In the last few years, we have got much closer, but before that we were like complete strangers. I think there was a time we literally hated each other, because she was rebelling and I was not going to stand for a child more or less telling me what I should do. She says she doesn't remember much now, but I'm sure there's little things she hasn't forgot. She still has her books upstairs from her foster parents. I've kept them, it would have been unfair to throw everything away. I think because she had a start in life

114

where she was coming from a conservative background where you don't have anything in your house that is not worth something, that's made her arrogant. The child was growing up with toys that have a value to them, and she expects that. Not everything she had was new, but they were quality. There were certain things about her personality which used to irritate me – the prim and proper way she had of doing things. If I threw my cardigan over the chair, she would pick it up and hang it up properly. We used to have some terrible rows, but now it's really nice, I can talk to her, although there is still a bit of coolness sometimes. That could be put down to her age – she's fourteen now. I find I'm always having to drill her, and sometimes she avoids having too much to say to me. I think it wouldn't annoy me so much if she had been with me from a baby. I think that break has made a stranger of our relationship, as it did with my own mother. My mother left me to come over here when I was five, and when I came to her, I came to a stranger. Once you make a break between mother and child, you become like two separate individuals. You can't make that contact. Even today, my mother and I don't have any relationship at all. We've just never been able to build a bond. I was going through puberty, and she couldn't cope with it. So really I have no relationship with her after being in care, and when you haven't had it, it's hard to know what you're building with your children. I think with the other children it's not so bad, but with my daughter there isn't a model, and I look at other mothers and their daughters and think this is how it should be. I know we'll never get like that. I think we will always respect each other though, and I say to my friends I don't care if she doesn't love me, as long as she respects me.

The 'benevolent' intervention of the Welfare State, which allows our families to be split up 'in the interests of the child' does not extend to our treatment once in care. In the short-term, our hair and skin care are neglected, our diet and cultural needs ignored; in the long-term, we can end up

115

living in total cultural isolation in white foster homes or residential institutions where no one is around to help interpret our experiences of racism. But the children's home is also a stop-over for young offenders, meaning that our experience of care can be a criminalising one. Once exposed to the influence of juvenile car thieves and house burglars, the likelihood that we will pick up the tricks of their trade is greatly increased. For Black women, therefore, the term 'care' represents an experience which is often the very opposite to that which is suggested.

But the uncaring arm of the State extends to other areas of our lives. Often when we enter the classroom we have our first experience of 'Big Brother'. The process of moulding and conditioning us to accept our role in society begins in the reception class, where any display of rebellion is viewed with alarm. Failure to conform is seen as evidence of our individual shortcomings, so first the child, then the family, and ultimately our culture is blamed. A whole range of racist stereotypes exist which confirm that we – and not the school or the society – are defective. Thus begins the process of social classification. We are 'hyperactive', 'disruptive' or 'maladjusted', and because it is 'in our nature' to be so, such labels can help other professional welfare agents to anticipate how we will behave for the remainder of our childhood. Once acquired, they become the justification for all forms of State interference, from visiting our homes uninvited to locking us away indefinitely.

Any display of anger or hostility serves to confirm existing notions of us, and to justify more severe forms of social control. So for the young Black woman who ends up in a detention or assessment centre, custodial care is much more than a temporary loss of liberty. It means being exposed to a way of life in which depression, hysteria, physical assaults and suicide attempts are regular occurrences. It is therefore little wonder that those of us who enter such institutions relatively sane frequently end up displaying precisely those symptoms which our incarceration was designed to cure.

I was thrown out of school when I was thirteen, and I

116

didn't get back to school until the sixth form. I missed out three years of schooling, and didn't have no tutors coming to my house. I know it's against the law, but it happens to a lot of people. My mother tried to get me back into school. She went to her MP, to the social services ... in the end they said I was mad and wanted me to see a psychiatrist. They refused to let me go back to school until I went to see one. In the end I did, because I was fed up and depressed being at home all the time and not talking to anyone.

I was sent to the adolescent unit, and there were people there for reasons like they couldn't get on with their parents or had problems at school. Some had anorexia nervosa, and there were a few who were schizophrenic. There were a lot of Black girls there at the time. It was a place where, if someone was crying, they put them in a straight-jacket and put them in a room with no windows. They took out the bed and just left a mattress. When it was time for you to eat, they just put the food through the door, and there were pails for you to go to the toilet in – in the same room. If you cried for any reason, say you wanted to get out, the next thing you know is that your wardrobe's disappeared and you're in there with your mattress until you've 'come to your senses'.

It was things like that which made me depressed. In the end I tried to commit suicide, because I didn't know any way out of that place. I was only in there for a month, but so much happened during that time, it seemed like ages. They used to drug us up all the time. They gave me some sleeping pills every night and some other tablets during the day. They stood over you to make sure you took them, but I pretended to swallow them and saved them up and hid them in my room. I didn't do it intentionally to take an overdose, but it got so bad that I took all the tablets one day and just lay down on my bed. It was dinner time, and everyone had come out of their room. When they realised I hadn't come down to eat, they came and found me. I was half gone already. All I remember was being told to stand up and the wardens holding me up and trying to walk me

117

up and down the corridor. I wanted to lie down, but they wouldn't let me. They called for the house doctor who tried to find out what I'd taken. Then they pushed a tube down into my stomach and filled a jug with half salt and half water and poured it down into my stomach through the tube. Although I was weak, I was struggling because I just wanted to die. The next thing I knew I was vomiting. They flung me into my room and took all my things out, stripped me and put me in an 'operation' nightdress. No one was allowed to see me for twenty-four hours and I couldn't leave the room. When I felt okay again I wanted to get out of the room, but they wouldn't let me. So I started banging on the door, and two nurses came and injected me to keep me calm.

The next day I sneaked out and managed to phone my grandmother to ask her to come and get me. She'd been trying to phone me, but they told her I wasn't allowed to speak to anybody. She took the first train up. They told her she couldn't see me, but my grandmother didn't take any notice of them. I was banging on the door and I heard her ask me if I wanted to come home, and I said, 'Yes'. They were arguing with her, saying that she can't take me home because she wasn't my mother. But she took me home though, there's no way they were going to stop her once she realised what was going on. I was fifteen when this happened.

It is experiences such as these which have led a disproportionate number of young Black women to leave school and enter a lifetime in and out of institutions. There, the symptoms we display – whether of stress, anxiety, depression or outrage – are just as likely to be mis-diagnosed, for all the established myths and stereotypes which affect social workers' judgements of our families and teachers' assumptions about our response to schooling are also held by psychologists and those who work in custodial detention centres. The widely-held assumption that Black women are aggressive, erratic and emotionally unstable forms the basis of a range of damning stereotypes, on which such people rely

118

to interpret our responses. Racism ensures that our ways of relieving tension are witnessed with alarm. As evidence of our lack of self-control and our refusal to conform, they serve to confirm our need for more drastic forms of treatment.

This treatment is rarely therapeutic. Therapy is, in any case, far too costly and time-consuming for the NHS to make it generally available. Instead, a course of debilitating drugs, sedatives, electric-shock treatment and confinement in institutions which have neither the staff nor the resources to achieve more than a temporary suppression of our 'symptoms' are seen as the answer. The result is often a cycle of dependency, both on the drugs and the institution, ensuring that the State's short-term solution is likely to become our long-term problem. When we protest that we are being sectioned under the Mental Health Act, imprisoned for indefinite periods, mis-diagnosed and given dangerous, mind-shattering drugs on a scale out of all proportion to our less than two per cent of society, the argument that we are 'more prone to stress and mental disorder' is used to justify our treatment.

For the working-class Black woman, it is true that avoiding high levels of daily stress is virtually impossible. The economic and social pressures of our class are acute because capitalism itself is in crisis, and we bear the brunt of that reality. But although we face the added pressures of being Black and female, Black women have no particular monopoly on mental disorder and our exposure to stress is not, in itself, sufficient to explain our over-representation in psychological assessment centres, prisons, psychiatric wards, and mental institutions. Black women have been dealing with pressure for centuries, and there is nothing in our collective experience or our genetic make-up which indicates that we have a lower breaking point or are more prone to mental illness and insanity. If anything, the reverse is true. We have always had to find ways of coping with pressure, and have often achieved this by redirecting our anger and frustration into battles with those authorities and agencies of the Welfare State whose function is supposedly to alleviate such

119

pressures. This well-worn strategy for survival has been one of our most effective forms of self-therapy, enabling many a Black woman to resist the sense of individual failure and impotence which can lead to mental breakdown. It is this very ability to challenge and resist which is at the root of our experience, however, for it is not the amount of stress we are exposed to but rather the ways we respond to that stress which underlie our negative dealings with the welfare, psychiatric and custodial agencies in Britain. When we come into contact with the police, social services or some other branch of the Welfare State, we are already more likely to be in a situation which is more fraught, angry or emotional. But even when we are in total control, any show of anger or frustration can become the evidence required to lock us away.

Section 136 of the Mental Health Act gives police and social workers all the authority they need to section us for disruptive or unsocial behaviour. Once in a place of safety – usually a police cell, in the first instance – we can be held without charge for up to forty-eight hours. Other sections of the act can then be used to detain us further, giving police doctors and psychiatrists total power to recommend drugs, electric shock treatment or solitary confinement, and to use any amount of 'reasonable' force which circumstances warrant. The majority of Black women who receive psychiatric treatment do so as a result of being sectioned under this act, often by people who have no expertise or training in the field of mental health.

In some prisons, where up to forty per cent of the women inmates can be Black, the use of tranquillizers is commonplace. Although most Black women are there for 'economic' crimes such as shop-lifting, prostitution, selling ganja or passing stolen cheques, many of them can expect to receive some form of drug treatment. This form of social control has an added, racist dimension, though. We are also prey to all kinds of victimisation and intimidation from prison officers, who – next to the police – are renowned as the most prejudiced and bigoted group of civil servants in the country and a breeding ground for right-wing racists.

When you first go into prison, you're give a medical

120

examination and a form to fill out stating your religion and diet. Because I'm a Rasta, I put 'Rasta' down under religion and 'vegetarian' under diet. The officers said that the Rasta religion was not recognised and that I wasn't entitled to a vegetarian diet. For the first week, I didn't eat and by the third week they were talking about sending me to the hospital unit. The prison officers were taunting me, giving me pork sausages for breakfast when no one else was getting them, and meat for dinner. I got so angry with all this that one day I just threw the tray over one of the officers. After that incident they sent me to the psychiatric wing where I was given Depixal, which is similar to Largactyl. I was also charged with assaulting a prison officer, because I'd thrown the tray. I insisted on going to the board of governors to demand why I was being treated as a psychiatric case. The doctors who'd examined me there had said I wasn't mad and that I shouldn't be in the unit. The governors ruled that I should be given a vegetarian diet, whether or not my religion was recognised, and that I should be allowed to leave my headwrap on. So I was sent back to the main part of the prison, where I had to do twenty-eight days solitary confinement for assault. Some of the prison officers were still hassling me about my religion. They kept up the abuse and harassment and kept calling me 'nigger', so it all came to a head again. I was having a wash and this woman officer kept shouting abuse at me and refusing to call me by name. I threw the soap at her and it hit her in the windpipe, so I found myself in solitary, even though the doctors had made it clear that they didn't think I was mad. The whole time I was in solitary confinement, I was in one of the rooms that were put aside for women who were severely mentally disturbed. Three of us were Black and there was one white woman. We were given Depixal and Largactyl three or four times a day, and when I refused it, which I tried to do all the time, by spitting out the medicine, the officers would come in, beat me up and stick an injection in my backside. I was on remand for five months and I spent nearly all of that time in solitary confinement.

121

My case was eventually heard in October that year, and I was sentenced to six months to two years in Borstal where I got exactly the same reception as I'd got in prison. So that sparked off the same chain of events. I was put into solitary confinement on the punishment block and although it wasn't the psychiatric unit, they still insisted on giving me Largactyl. I refused to take it and they beat me up. I got this huge blister on my foot as a result of one of these beatings, and they refused me medical treatment. My foot became septic, and when my mother visited me and heard what had happened, she was so angry she wrote to the Home Office and eventually they did give me treatment, but I've still got the scar.

At first, the other Black girls there were against me, because they thought I attracted trouble, but they got to see that I was being victimised. The officers wouldn't even let me have a Bible. The Black girls began to support me because they saw that I was entitled to follow my religion, to wear my wrap and not to eat meat. The officers accused me of inciting them to riot, so I was sent back to prison again. Rumours that I had started a riot followed me, and I found myself under psychiatric treatment. The doctors who saw me there said that I was a 'management problem' and that I wasn't mad, and although I was eventually moved, the prison officers still carried on beating me up and giving me drugs.

I was released shortly after the death of Richard Campbell. That case must have influenced their decision to release me, because I didn't serve my full term even though I had all those cases of assault on my records. After the news of what had happened to him, two white girls who were on my corridor were caught trying to smuggle a letter out saying that I was being mistreated. I was put in the punishment block because the authorities thought I'd put the two girls up to it, but I didn't know anything about the letter at the time. They released me soon afterwards, probably because they were worried about the publicity that Richard Campbell's case had attracted. They know that Black women prisoners are

122

abused and given drugs, but the officers get away with it. The prison system treats all women prisoners as if they're mad because they can't see how women would be in prison unless something is wrong with them. They've got this belief that Black women are violent or 'savage', as they'd put it, and that therefore we are mad. When I was in prison in the ordinary block, I'd say that more than half of the Black girls were being given Largactyl. There's so much racism in prison. When I was there, for example, there were some Muslim women inside and they treated them just as badly. They wouldn't respect their religion and they weren't given a copy of the Koran. Their diet wasn't taken seriously either, and they gave them pork and sent Catholic or Church of England vicars to see them.

It's up to prisoners to organise in the prisons, though, because all this is going on behind closed doors and no one from outside gets a chance to witness it. Black prisoners have got to organise in this country, like they have in the States, if this kind of abuse is ever going to be stopped.

The Black woman's experience of prison can only be seen as a confirmation of the State's own paranoia when faced with a people who refuse to be cowed or contained. Prison and the attempted manipulation of our minds by drugs are a last resort, when all other forms of social and State control can be deemed to have failed.

But our experience of prison does more than expose the ultimate brutality of the British State. It also confirms a positive phenomenon, which no amount of State intervention or institutionalised racism has been able to repress. It provides evidence of Black women's stubborn will to fight back. Although we know that some of us do succumb to the pressures of the system, weary of the daily struggle to survive, our individual and collective acts of defiance and resistance are proof that Black women are refusing meekly to accept relegation to the ranks of the living dead.

4

Chain Reactions: Black Women Organising

The voices of Black women who have suffered because of racist and discriminatory practices in this country speak on every page of this book, so in this chapter we have concentrated on our *organised* responses. We have always been active in our community: we began by forming ourselves into small church, social and welfare groups, which were our spontaneous response to the isolation and alienation we faced when we first arrived in the Mother Country. But as our community found its feet, we organised ourselves into more formal political organisations, and worked alongside Black men to further the aims and defend the rights of our people. Later, it became necessary for some Black women to organise themselves independently, rejecting the notion that the concerns of Black women are secondary to those of our race. All three forms of organisation have survived into the eighties with equal credibility. Although we have not always agreed on the most effective way to develop our political strategies, we have nevertheless proved our capacity to take up our own specific concerns without losing sight of our commitment and accountability to the Black community we represent.

124

In this section we have chosen the campaigns, groups and individuals mentioned in the following pages, not because they are fully representative of all we have achieved, but because they are typical and they represent the level of commitment to our community which has characterised Black women's political activities throughout Britain.

Traditions of Resistance

Our long tradition of resistance can be traced back through the centuries to its origins in our African past. Our stubborn refusal to accept a state of bondage, both under slavery and in contemporary Britain has often been hidden behind stereotypes of passivity and acquiescence. Such images of Black women as downtrodden victims may well disclose one dimension of the realities we have lived through, but they fail to reveal the fact that our very survival has depended on our militant responses to tyranny.

From Queen Moo of Egypt, who engineered the building of the sphinx on the banks of the Nile, to the Amazon warriors of Dahomey, who removed their right breasts in order to improve their accuracy with the bow and arrow, our history is steeped in legends of powerful Black women fighters and leaders. African warrior-queens, such as Nzinga, who fought the early encroachments by the Portuguese at the beginning of the seventeenth century, and the Queen Mothers who wielded such power and influence during the Ashanti wars against the British, are revered and immortalised in Africa's oral history and folklore. Their pride, courage and spirit of resistance is the heritage which African women took with them to the Americas. It was this heritage which ensured that there would always be women among the slaves who resisted and rebelled against human bondage.

Because our participation as women in the struggles against slavery is poorly documented, the extent of our contribution can never be fully established. Nevertheless, the existing evidence makes it clear that Black women resisted with great vigour, using every tool available to us. With the ingenuity of all oppressed peoples whose survival is threatened, we turned our every activity into a potential act of subversion. Through our efforts, resistance itself took on a new definition, embracing everything from quiet subversion to open rebellion.

The African tradition of breastfeeding through infancy was just one of many ways in which Black women succeeded in disrupting the slavers' attempts to extract and exploit our labour. As an effective (though unreliable) form of natural contraception, it successfully disrupted many a slaveowner's efforts to force his women slaves to breed; and because feeding a child is both frequent and time-consuming, nursing mothers were often able to reduce the number of hours they worked in a day. Above all, it was an activity difficult to punish, and as such it was a particularly effective form of passive resistance.

Black women who worked as domestic slaves are frequently described by male historians as having had an easier time under slavery because of their privileged position over those who worked in the fields. But many women who worked in the master's house were both devious and defiant and had no interest in preserving the status quo. Their acts ranged from daring attempts to poison the food consumed by the household to using their access to books and newspapers to teach themselves to read and write in secret, thus becoming a source of news and information to fellow slaves. This activity was particularly significant, since every effort was made to prevent us from learning to read or write the language of our captors. The argument of intellectual inferiority was used by the slavemasters to hide their real fears that, if armed with book and pen, we could successfully challenge the religious, scientific and philosophical myths which were used to justify our state of bondage.

Such acts were truly courageous, for all forms of subversion, whether overt or covert, were punished with equal force if detected. Corporal and capital punishment were a well-entrenched feature of slavery, for it was the power to intimidate and terrorise which ultimately enabled the system to survive as long as it did. Black women were punished as harshly and as frequently as men for a variety of

126

offences, which ranged from poor productivity in the fields to burning the dinner. For daring to resist, we risked whippings, torture, amputations, shackles and stocks, sale to another plantation owner, and execution. We received no concessions on account of our sex and were 'equal under the whip' with one dubious exception – that if pregnant, we should not be executed until after the birth of the child. So brutal were the floggings and so sadistic the other forms of terrorisation, that many Black women were permanently disfigured, sometimes for the most trivial of 'crimes'. But despite this severity, we refused to be intimidated, and the proof of our militancy lies hidden in the planters' own records.

When the British government attempted, in the early 1820s, to outlaw flogging and thereby 'prove' its liberalism to those who opposed slavery, the planters were unanimous in their fear of the consequences. Arguing on their behalf for retention of the whip. Sir Ralph Woodford, Governor of Trinidad, claimed that it was the slave *women* who were 'most prone to give offence' and for whom the whip was therefore the most effective means of control. The Barbados Council, in 1823, echoed this argument, claiming that 'Black ladies have rather a tendency to the Amazonian cast of character'! Their fears proved justified. Within a year of the whip being officially abolished Woodford wrote to the Colonial Secretary in London, complaining that the women slaves had become unmanageable. Referring to countless incidents 'of insolence and insubordination [which] occur frequently among the female slaves', he lamented that he no longer possessed the authority 'to repress the violence of turbulent women'. In the space of two years in Jamaica (between 1824 and 1826) nearly double the number of women slaves as men received punishments worthy of court record. These records also cite endless cases of insolence and defiance by Black women towards overseers and other whites.

Our refusal to bow down was not confined, however, to individual acts of insolence and subversion, as history bears witness. The period of slavery is littered with rebellions and

127

uprisings successful and otherwise, in which Black women performed an important, often crucial role. The Maroons of Jamaica, for example, included countless women who had escaped from the plantations to live in the hills as guerillas. Nanny of Maroon Town is one such woman we can claim for posterity. She was renowned for her skills in organising and directing campaigns during the Maroon Wars of 1733, using the 'abeng' (or maroon horn) to communicate messages from one group of guerillas to the next. Her influence is said to have ensured that women and children were greatly respected within the Maroon communities, particularly significant since by the end of the eighteenth century there were more women than men living in the Maroon settlements. Nanny's role was very much in the tradition of her African foremothers, the Ashanti warrior-priestesses who performed essential tactical and spiritual functions during warfare. She has gone down in history as a revolutionary fighter and leader.

Cubah, 'Queen of Kingston', is another Black woman whose story confirms our militant resistance to slavery. She played a central part in plotting what would have been one of the biggest uprisings ever to take place in Jamaica, in 1760, involving the simultaneous revolt of at least six parishes. When the plot was discovered, Cubah was captured and deported to another island, but undeterred she made her way back, to be finally captured and executed.

Black women such as Cubah and Nanny are not only worthy of a place in history because of their own courage and determination. Their real significance to us lies in the fact that they represent the many, many thousands of anonymous Black women who, in their own way, challenged and resisted the barbaric system of slavery.

Black Women Organising in Britain in the 1950s and 1960s

The Britain which Black women entered in the late forties and fifties was a hostile, unwelcoming environment. The British people, nurtured on notions of white superiority and

128

steeped in racist ideology, ensured that our reception was a cold one. Women like Una Marston, who had come from Jamaica in the 1930s, felt its sting. Incidents of racialist abuse so enraged her that she wrote this angry poem in *The Keys*, journal of the League of Coloured Peoples:

> They call me 'Nigger'
> Those little white urchins
> What makes me keep my fingers
> From choking the words in their throats?

This we refrained from doing. Instead, we went on to fight in Britain's war effort, losing both life and limb in a war which was allegedly fought in defence of ideals of freedom and democracy. The British people, aided and abetted by white American servicemen, many of whom travelled here with their own uniquely American brand of racist poison, responded with petty insults, hypocrisy and a whole panoply of disciminatory practices, which would soon become known by the rather quaint name of the 'Colour Bar'.

Our earlier visions of the Mother Country meant that many of us were amazed and disillusioned by the treatment we received. Women from the Caribbean who served in the Auxiliary Territorial Service found themselves widely abused and insulted. Others, like Amelia King whose family had been in this country for three generations, were refused entry to the Women's Land Army because they were Black. When the war ended many Black women came to join men who had fought for Britain, thinking that their service to the Mother Country would be rewarded in the form of a better future:

> I was only very young at the time, but I remember the telegram coming to St Vincent just before the end of the war, saying that my father had been injured in Egypt. It was a terrible shock to the family. He was sent back to England to convalesce, and he stayed there for eighteen months recovering from his back injury. While he was here, he started reading Law and when he got out of the hospital he registered and took his exams. That's when he decided to send for us. Why not? He'd fought and almost

129

died for this country. We came over in 1948 – not on the *Empire Windrush*, which carried a lot of returning ex-servicemen, but on the *Empire Trooper*. On that boat there were a lot of families like ours who were coming over to join their menfolk – and of course at that time nearly all the West Indian men in Britain were ex-servicemen.

But even as the rewards were being shared out to those white workers who had served in the defence of this country, Black men and women were being attacked and spat on in the streets. In 1948, on the streets of Liverpool – only a few weeks after the *Empire Windrush* had docked at Tilbury – the white community, with the support of the police, turned on its 8,000 Black residents, many of whom had so generously defended Britain against German fascism, in a show of open hostility. Black homes and clubs were raided, and pitched battles were fought in the streets between whites and Blacks, most of whom had ties with Britain which went back for centuries. Yet even though the presence of Black people was blatantly unwelcome, Britain was still desperate for our labour; and as the 'riots' raged in Liverpool, new workers continued to trickle in.

Discrimination in the job market and the British misconception of our skills meant that we were directed into the worst jobs. These poor conditions, long hours and back-breaking routines could have been eased with decent accommodation. But the 'Colour Bar' excluded us from this, and we found ourselves at the mercy of racketeers.

I was living in a small room which was draughty and cold and had one little paraffin heater. If you slept with it on, the next day your nose would be blocked and you'd feel drowsy. The bathroom – and I was lucky to have one – had no heating at all. There was no geyser and you had to heat buckets of water if you wanted a bath.

It was to alleviate these miseries that we first began to look for a collective means to make life more bearable. Women figure strongly in the initial and predominantly informal efforts we made to establish our communities and maintain

130

ourselves. The hairdressing salon, for example, served many Black women as a meeting place and more often than not the 'salon' would be based in somebody's front parlour, since no European hairstylist would cater for our particular needs. Going along to have your hair pressed or relaxed was a social event, an opportunity to meet and exchange stories with other women. And the woman who was the best source of information was, of course, the hairdresser who was well-placed to give advice, support and reassurance to others. Most significantly, we organised the 'Pardner' system through which we saved regularly and collectively. By withdrawing the money we pooled on a rota basis, we gave ourselves access to much-needed funds:

It was mainly women who set up the pardners. Nine out of ten of the pardners schemes had a woman in charge of them. It was done on a village or family basis. Whoever's needs were greater, they got the deposit on a house. It was the woman who held on to the money and paid down the deposit, but still no home could be put in her name. Later people started to have selling parties. It helped to pay the mortgage, but it also provided us with somewhere to go. That's why they started.

The Pardner system has survived up to the present day as a widely-used and efficient community money-lending and savings scheme. But in those early days, it provided us with the only regular and available source of funds when a lump sum was needed as a down-payment on a mortgage or to cover the cost of our children's air tickets. In the absence of friendly building societies or sympathetic bank managers, self-reliance was a common objective and served to bind us closer together as we strove to establish our communities.

Through our embryonic churches, too, we gave the help and support to new immigrants which the British government and people had failed to offer. The churches provided Black women with one of our main sources of support and sustenance, offering some continuity with the forms of social and community organisation we had known in the Caribbean. For many of us, these churches offered the only form of recreation we had to relieve the pressures of our working lives, and to support an otherwise bleak existence.

They organised the churches because of our exclusion from the Methodist and Baptist churches. We used to hold the services in our own front-rooms. I used to think those church women were feeble-minded, allowing the church to have so much influence over them. But when I heard the same women on the platform, I realised that they had found the place where they could channel their energies, and they were no longer feeling alienated and excluded. Even so, within the church organisation they were delegated to carrying out the women's role, doing the cooking for the functions, things like that.

It is in the church communities too that the origins of some of our earliest social and welfare organisations are to be found.

Political organisation was not paramount at this time, because Britain was still regarded by most of us as a temporary home. Very soon, however, the increasing ferocity of racist attacks galvanised us into organising in a more overtly political way.

The ideology of racial superiority had become more virulent at the beginning of the fifties, forming the basis for a score of fascist organisations. The British Union of Fascists, the League of Empire Loyalists and the British National Party are just a few of the better known ones. They infected the whole climate in the areas where we lived, and were frequently known to descend on our communities in gangs, Ku Klux Klan style, shouting 'Let's get the Niggers'. Racial tensions not only limited our social lives, but ensured that we relied almost exclusively on our relations with people at work and on women and men in our immediate communities for emotional support and friendship. They also forced us to rely on our own resources to meet our social needs.

In Manchester, there was already a small Black community that was able to buffer the shock of arrival here. The women were most vulnerable to racist attacks. The few resources we had on Moss Side, we shared. The

132

Black women set up childminding because there were no nursery places for us. We needed housing, so we tried to do something about that, too. There was no demand from us on the housing department, because the authorities were racist.

The arrival of increasing numbers of Black men, women and children was seen not only by fascists but also by the general public and the media as a threat to the 'British way of life'. In particular, Black women became an easy target for individual attacks in the long-established communities of Bristol, Cardiff, Liverpool and Manchester, as well as in the areas we had recently settled.

To begin with there were very few Black women around. They didn't really come onto the scene until the mid-fifties. That was when the real hostilities began. With our arrival, they found a place where they could focus all their psychological hatred. They knew that if they attacked a Black woman on the street with her kids, she wasn't in a position to fight back.

Verbal taunts and sporadic street clashes marked the ever-worsening relationship between Black and white people throughout the fifties.

In those days, there was a lot of racism with the teddy boys. I used to work in Effra Road, and one day I was going to work and it was very foggy. I knew these chaps behind me were white. Then one of them came up alongside me and felt my hair. My hair was straightened at the time, and he said, 'This one's hair feels white, so leave her alone.' Then one of the others shouted, 'There's a nigger, over there.' Whoever it was, she really got some kicks – you could hear her screaming. But things like this helped us to band together. We were all West Indians! When the teddy boys beat up a Black person from another island, some people would wait until a white person came into our area, pick up the milk bottles and beat them up. It was vicious but they were desperate times.

Finally, in August 1958, large-scale confrontations broke out on the streets of Nottingham and London. Black women and men were attacked for days on end; petrol bombs were thrown into our homes. These attacks were often preceded by a letter or a verbal warning, saying, 'We're going to get you tonight if you don't clear out.' As a consequence we united and fought back. Black women could be seen standing firm, machetes and bottles in hand, side by side with the men, defending ourselves in the 'riots' which were entirely of the British people's making. To us, it was not merely a question of self-defence, but a struggle for survival. As a people we had to move fast.

Black organisations began to be formed around the need to protect our emergent communities. Having witnessed the failure of the police to offer us 'impartial' protection, even the more moderate organisations pledged to devote themselves to our communities' self-defence. Events reached a climax with the stabbing of Kelso Cochrane in 1959 on the streets of Notting Hill. Even though murdered in broad daylight, no witnesses came forward and his funeral became a demonstration, attracting Black people in their hundreds from across Britain. As a consequence, our organisations became stronger, more radical, and less concerned with simple welfare issues. As we entered the sixties, the fight against 'racial prejudice', whether perpetrated by individuals or the State, became the main priority for Black people up and down the country.

As we began to focus on how to defend our communities here, however, we did not lose sight of what was happening 'back home'. Our struggles in Britain were mirrored by those of the movements for self-determination in our countries of origin. As we sought out ways of establishing our rights here, we also supported the independence struggles which were being waged elsewhere. Our very presence here was the result of Britain's colonial legacy, and though resident here, our ties with the families we had left behind in the Caribbean were strong and binding. The added fact that the anti-colonial movement had had such a long tradition in Britain, through overseas student associations and the

134

presence of progressive Pan-Africanists, ensured that we looked beyond the immediate horizons to link our fate with Black people elsewhere. The West African Students Union, for example, had as its explicit aim 'to oppose race prejudice and colonialism'. Similarly, the moderate and more cautious League of Coloured Peoples was pledged to improve 'the welfare of coloured peoples in all parts of the world'. 1944 had witnessed the birth of the British section of the Pan-African Congress (PAC) which, though based in Britain, agitated for independence in the colonies and maintained strong bonds with local movements in our home countries. Then, as now, the most enduring of our political platforms were those which understood the links between the two aspects of our single struggle, expressed by the PAC as a demand for 'democratic rights, civil liberties and self-determination' for all Black peoples the world over.

Black women played a positive and substantial role in these formal organisations, despite the fact that we were frequently overshadowed by the men. Stella Thomas, for example, was a founder-member of the League of Coloured Peoples, even though the tendency is to identify the organisation with Harold Moody. Una Marston, schooled in the social, cultural and political life of Jamaica, became the organisation's secretary. She contributed regularly to its journal, and became a prominent speaker, worldwide, on the position of Black people in Britain. It was left to women like these to raise and speak out on the Black woman's perspective. At the Fifth Pan-African Congress in 1945, Amy Garvey had to ask why there had been so little discussion of the Black woman, whom she described as having been 'shunted into the social background, to be childbearer'.

Perhaps the woman who best epitomises the fine fighting spirit of the Black women activists of the fifties is Claudia Jones. A little of her story is told here, because her life and beliefs demonstrate the important role that Black women like her have played in Black struggle in this country.

Claudia Jones

Claudia was born on 21 February 1915 in Trinidad. When she was eight, her family moved to Harlem, USA where she experienced first-hand the brutal realities of American racism. Through her family's poverty, she learnt only too well of the conditions under which Black women, the unemployed and domestic and factory workers lived. It was this sharp and painful experience which led her into politics. She worked for the Young Communist League, as the editor of its newspaper, and became passionately involved in anti-racist work, such as publicising and campaigning in the Scotsboro case. (This trial, which spanned four years (1931-35) received worldwide notoriety. Nine Black men accused of raping two white women were sentenced to death, resulting in a huge and much-publicised campaign for their release. After a retrial, the charges against five of the men were dropped, but the remaining four received the equivalent of life imprisonment – despite the fact that one of the women later recanted her story.) She was a strong supporter of Black women's involvement in such struggles, which she saw as a major source of our own liberation. Because of her firm and positive stand against racism she came under attack during the McCarthy 'witch-hunts' which characterised the Cold War period. In 1951, she was arrested and charged with 'un-American activities'. She was imprisoned for a year and finally deported, despite a massive international campaign in her support.

Consequently in 1956, Claudia came to Britain. Already conditioned to the racism she had experienced in the States, she now saw it in operation in Britain – a more subtle brand maybe, but no less effective. What she saw of Black people's plight in Britain sharpened her awareness of the way racism works the world over – and of the need to fight it. She threw herself into the task, involving herself in the work of organisations and campaigns which were busy fighting British racism at every level – in particular, discrimination in housing, jobs and education, but also the very immediate issue of racial attacks. She worked closely with Amy Garvey,

136

launching the *West Indian Gazette* in 1958, as the first campaigning Black newspaper. Also in that year she assisted those arrested while defending themselves in the Notting Hill 'riots'. The *West Indian Gazette* was to become a vital source of information for Black people, serving, in Claudia's own words, as 'a catalyst, quickening the awareness, socially and politically'. It was produced with very limited resources, but received material and other support from famous radical Black patrons such as Paul Robeson, who performed at its fund-raising functions, and from prominent West Indian women like Nadia Catuse, Corrine Skinner and Pearl Prescod, who were Claudia's contemporaries.

In addition to her anti-racist work in the Black community, Claudia held a very strong and clear anti-imperialist position. In an article in *Freedomways*, a Black American journal, popular during the Civil Rights era, she wrote in 1964:

> The citizens of the 'Mother of Democracy' do not yet recognise that the roots of racialism in Britain were laid in the eighteenth and nineteenth centuries through British conquests in India, Africa and great parts of Asia, as well as the British Caribbean. All the resources of official propaganda and education, the super-structure of British imperialism, were permeated with projecting the oppressed colonial peoples as lesser breeds, as 'inferior coloured peoples', 'savages' and the like – in short, 'the white man's burden'. These rationalisations all served to build a justification for wholesale exploitation, extermination and looting of the islands by British imperialism. The great wealth of present-day British monopoly capital was built on the robbery of coloured peoples by such firms as Unilever and the East Africa Company to Tate & Lyle and Booker Bros. in the Caribbean.

In her lifetime, Claudia gained an international reputation, visiting Japan for a conference on the banning of nuclear weapons; China, for a meeting with Mao Tse Tung; and Russia, to speak with women activists there. In Britain, she joined the hunger strikes outside the South African embassy,

137

in the campaign to free Nelson Mandela. In solidarity with Black Americans who marched on Washington in 1963 to demand Civil Rights, she also led a British Freedom March to the US Embassy. In addition, she demonstrated her support for white workers in this country by addressing numerous trade union meetings and actively engaging in discussions and demonstrations in support of workers' rights. She was also ready to give support to Black people in her own community, and her politics were a source of inspiration to, and influence on, all those who knew her.

I first met Claudia in the early sixties. I had not been long in this country, and was experiencing the worst of British hospitality. I was in the launderette, and she must have noticed me sitting there alone, depressed and on the verge of tears. She had been reading, and she put her book to one side and came over to talk to me. I told her about the problems I was having at the time over accommodation – I was living with my three very young children in one room on hardly any money. She was very sympathetic. She showed me where she was living in the next street, and I remember her telling me that all Black people throughout the world were going through the same kind of experiences. Then she helped me to claim Social Security, which I hadn't known how to go about. Claudia was always like that. She could talk to you in political terms, and explain things very clearly, but she was also there with the practical help, too.

After that, she came to visit me quite often. She was a wealth of knowledge and she explained a lot of political matters to me. She stopped me from going around thinking that what was happening to me here was my fault. This really encouraged me to do some thinking and some reading for myself. Whereas before I had used to read a lot of fiction, I now started to read some serious books. Claudia even gave me a booklist! This was the beginning of my involvement in politics, because I became interested in what she was doing and started going along to meetings. I had even planned to work on her paper

138

[*West Indian Gazette*] and she was going to help me to sort out the childminding. But sadly, after she came back from a visit to China at the end of 1964, she died. It was very sudden, and a great loss to us. I went to her memorial service, and saw how many there were who knew and respected her. She was a great woman – a good woman, a real fighter.

In 1964 Claudia's efforts were cut short when she died in her sleep in Christmas Day as a result of a stroke. Her funeral was a testimony of the many who knew, loved and drew strength from her. In the words of Paul Robeson, Claudia Jones 'continued in her day the heroic tradition of Harriet Tubman, of Sojourner Truth – the struggle for negro liberation and women's rights, for human dignity and fulfilment'.

One of the main areas of Claudia Jones's work, which was left for others to continue, was agitation around the 1962 Commonwealth Immigration Act. In the aftermath of the street confrontations of 1958, dubbed 'riots' by the media, the British government gave open sanction to racism and legitimised public assumptions that Black people were the 'problem'. The logical extension of this argument was that our numbers needed to be controlled. The Act was designed to regulate the numbers of Black people entering Britain by allocating us specific immigration categories. Men and women applying to enter Britain were given vouchers, depending on whether they were professionally qualified, skilled or unskilled. By 1964, no Category C immigration of unskilled workers was allowed. The effect of this was to split our families, particularly where we had applied for our older children to join us here. A direct consequence of this was that many Black women decided to send for children who had been left behind in the Caribbean, out of fear that they might be permanently prevented from visiting or joining families here. As Britain's economic boom began to decline it seemed that she no longer required our labour – or our 'superfluous appendages'.

139

The 1962 Immigration Act revealed that the government was more than prepared to institutionalise the rampant racism of its citizens. Other organisations felt emboldened to put their own racist views on record. The police, too, were becoming more openly hostile, both ignoring and initiating attacks on Black people. This created rifts which would widen over the years and result in open antagonism between our community and the 'forces of law and order'. The very first documented evidence of police brutality, 'Nigger-Hunting in England', was delivered to the West Indian Standing Conference and later published in 1966, confirming what was already a widespread experience for Black men and women alike although it provoked little reaction among the British people, who saw 'Dixon of Dock Green', the friendly local bobby, as the typical British policeman.

It was developments such as these which spurred our communities into greater mass organisation. A variety of Black organisations was set up during the early sixties whose brief was to organise against both discriminatory legislation and racist practices. In 1965 many of these newer groups came together with those which had been longer established in the federal structure of CARD (Campaign Against Racial Discrimination), an organisation which linked Asian and Afro-Caribbean activists with Labour Party liberals. It was a contradictory and complex alliance that was doomed to fail as the variety of politics within it came to the fore and clashed. Its demise was greeted with relief by the establishment which feared that the influence of events in the States would cause it to metamorphose into a militant Black Power organisation – a distasteful development in their eyes. Even so, the occasionally uncompromising attacks on racism which CARD initiated clearly presaged the next stage in our political development as a community – the movement for Black Power.

Black Women and Black Power

In many respects, the organisations which ushered in the Black Power era were a continuation of their predecessors in terms of their preoccupations and concerns. However, in their inspiration, ideology and practice, they differed radically. Racist attacks and police brutality continued to be a major concern, as was the position of Black people worldwide. There was now an even closer bond, however, as the links were made between Black people throughout the diaspora who shared the status of oppressed minorities and resisted under the revolutionary slogan 'Black Power'. These ties were strengthened by the visits from America of those who were involved in the struggles there – Malcolm X, Stokley Carmichael, and even Martin Luther King at an earlier date. Later, many others would come to give their support to our struggles here in Britain, but in the mid sixties it was these leaders who gave us inspiration, and helped renew our sense of pride and dignity.

Among the new organisations was UCPA (United Coloured People's Assn), formed in 1967. This was a particularly important organisation, for it spawned several more vibrant and radical successors in later years, some of which still exist in one form or another today. UCPA took on the rhetoric of Black Power, incorporating Black pride but extending it into a demand for social justice for all.

From UCPA came such organisations as BUFP (Black Unity and Freedom Party) and BPM (Black Power Movement), producing their respective papers, *Black Voice* and *Freedom News*. The former took a more consciously internationalist and Marxist stance, but both chose to work around police brutality and the mis-education of Black children in schools. In individual campaigns against police harassment and the ESN mobilisation of parents, they proved to be very successful. Their most important effect, however, was to mobilise hundreds of young Black women who had had no former contact with political organisations, but who felt that the message of Black Power spoke to their immediate situation.

I first got involved in a Black Power organisation after being on the fringes for some time. I'd been involved in one or two cultural groups for a while, but it seemed to me

141

that they'd been talking about 'Black is Beautiful' for too long, as if it was the only slogan we should be relating to. I wanted to take my politics a bit further than that – to make some kind of immediate contribution. Every day you'd be hearing about assaults on black people, either by the police or by the courts and I wanted to get involved with a group that was serious about taking that on.

Thus, by the beginning of the seventies, Black nationalism had given birth to organisations and pressure groups in Black communities up and down the country. Their common purpose – to organise and agitate for the rights we had so long been denied – was pursued with a new militancy. Demonstrations, boycotts, sit-ins, pickets, study circles, supplementary schools, day conferences, campaign and support groups – all had become commonplace activities, exposing both young and old to their politicising influence.

I was still at school when I first woke up to what was going on. A lot was happening in America at the time – the Panthers were being shot, people like George Jackson and the Soledad Brothers were being put on trial ... it was really getting heavy over there and it seemed as if we were all under threat, even here. Then the Mangrove 9 went on trial, and we began to realise that it *was* going on here already. [The 'Mangrove 9' refers to the trial of nine Black activists on charges arising out of their participation in a demonstration in 1970 in Ladbroke Grove, London. Seven of them were acquitted of the main charges.] Everybody thought that it was a political trial. People believed they were framed because they'd helped to organise a demonstration in the Grove against police harassment of Black people who used the Mangrove Restaurant. So for me it was something to do with the times. I felt that the whole of society was going through a radical change, and I wanted to play my part in that. Even though I was only sixteen I realised that there was a lot I could do.

Never before had there been such an obvious level of fervent

142

activity and debate around the issues which affected our day-to-day lives in Britain. Racist immigration laws, second-class state education, treatment by the police, discriminatory housing and employment policies were being exposed, confronted and denounced in every community where Black people figured.

Young Black women joined these initiatives in force, and the effects of their politicisation began to be felt, particularly in the schools.

We started with Black Studies. We went to the Head and asked her to let us set up a Black Studies debating society. She was really shocked and upset by it all. She kept saying, 'But why, we're all one here.' So we went off to join the Black Studies programme at Tulse Hill School, until she gave in. That's when we began to come into our own. We started with the Black berets and carried it through, right down to Black socks and shoes! That's also when I went to my first Black meeting. I heard a Black woman speak there, and I was really impressed with her. Seeing a Black woman up there on the platform made me feel even more enthusiastic.

In some organisations, like 'the Fasimbas' in South London whose emphasis was on culture and education, we formed more than half the membership. Our lives were taken over by political activity.

I flung myself into the work we were doing. We had street collections and we went out selling the organisation's newspaper. We also went on 'door-to-door' in the evenings, when we used to team up and work with a more experienced member of the group, talking to people in the community about what was going on locally and how we should be organising. We went on lots of demonstrations, too, like the Immigration Demo of '71, and we picketed various police stations and courts. Being active filled my life, every evening and weekend.

The attitude of the 'brothers', however, often undermined our participation. We could not realise our full organisational potential in a situation where we were constantly regarded as sexual prey. Although we worked tirelessly, the significance of our contribution to the mass mobilisation of the Black Power era was undermined and overshadowed by the men. They both set the agenda and stole the show:

On the whole, the relationship between the men and the women was down to the fact that it was a youth group. Most of the people in it were young and unattached, and all their time was taken up with the work they did for the organisation. So you had the thing where every new woman member was regarded as easy prey. Some of the brothers were called 'flesh heads' because people knew what they were about. It didn't mean that they weren't serious in their work but it just meant that they had a leisure-time sporting activity which was chasing women. In that atmosphere, you felt vulnerable and exposed as a woman. The men certainly didn't understand anything about women's oppression. In fact, they didn't have the faintest clue about it. Nearly every one of them was a die-hard sexist. Some women were badly mistreated, but the way the leadership tried to deal with it was similar to the way they tried to get new ideas through to the membership generally. Brothers were hauled up and disciplined when what they needed was political education – to read, study and discuss the woman question and to confront their own sexism. No attempt was made to seriously take up women's issues, they just weren't considered immediately pressing.

Certain things did refer to women in a way, like the all-women picket of the Old Bailey during the Mangrove 9 trial. But this wasn't about recognising women as a force in their own right, it was more about raising publicity for the campaign. Otherwise, even though there were quite a few sisters around who were active in the organisation, when it came to making any decisions, things were dominated by the men. We had very little say in anything, to begin with. The brothers used to be busy making all the decisions, taking all the initiatives, and we got to take the

144

minutes, make the coffee, that sort of thing. If we ever got a mention, it was usually only to ask why more sisters weren't coming to meetings! There was this romantic image of African womanhood around at the time, and although a lot of us were beginning to take on the idea that Black women were strong and had a role to play in the struggle, many of us still hadn't reached a stage where we could challenge the idea that we should walk three paces behind the men. That's why Angela Davis was such an inspiration to Black women at the time. She seemed to have liberated herself mentally and fought in her own right, showing us all a lead. Angela was a very positive development, where Black women's image was concerned, because hers was less romantic than the one which had been held up until she came on the scene.

As a result of the sexism we encountered, and because of the powerful influence of sisters like Angela Davis, Black women within such organisations were moved to begin to examine our own role in the Black struggle. Although our early, hesitant questions were firmly couched in terms which did not challenge our role as women within the family, they nevertheless represented the first efforts of Black women to speak up on our own behalf.

But changes were on the horizon which would spur us to take this analysis much further. At an organisational level, the limitations of cultural nationalism which did not take account of class were beginning to be recognised. Many organisations were moving from an obviously cultural-nationalist position to adopt a more overt class line, as shown in this extract from *Uhuru*, the journal of the Black People's Freedom Movement in Nottingham:

Black organisations, whilst rightfully standing up for the Black *man*'s [our emphasis] dignity in every possible way, should nonetheless move away from Black Power concepts and see the whole issue in class terms. The race-class struggles of Black people are not antagonistic. They are one and the same thing.

145

This was all very well, but the dignity of Black women was meanwhile being ignored.

Many members, however, would not accept this shift away from Black Power towards class considerations. It had been the guiding force in their politics. They had joined these organisations on the tide of Black Power, and ideological developments such as these did not conform to their understanding of what Black struggle was all about. This was due in part to the failure of the (male) leadership to ensure that the membership grew with them politically. The young Black women and men who had supported them with such enthusiasm and commitment could not understand their arguments, particularly when white dockers were marching on Parliament in support of Enoch Powell's racist call for mass repatriation in his 'Rivers of Blood' speech in 1968. As the organisations began to shift under the strain of their own ideological contradictions, the support of women members was consciously sought to strengthen the membership and new women members were actively encouraged to join. Black women had already begun to consider our own special situation, however, and our response was to call more loudly for our own liberation:

POLITICAL UNION

You call me 'Sister' Brother,
yet it seems you speak with the empty kernel of the word,
and sometimes
when you talk to me
there lingers after
a void
far more empty than existed before.
When you hear my anguished silence and are reassured by
   it
     then I know that your strength depends on my
       becoming weak
     that you have not questioned
     the bars, deeply entrenched,
     of the barbed cage, externally defined
     that is the oppressor's role you so emulate.

146

When you look above the waist
    see my face
    touch my skin,
    nestle on my breast as though
    to reclaim the ease of infancy
then I know
    that you have concretised my body
    in your mind, into a temple
    for your fantasies.
When you fraternise with my sisters while demanding my
    fidelity
then I know that you yourself are unfulfilled.

Many times you have seen my nakedness
    but not noticed my eyes
    as you surround me in your taunting caress.
Can you, physically a part of this body
Try to see, inside this body
    the joy and pain at once housed side by side?
Can you stop wearing me, playing me
    stop strumming my emotions?

You call me 'Sister' Brother,
    yet I know
    that it is simply a psychological lever to prise apart
        my legs.
'Sister, make coffee for the movement,
Sister, make babies for the struggle'
You raped my consciousness with your body
    my body with reason,
    and assuage your unconscious guilt by oral politiking
                    make believing
'Sister, Sister'.

When you yourself acknowledge the Occidental fetters
    that truss you,
When you yourself see the hidden fenders that seal the
    seal
over your mind's eye
against me

147

When you can see that my political significance is
a vertical one
that my contribution is
a vanguard one
and you can see my total
Then you can call me Sister
Then you will be my Comrade.

Iyamide Hazeley

Coming Together as Women: The Development of the Brixton Black Women's Group

The early seventies saw the first Black women's caucuses being formed within the Black Power organisations in London. Because they were an attempt to bring more women into the political arena, their approach was to appeal directly to Black women's issues. The women's caucuses would ultimately find that they could not fulfil their function of attracting large numbers of new members, but they were extremely successful in another respect. They enabled Black women who had shared similar political backgrounds to come together, as women, for the first time ever. Here we began to discuss our common experiences of racial and sexist oppression, and as we began to forge the links, we were unknowingly laying the foundation of the Black women's movement which would emerge in the years to follow.

A lot of people think Black women began to challenge what was happening in mixed organisations because we were influenced by what was going on in the white women's movement. But I think we were influenced far more, at the time, by what was happening in the liberation movements on the African continent. There were more and more examples of Black women who were active in revolutionary struggles in places like Angola, Mozambique, Eritrea, Zimbabwe and Guinea-Bissau. And those sisters weren't just picking up a gun and fighting – they were making demands *as women*, letting it be known that they weren't about to make all those sacrifices just so

148

that they could be left behind when it came to seizing power. So although we had begun to form women's caucuses and women's study groups, what Samora Machel had to say about women's emancipation made a lot more sense to us than what Germaine Greer and other middle-class white feminists were saying. It just didn't make sense for us to be talking about changing life-styles and attitudes, when we were dealing with issues of survival, like housing, education and police brutality.

We formed the Black Women's Group in 1973. We didn't even bother with a name. We were just the Black Women's Group. We came mainly out of Black organisations. Some had left and some were still there, but on the whole the organisations we came from were in the process of disintegrating. There were a lot of charges and counter-charges, which I felt had nothing to do with me or my struggle. I had begun to meet in the previous months with other Black women in the caucus meetings. Straight away we got accused of 'splitting the movement', of weakening organisations which were already on the way out. The brothers gave us a hard time over that. Some sisters felt very strongly that we should stick it out within the organisations and try to strengthen the women's position within them. But for most of us, setting up an autonomous group for Black women was really necessary at the time.

From the discussions we had, we were aware that there were issues that related to us particularly as Black women, like women's work, our economic dependence on men and childcare, which we could organise around. It was a chance to put them at the top of the agenda for the first time. We didn't want to become part of the white women's movement. We felt they had different priorities to us. At that time, for example, abortion was the number one issue, and groups like Wages for Housework were making a lot of noise, too. These were hardly burning issues for us – in fact they seemed like middle-class preoccupations. To begin with, abortion wasn't something we had any problems getting as Black women – it was the very reverse for us! And as for wages for housework, we were more

149

interested in getting properly paid for the work we were doing outside the home as nightcleaners and in campaigning for more childcare facilities for Black women workers.

We helped to set up and maintain the first Black bookshop in Brixton, and joined the Railton 4 Campaign over police harassment. We also mobilised the community in Brixton against the practice of setting up disruptive units and helped in the campaign for parental rights. As the first autonomous Black women's group of its kind, certainly in London, there were no models for us to follow, no paths laid out. We just had to work it out as we went along. We were very wary of charges that we might be 'splitting the Black struggle' or mobilising in a vacuum or imitating middle-class white women. These were the kinds of criticism Black men were making at the time. We couldn't be – in fact, we never were – anti-men, in that sense. But it was so good to be in a group which wasn't hostile and didn't fight all the time. That sense of autonomy, of woman-purpose was something everybody felt at the time, though. The attack was that we were all just a bunch of lesbians, implying that we had just got together to discuss our sexual preferences and weren't serious about taking anything else up which had relevance to the Black community. We were determined to prove them wrong on this, because it was a label which really undermined what we had set out to do at the time. We would not have called ourselves 'feminists' by any means – we didn't go that far for many years. It took us a long time before we worked out a Black women's perspective, which took account of race, class, sex, *and* sexuality.

But it wasn't just a case of making links and maintaining our credibility within our own immediate community. We also made some important contacts with organisations outside Brixton, which influenced our politics. There were groups like ASU (African Students Union) and the African women's study groups which had been formed by women from Ethiopia, Eritrea and other Third World countries. We also had links with the ZANU

150

Women's League, so we were in close touch with what was happening to Black women within the liberation struggles on the continent. And then, of course, there was OWAAD [Organisation of Women of Asian and African Descent] which we contributed a lot to in the early days, because there was such a need for Black women to make contact with each other on a national basis. We organised joint activities and maintained links with these groups, in some cases for quite a few years. I think they all made a really positive contribution to our political perspective, as it developed.

Groups like the Brixton BWG were just one of the strands which, when woven together, helped to bind the political practice of the Black community as a whole. They were in many ways simply a continuation of the Black groups which had existed ever since our arrival after the war. Black women were just as committed to the task of fighting racism both locally and internationally, but brought the important new dimension of feminism into our struggle.

Olive Morris

One of the founder members of the BWG was Olive Morris, who in her very short lifetime made an invaluable contribution to Brixton BWG, OWAAD and the Black communities in both Brixton and Manchester. Like Claudia Jones, she represents the kind of Black women who, over the years, have thrown themselves into the struggle in this country and made an indelible, if anonymous, mark.

Olive Morris's short life was similar in most respects to the lives of the majority of West Indian women living in Britain today. She came to Britain at the age of eight to live with her parents, and went to a secondary modern in south London where she experienced all the inequalities and injustices of the British education system. She left at sixteen with no qualifications, but undeterred, she went on to college to study 'O' and 'A' levels, while at the same time holding down a full-time job.

151

It was during this phase of her life, when she was only seventeen years old, that Olive carried out her first conscious political act, one which was to lead her into organised political activity for the rest of her life. This was in 1969, when she went to the aid of someone who was being harassed in the street by the police. His crime was to have been driving an expensive car, which the police found suspicious enough to warrant an arrest. As a result of her intervention, Olive herself was arrested and taken to the local police station, where she was made to strip and was brutally assaulted. The incident did not intimidate her, however. It simply strengthened her opposition to racism and injustice.

Olive went on to join the Black Panther movement, and it was here that she began to develop the political ideology which would determine her future actions. She gave a total commitment to the organisation's work and development, and participated in nearly all of the battles which formed part of the community's everyday life. She was in tune with the needs of the people, and always showed herself willing to take the initiative and act. This was certainly the case with the squatters movement in Brixton, when she organised with others like herself to squat because there was nowhere to live and no hope of a council flat. She became well known in the community for her willingness to help other Black people who were facing difficulties, whether with the schools, the police, housing, social security officials or the courts – whatever the issue, she was never too busy to offer support. For Olive, it was not just a case of doing things for those who couldn't do it for themselves: it was her way of involving people in the struggle, showing by her own example the will to resist and to challenge.

After the decline of the Black Panther movement, Olive worked with some other Black women in the area and with a group of brothers to set up Sarbarr Bookshop, the first Black self-help community bookshop in south London. During this same period, she helped form the Brixton Black Women's Group, to which she made a lasting contribution. The political perspective she brought to the group helped it to develop a coherent political ideology, based on the needs of ordinary Black people in the community, which made clear links with other anti-imperialist struggles. She worked relentlessly to translate these ideas into practice, and most of her political work was done at grassroots level.

In 1975, she went to Manchester University to study for a social science degree. This in itself was an important step for Olive, who believed in education for the people. For her, going to university was not a status symbol, but an example to many young Black people of how to fight and win against a system which tries to push us to the bottom of the education pile and force us to compete against each other.

Unlike many students, Olive did not separate her work at the university from the struggles which were being waged in the rest of the community. In her work with the Manchester Black Women's Co-operative and the Black Women's Mutual Aid Group, which she helped to set up, she participated fully in the Black community's battles in Moss Side. Committed to furthering education rights for Black people, she campaigned with Black mothers for better schooling for their children and helped to set up a supplementary school and a Black bookshop in the area. Because she was an internationalist, she also worked at the university within the National Co-ordinating Committee of Overseas Students. She provided an essential link between international, community and women's organisations, drawing the parallels between our experiences here and in the Third World.

In 1978, Olive visited China. The trip was of great significance to her, for she saw China as one of the countries which Third World peoples could learn a lot from, and which could serve as a model for us in self-help and self-reliance. The lessons she learnt there were shared with everyone she worked with on her return. Sharing knowledge was always her practice.

Olive had always identified the relationship between the struggles of people in the Third World and those of the white working class. She recognised that it was a fight which had to be won through the contribution of both groups, and that we would need to work together if we were to bring about any

153

meaningful changes. It was this awareness which was her greatest contribution to the political development of those she worked with.

When she returned to Brixton in 1978 after completing her studies, the work she had begun while in Manchester to launch OWAAD was taken up by other women in the Brixton Black Women's Group. It was then that she began to suffer the symptoms of the cancer which killed her within the year. In her fight against leukemia, she displayed the same courage she had shown throughout her life, and when she died on 12 July 1979, at the age of twenty-six, she had already made her mark. She was mourned by all sections of the Black community, and by many others from outside it whose lives she had touched.

Olive and I went to the same school. Even then she had that streak in her – in school, they would have called it rebelliousness or disruptiveness, but it was really a fearlessness about challenging injustice at whatever level. This made others very wary of her, she was so obviously a fighter. I saw her once confronting a policeman – it might have been when she was evicted. She went at him like a whirlwind and cussed him to heaven. And this policeman looked really taken aback, he didn't know how to deal with someone who had no fear of him. He was meant to represent the big arm of the law. But because she was angry and she knew he was in the wrong, she didn't hesitate.

She would take anybody on like that, even people in organisations if she thought that someone needed to expose their hypocrisy for mouthing slogans and living a lie. Because of that, a lot of them saw her as a pain in the neck, and she was too! She'd fight them physically, if it was necessary. If you moved with Olive, you couldn't be a weak heart. She gave a lot of support to so many sisters though, when they came under pressure from the brothers at meetings or wherever. She was a real example. You didn't see it then, of course, but that fearlessness of hers, and that genuine commitment she showed to the work she

154

did made her stand out, made her special.

I remember when Olive was in Manchester, I went up to an education meeting she was organising with the Manchester Black Women's group, and it struck me at the time how at home she was away from home. She had gone up to the university to study, but she made contact with people so easily that before you knew it she was right in there with the Black women in Moss Side, organising with them, taking things on. She could easily have found a student clique on the campus, but instead she sought out her people and just carried on the work we'd been doing in Brixton. But then she always was hot on personal commitment – not just showing willing, but showing determination. Her life is a kind of symbol to the people who knew her. People like Olive inspire you to resist.

At her memorial ceremony in Brixton a few weeks after her death, several hundred people came to pay testimony to her remarkable courage and her fighting spirit. Those who knew her were left with her vision of a new society, and the lasting memory of one more Black woman who was not afraid to fight back.

The Struggles of the 1970s

There were many Black women like Olive who emerged during the seventies. It was a time when Black women were becoming increasingly visible and active. We were involved in tenants' and squatters' campaigns, in the struggles of our community against the abuses of the education system and in a variety of defence campaigns which arose out of our daily battles with the police:

I was on my way with another sister to a meeting when we witnessed a pregnant Black woman being bundled into a police car. My friend and I rushed over because she was shouting for someone to help her. The police grabbed her, but I took her other arm and there was a real tussle and a lot of shouting. They threatened to arrest us too but they didn't. When they drove away, we followed them down to

155

the police station and tried to make some enquiries. The sister they had taken in had only been passing them on the street, from what we could tell, but they refused to tell us what they were charging her with. So we went off to the meeting, rounded up some of the people there, made up some placards and went back to the police station to picket it until they released the woman. That kind of response was necessary simply because they were picking Black people off the street like that all the time and we were getting fed up with the way the police got away with it.

It was not only the young Black women who were involved in the Black Power organisations and already had a taste for militancy who took part. Black women of the previous generation, many of whom had a long history of struggle against racist attacks and police brutality, were finding ways of expressing the anger they felt, too. The treatment of their children at the hands of the police, education authorities, employers and the courts spurred them on to organise in a more overtly political way, often with the encouragement and support of the children themselves:

My daughter used to come home and tell me about the meetings she was going to and the ways they were taking things up and I found myself getting more and more interested. I started going along to some of the meetings with her, and to my surprise I found that it wasn't just the young people who were turning up. My daughter really encouraged me and it began to rub off on other areas of my life. For example, I joined the union and started getting involved in things that were happening to Black people at my workplace.

Black schoolgirls were making their contribution, too. They rebelled against their experiences at school, helping to initiate boycotts of classes to further their demands for a better educational deal. We were striking, demonstrating, picketing and speaking out with a newfound urgency – and whatever our age or our level of political awareness, Black women seized the opportunity to make our voices heard.

156

We were refusing to bow down to another decade of institutionalised racism, and it was because of the militancy of our people's response that successive governments constantly sought out ways of containing and controlling our presence here. But only a thin veneer of legality disguised the real motives behind the racist laws and practices which became characteristic of the seventies. In 1971, for example, a new Immigration Act legitimised the notion that Black people were second-class citizens. By classifying all those who had no formal blood ties with Britain as 'non-patrials', the State took away our right to enter Britain and made it clear that we had no entitlement to equal treatment, once here. The 1971 Act was followed by a series of Immigration Rules which went almost unnoticed by the media, but which affected all Black people severely, particularly Black women. The 'Sole Responsibility' rule, for example, was directly aimed at preventing our children from joining us here.

People have tended to think of Immigration Laws as only affecting the Asian community, but this isn't the case. The 'Sole Responsibility' rule directly affects West Indian women, particularly if they're single parents. It's really difficult for a Black women to bring her children here if she's not married. She has to prove that her children *have* to join her in Britain, that she's the only relative who is in a position to look after her own children. But parents are supposed to look after their own children, it doesn't matter whether they've got hundreds of relatives, all of them millionaires. The fact that we've been separated from our children in the first place is down to purely economic factors. We got here, the streets weren't paved with gold, we're in lousy jobs, the worst housing, and still they want to keep us apart from our kids. Just because a relative has been bringing up your child, it doesn't mean they're going to be prepared to do that for you indefinitely or even able to do it financially. When Black women left their children, it was a temporary measure. But in order to get them into the country, you have to show that contact with the child has been regularly maintained, *specifically in the form of*

157

visits. Now, if we'd had that kind of money, we wouldn't have had to send for our children in the first place! When the adjudicators are making judgements about whether or not a Black women has 'sole reponsibility' for her child, they push the argument that in the extended family unit in the Caribbean, everybody has the responsibility for being a parent. This is how stereotypes are used against us – they just get written into the law. We really have to be on our guard.

Such legislation confirmed our suspicion that the main object of immigration controls was racist – particularly since no comparative rule has ever existed to regulate the entry of EEC citizens to Britain.

When unemployment took a sharp turn upwards in 1974, compounding the discrimination we already faced in employment and education and speeding up our steady relegation to the dole queues, the inherent racism of the Immigration Act became even clearer. Now that Britain no longer needed our labour, we had officially become 'persona non grata' – and that included our children.

Many of our struggles in the seventies were centred around ways of protecting ourselves and our communities from police violence and the racism of the courts. The flimsiest of evidence from the police was repeatedly used to impose severe penalties on us, for the most minor of offences.

We first heard the story of how the police were harassing one of the local youths from his mother. She told us how he had been coming home one night from a party when the police stopped him and asked him where he was going. They called him 'sunshine' or something, and when he said, 'My name's not sunshine,' they laid into him and beat him up. They charged him with resisting arrest. When his mother told us what had happened, we decided to take it up, because it was just one of many incidents like that which we were hearing about every day. This triggered off a lot of activity. We fought the case by supporting his mother in making a complaint against the

158

police. She was already a member of the group, but other Black women became involved simply because they wanted to support our action. We picketed the local Police Station and called in the local press. Then we got involved in a People's Enquiry, gathering information and evidence on the courts, the police, our housing situation, employment and education practices – everything which affected the Black community in our area. A lot of Black people came along to give evidence on how they had been dealt with by the local police and we helped to compile a report. At that point, we felt that all our involvement with these pressing issues called for a linking up with other local groups, some of which could take up particular issues and take them further. In this way, we would be free to move on to other equally pressing concerns affecting Black women and our community generally, and avoid getting bogged down with trying to take on too much. This was particularly important because we were only a handful of Black women, with no resources of our own, and we faced the usual problems of trying to be active and having to be mothers, cooks, cleaners and go out to work to earn our living.

Black women were responding to the growing criminalis-ation of young Black people. Even when our children were at school, we could expect the police to be called into the playground to break up fights or to sort out minor incidents. Small Black children, too, would be brought to court for stealing a packet of sweets or a toy car, evidence of the police's contemptuous attitude towards Black parents' ability to discipline our own children. It was as a result of these experiences of a racist police force that Black women began to organise both against specific incidents of abuse and against legislation like the 'SUS' law which legitimised police brutality.

By resorting to the use of a clause in the 1824 Vagrancy Act, an old and obsolete law which had remained dormant in the statute books for years, the police were able to stop, search and arrest anybody on the basis of a mere suspicion.

Because it was our children and community who were victims of this law, Black mothers were in the forefront of campaigns like the 'SCRAP SUS' initiative. This began in a Black woman's front room in Deptford and eventually swept throughout the Black community, uniting the generations in a call for the law to be scrapped.

Some of the women began meeting with other Black groups to talk about the SUS law – particularly with the women who had organised in Deptford. Out of these meetings, we formed the SCRAP SUS campaign. Over the next few months, we held a series of public meetings and demonstrations, wrote to the press, organised a petition, made badges – everything we could think of to publicise the SUS issue. It was important to us that the television and newspapers should acknowledge how the SUS law was being used by the police against Black kids. Eventually they began to take a very unusual interest in our grievances and they got reported quite widely in the media. That's how people outside the Black community got to know about SUS. Black mothers covered the groundwork which made SUS into a public issue. It was only after this that the local Community Relations Council decided to get off their backsides and get involved in it too. Before that, they didn't want to know.

As Black women channelled the anger we felt at the criminalisation of our children into defence campaigns the role of the police was called into question publicly, in a way that had rarely been witnessed before. Nevertheless, when open clashes between police and Black people took place outside the factory gates at Grunwick and at the centre of the Notting Hill Carnival, in 1976 and 1977 the media and the politicians were unanimous. With unashamed partiality, they blamed us for the violence and engendered public sympathy for the 'beseiged' forces of law and order.

Black women were also active in housing campaigns. At the hands of unscrupulous landlords or racist local councils, we faced – and still do face – the worst housing conditions in Britain. By 1978, the proportion of Black people living in

160

homes without baths, running hot water or an inside toilet was more than twice the national average, and three times as many Black families as white were living in sub-standard privately furnished accommodation. Because of the discriminatory policies of local authorities, growing numbers of Black women were being housed in high rise blocks on 'problem' estates – particularly if they were single parents.

The consequences of these housing policies are still acutely evident today. When, in 1984 Hackney Council claimed that it had just discovered racism in its housing department, most Black people simply shrugged their shoulders and said, 'So what?' We knew that we had suffered discrimination in housing ever since our arrival in this country, and that this was only the tip of the iceberg. But then as now, we found ways of fighting these policies of ghettoisation: with the same determination to fight back as we had shown against the police, Black women organised both individually and collectively against the housing policies of racist councils. In the early seventies, Black women led the tenants in their fight to be transferred from their homes on a London estate. They organised rent strikes, demonstrations and an occupation of the Town Hall in their struggle to demand better housing.

We all came here as homeless families. Nearly all the tenants were Black. When I came here, as with most people, I came for six weeks to six months. The longest time we were supposed to stay was eighteen months, but a lot of the people had been there for three or four years, and no one in the council was doing anything about it. Then, in 1972, the council wrote us all a letter stating that from April that year, we would be proper council tenants. Everyone was mad because that meant we were here for keeps and they weren't planning to transfer us anywhere. Everyone was dying to get out. People were getting offers of places which were in worse condition than the ones we were already in, and they were taking them. A lot of the flats had no electric points and no heaters, but the council had been promising for months to start the work and nothing had happened. This was what led us to organise

161

the rent strike and to occupy the Town Hall. We took the children down and let them loose. After that, they had to sit down and talk to us.

After we went on the rent strike, some tenants started asking why the council should move us from here into smaller places in the first place. We were certain that there were a lot of people who wouldn't mind staying on the estate if the facilities were modernised, and we wanted to know why the council wasn't prepared to do that. They were going to move people out and board up the whole estate. So we did a survey asking who would like to stay if the facilities were improved, and whether, if they were moved out for that purpose, they'd like to come back. We sent the results to the council.

When the council wants to modernise its property and needs you to move, they're supposed to give you a Home Loss Grant which is the equivalent to three times the rate of the value of the property. Some people didn't get anything though, the council just took it all back in settlement for rent arrears. Rent arrears – for a slum like that! We thought they would empty one block at a time, but suddenly they started emptying the lot. They made sure that the group who had formed the tenants' association got acceptable offers, but I think that a lot of people regretted leaving, because the places they got were no better than here.

Meanwhile, our housing situation and our treatment by the police were being compounded by the treatment our children were receiving in schools. Inner-city education authorities, such as the Inner London Education Authority, were setting up disruptive units and developing other ways of combatting our rebellions in the classroom in their effort to contain those of our children whom they now considered 'unteachable'. Black children were being thrown into these 'sin bins' in numbers out of all proportion to our three per cent of the population. And this over-representation spilled into the detention centres and the prisons, into unemployment statistics and mortality rates, and into computerised police criminal records.

162

As our community came under greater seige Black women would play an increasingly central role in the fight to defend ourselves and our children from the onslaught. As mothers and as workers, we came into daily contact with the institutions which compounded our experience of racism. We were the ones who rushed to the police stations when members of our family got arrested. We were the ones who had to take time off work to confront teachers and the education authorities about the mis-education of our children. We were the ones who cleared up the debris when police entered our homes uninvited to harass and intimidate us. We were the ones who battled it out with the housing authorities, the Social Services and the DHSS, as we demanded our right to decent homes and an income above subsistence level.

At our meetings we started by trying to educate ourselves, first of all, by looking at our rights – for example, our rights on arrest, our housing rights, that sort of thing. Also, our children's rights, particularly in education, because there were a lot of suspensions of Black kids in our area taking place. Out of our discussions – particularly about the attitudes of Black mothers when their kids got picked up by the police or suspended by the schools – grew the idea of making a video. We felt that to have such a tape would be one way of challenging some of these attitudes, because we could show it at meetings and use it as a basis for discussions. We wrote and filmed three short plays, based on three actual cases we knew of. We used the plays to illustrate some of our own attitudes and some of the reactions we knew were common among Black mothers at the time, when confronted with the police, local authority workers and teachers. The first time we showed the tapes was at a public meeting, which we held jointly with the Afro-Caribbean Women's Association in Deptford and with some sisters from the West Indian Women's Association in Walthamstow. This is how we started to make links with some of the other Black women who were getting organised in the London area.

163

We bore the brunt, too, of the increasingly drastic cuts in health and social services, welfare benefits, housing programmes and childcare facilities. In every area of our lives, we found ourselves on the frontline in our community's battles to confront racism and repression. It is therefore no coincidence that at the end of the seventies, a strong, vibrant, militant movement of Black women emerged – a movement which would play a leading role in the Black struggles of the 1980s.

Organising into the '80s

The Organisation of Women of Asian and African Descent, or OWAAD as it came to be known, was undoubtedly one of the most decisive influences on Black women's politics in this country. As the first national network of its kind, it brought Black women together from all parts of Britain.

OWAAD's lifetime spanned only five years, from its foundation in 1978 to its demise in 1983. During this time, it captured the imagination of many Black women and succeeded in bringing a new women's dimension to the Black struggles of the eighties. Its national conferences, held annually from 1979 to 1982, along with its day-schools, special project committees and its newsletter *FOWAAD*, served as essential points of communication for Black women, presenting us with our first opportunity to meet as women on a national scale, to exchange ideas and lend each other mutual support. Because the organisation emerged at a time when Black women generally were bursting to articulate their own experience of oppression, it was in a position to channel this energy and anger, providing a focal point for those women who were active in the community, or needed information and practical support. As a direct result of OWAAD's influence, the number of Black women's groups grew dramatically in the space of a few years, not only in London, where it was based, but also in Black communities in other parts of the country. No longer prepared to play second fiddle to the men when our communities came under attack, Black women became visible and audible as never before.

164

True to the tradition of many Black political initiatives, OWAAD's origins lay in the efforts of a handful of Black women. Their aim was to create and promote a national network of Black women, something which had been missing in our struggles until then. When the organisation was formed by a small group of Black women students and activists, its base was narrow; but within a few months, it had succeeded in mobilising large numbers of Black women, embracing any woman who agreed with its basic objectives.

OWAAD was formed after a group of about fifteen of us met at Warwick University in February 1978. We'd come together to discuss how we could mobilise more sisters to take part in the African Students Union, which we all had connections with. The women who came to that meeting represented a number of Black women's groups which were around at the time, like the ZANU Women's League, the Ethiopian Women's Study Group, the Eritrean Women's Study Group, the Black Women's Alliance of South Africa, and the Brixton Black Women's Group. When we started talking about forming a women's caucus in ASU, the African sisters just told us, 'Forget it'. They had a lot to say about what it was like to be a minority of women within an all-male organisation because most of them had already withdrawn from that set-up. By the end of the day, we came to the conclusion that we'd have to go it alone, by forming ourselves into an autonomous organisation which was independent and committed to prioritising African and Afro-Caribbean women's issues. [OWAAD adopted its position on Afro-Asian Unity six months later, in August 1978, and changed its name accordingly. However its practice and composition reflected the fact that Afro-Caribbean women were in the majority, and the question of how to organise across both communities became one of OWAAD's most controversial discussion points.]
A small group of us began to meet regularly in London to follow up that decision. To begin with we maintained the links with ASU and saw ourselves as a 'sister'

165

organisation. We went along to their Annual General Meeting in Manchester the following month and lobbied the brothers to support us. We even got them to make a donation of £50 to OWAAD, to help us fund our publicity. Olive Morris was one of the sisters who came along to that meeting, and she won the day for us. She just jumped to her feet and cussed the brothers out whenever any of them came up with an excuse for not supporting us!

The first few months was a time of a lot of intense, sustained activity, a lot of learning from each other and thinking things through from scratch. We had to decide on our aims and on what we were going to prioritise. It wasn't just that easy to bring African and Afro-Caribbean women together, because we all came from different experiences of racism. The African sisters wanted to concentrate on things like supporting the liberation struggles and publicising what was happening to the women in them. But those of us whose roots were in this country wanted to take up Black women's issues here. In the end, with more and more Afro-Caribbean women attending and arguing for that position, the African sisters drifted away and went back into the national support groups.

Over the months, as more and more women started to come to meetings, we worked out a structure and set about the task of developing a national network. Some Asian sisters had started to come along, and they argued very strongly that we should be organising jointly. That's how the name got changed. The following month, we organised the first national Black women's conference to be held in this country, which was a real high point for Black women's politics, because it was the first time we had come together as a group to talk about our own priorities and start working on some strategies for dealing with them.

Three hundred Black women attended the first OWAAD conference in March 1979, and its effects were to ripple through the community for several years to come. The

166

variety of women who participated in terms of age, background and politics ensured that the mood would be conveyed back into our communities at every level.

That was the thing about the first OWAAD conference. It really broke down that isolation, because Black women realised from going there and seeing all those other women that there were a lot of us in the same position. So a lot of the difficulties we had had as women started to be shared and discussed. I remember being really struck by the number of Black women who were there – it must have been several hundred of us. I'd never realised that there were so many Black women who were articulate, organised and aware of what was going on. I was on a high for weeks afterwards.

Many women were inspired to go home and set about the task of forming local Black women's groups, some of which were to outlive OWAAD by several years. Others took back the demands which had come out of the conference, and began to organise with men around issues like 'SUS' and education.

After the first OWAAD conference in 1979, which some of the women in our group attended, we really began to tackle the education issue. We decided to form a sub-committee, whose task would be to set up a local education pressure group. This was because education had emerged as the most burning issue at the conference, and we were already concerned to do something about the high suspension rates of Black kids in Haringey. So we called a public meeting and the Haringey Black Pressure Group on Education was formed. The pressure group involved quite a few of us, plus local parents, teachers, youths and so on. The first thing we did was to try to find our more about what was going on in our local schools, how many Black children were getting suspended, and what the suspension procedure was. We used the local press to publicise the results, and ended up being asked to a meeting with the local Education Authority, which wasn't productive at all.

167

Their main concern was to sound us out and find out how serious we were. Then they went and issued a confidential document to local schools, urging them to set up disruptive units, or 'sin bins' as we called them, which was their way of hiding the suspension figures behind the school gates. So we spent a lot of time visiting local parents, leafleting the community, writing to local schools to let them know our feelings about disruptive units, and generally raising it as an issue within community. We gathered a lot of information through these activities – for example, we found out that about eighty per cent of the kids in the local maladjusted school were Black, which proved our fears about how these disruptive units would work against the interests of Black kids. To cut a long story short, we eventually won that battle, and the idea of disruptive units being attached to every secondary school in the borough was dropped. That was a really important victory for us.

Other women who had attended that first conference singled out specific concerns, like the racist use of Depo Provera which the women's movement had so far failed to pursue, or put their energies into campaigns against police brutality and immigration abuses.

There was the Shirley Graham case, which the East London Black Women's Organisation got involved in and which we eventually won. [Shirley Graham, a Jamaican by birth, was detained for five days in August 1981 and subsequently threatened with deportation, on returning to Britain after a short trip abroad. Her family had lived and worked in Britain for over twenty years, and she herself had been resident in this country since 1974.] We held public meetings and did a lot of fund-raising with other groups in the community. One of the local schools even put on a play to raise money for Shirley's campaign. We went up and down the country, giving talks to other immigration and anti-deportation campaigns. Shirley Graham herself did a lot of public speaking, and her experience politicised her. We worked intensively for a year with petitions, letters to MP's, the whole works. After that, we had umpteen letters from people from all over the country, experiencing immigration problems or being threatened with deportation. I mean, it's a really big issue for Caribbean women, although it's not presented as such. Shirley, for instance, was detained by immigration officials who delayed in giving her the medication and special diet she needed for her diabetes and high blood pressure. She might have been kept in detention until she was sent back if her cousin hadn't come into the Law Centre for advice.

It was not the originality of the issues which we raised, but rather the confidence we had gained in articulating them *as women* which gave rise to the intensity of activity which followed.

By the end of its second year, OWAAD had created a coordinated network of groups and individuals, representing Black women's groups, projects, campaigns and concerns from across London. Because of the practical difficulties of liaising with women outside London, the national network which was one of OWAAD's aims remained very informal, and London remained the focal point of most activities. Nevertheless, OWAAD did succeed in reaching large numbers of Black women in others parts of the country, either directly through its conferences, or indirectly through the newsletter, *FOWAAD*, and through the example of our political practice. Above all, we strove to develop an internal organisational structure which was non-hierarchical, enabling Black women to determine their own priorities and the level at which they would pitch their contribution. By devising a system of rotational representation, to take account of childcare demands and other commitments, it was possible for women to choose whether and when to participate in the overall running of the organisation. Although the system was by no means flawless, it represented a new and self-determined approach to political organisation which remained unhampered by leaders or appointed spokeswomen.

169

As we entered the eighties, Black women were active around nearly every major community issue. With our fingers on the pulse we were in a position not only to respond to the State's assaults on us, but also to anticipate them in advance:

In 1980, they had a Test Census in Haringey to sound out the response of Black people to having an 'ethnic' question in the 1981 National Census. That was something else we felt we had to take on, because our reaction would be used to justify a national head count of Black people, and we felt that this was a dangerous move on the part of the government, especially since these kinds of statistics have never been used to improve things for us. We took that on by joining with other groups in the borough who were concerned about the question, and organised a boycott of the question when the test census was conducted. We also made sure that the local and national press knew our feelings about it, and we got a lot of coverage of the issue which helped alert other Black people to what was being planned.

The fact that we were active and involved was not, in itself, unprecedented. What was unprecedented was that Black women had begun to articulate demands *as an organised body*, with the assurance which could only come from a strong sense of self-knowledge and mutual solidarity:

Our group organises on the basis of Afro-Asian unity, and although that principle is maintained, we don't deal with it by avoiding the problems this might present, but by having on-going discussions.

When we use the term 'Black', we use it as a political term. It doesn't describe skin colour, it defines our situation here in Britain. We're here as a result of British imperialism, and our continued oppression in Britain is the result of British racism.

Obviously we have to take into account our cultural differences, and that has affected the way we are able to organise. It can be very difficult for Asian sisters living at

170

home to actually come to meetings and get involved with organising; they may fear being ostracised by their family, for example. Some sisters left their families because they identified those restrictions as oppressive. Arranged marriages was something we took on quite seriously. Some Asian sisters left the group as a result of having to accept an arranged marriage, but others have rejected that kind of intervention in their lives. They argue on the grounds that if we're involved in a Black feminist group and we take ourselves seriously, that means questioning and sometimes rejecting aspects of our culture which oppress us, and that includes marriage and the family. We don't actually take that position as a group, though. We accept that individual Black women have to work out that contradiction for themselves and as far as we're concerned, we're there to support them, not to tell them to get in line.

Despite the differences in our histories and our culture, the racism in this society affects the Black community as a whole. Afro-Caribbean as well as Asian women are victims of deportations and Home Office surveillance tactics. Look at Cynthia Gordon. Asian youths as well as Afro-Caribbean youths are harassed and victimised by the police. During 1981, the most serious of all charges made during the uprisings were made against Asian youths in Bradford. Then there's the racism in the Health Service – the use of stereotypes by the medical profession when dealing with reproduction, fertility and family planning issues – this affects all Black women here. We're fighting the issue of racism and sexism in British institutions – we're all victims of that oppression, even though we may experience its effects in different ways. Black women can't let those differences stand in the way of our resistance, though.

The principle of Afro-Asian unity was expressed within our communities by the way we were organising together, and although the practice was more problematic than the theory, Black women proved that it could be done. While

171

some women were organising against virginity testing at Heathrow Airport, others were campaigning against ethnic record keeping and the dangers of racist statistics and secret files. When Asian women went on strike at Futters in 1978, women from OWAAD supported them on the picket lines. When the Tories introduced their White Paper on Immigration and Nationality in 1979, women in OWAAD campaigned to expose its inherent racism and sexism. When hundreds of Black people were injured and Blair Peach bludgeoned to death during a demonstration against the National Front in Southall in April 1979, women from OWAAD were involved in the defence campaigns of those who had been arrested. When Akthar Ali was stabbed and murdered in July 1980 by a gang of East London skinheads, and when Richard Campbell died that same month in a remand centre, women from OWAAD participated in the community's campaigns to discover the real circumstances of their deaths. And when State harassment reached a new peak in 1981, Asian and Afro-Caribbean women came together in their hundreds in London to demonstrate their opposition to the racist tactics of police and immigration officers. Although many of these initiatives came directly out of the bonds we had formed in OWAAD, they were not solely dependent on its existence. Black women's central role in our communities' struggles has ensured that we are always there when there are battles to be fought. OWAAD's singular achievement, however, lay in its ability to present Black women in Britain as a united front, lending our actions greater weight and a sense of common purpose which was unprecedented in the history of Black struggle in this country.

Organising together as Black women did not develop simply from working and campaigning at a practical level. Our confidence grew out of our sustained effort and collective willingness to grapple with definitions, to assess and re-assess our priorities and constantly to seek out ways of ensuring that our politics represented the aspirations of our people. Conferences, day schools and meetings frequently brought forth fiery debate. But this was because Black women were discussing questions which were of

172

crucial importance not only to us but to the communities to whom we were accountable.

As the Black women's movement took shape and form, the relevance of feminism to our struggles became an increasingly contentious issue. OWAAD was built on the long-standing tradition among Black women of organising together within our community. The basis of that organisation, however, was not necessarily a feminist one, and some Black women have always rejected the term outright:

We're not feminists – we reject that label because we feel that it represents a white ideology. In our culture the term is associated with an ideology and practice which is anti-men. Our group is not anti-men at all. We have what I'd describe as a 'controlled' relationship with them. When we have study sessions on Black history and culture, men come along. Other meetings however are exclusively women's meetings. We do prioritise women's issues and we don't confine our work to meetings – we work on those issues all the time. When we discuss, organise, campaign on that basis we are placing our oppression in the context of racism and imperialism. We're not just addressing women or Black women. We recognise that as Black people, we have a collective responsibility for each other. We want to show that in a concrete way, by the way we organise in the community and the issues we take up. At the same time, we're giving space to things that particularly concern Black women, because for a long time these have been ignored or neglected. We don't alienate men because they put down Black women, because we recognise that the source of that is white imperialist culture. We've been able to work with and to support other African and Caribbean organisations in this area, despite political differences with the men, because the reality is that it's not a Black man's struggle or a Black woman's struggle, but a Black people's struggle. Often other groups find the concept of women organising very threatening, but we try to show them that our organising

173

is positive. We're working together by different routes. We want to show people sisterhood in operation, something that's a forward movement, not a divisive one. We take our responsibility to the community very seriously.

The belief that feminism is 'anti-men' and therefore divisive and counter-productive is not the only reason why Black women have traditionally organised outside the women's movement. The failure of white feminists seriously to address women's issues which are to do with race and class has been a barrier which relatively few Black women have been prepared to cross:

I think if you're a Black woman, you've got to begin with racism. It's not a choice, it's a necessity. There are a few Black women around now, who don't want to deal with that reality and prefer sitting around talking about their sexual preferences or concentrating on strictly women's issues like male violence. But the majority of Black women would see those kinds of things as 'luxury' issues. What's the point of taking on male violence if you haven't dealt with State violence? Or rape, when you can see Black people's bodies and lands being raped everyday by the system? If women want to sit around discussing who they go to bed with, that must be because it's the most important thing in their lives and that's all they want to deal with. In my mind, that's a privilege most of us don't have.

I'm not dismissing the women's movement. A lot of the gains white women have won have been very relevant to Black women. Black women do have to deal with things like rape and domestic violence, and Black men are as sexist as the next man. But it's a question of where we pitch our level. If you're talking about racism, you're talking about survival issues. Black women have to put everything in that context. Where the women's movement is concerned, there are some women trying to do that, particularly Third World and Irish women. That's because they've got a perspective on things which women who come from a cushioned, middle-class background don't have. But on the whole, they're in the minority, and the women's movement has acquired the image of the people who are running it. That's why, if you go to their conferences, they'll skirt around the issues, or make excuses for not dealing with them. They're always asking the Black women to tell them what to do about their racism, but if they went out and got involved in things which involved them taking on racism, they'd soon learn.

The best example of this is in the women's peace movement. They've got all the openings there – the uranium mining in Namibia, the nuclear testing that's been going on on the Aborigine's land, the police powers to brutalise people on demonstrations – yet they can only see the anti-nuclear issue in terms of protecting their own backyards. It's as if they've just discovered imperialism, and they're only worried about it because it threatens their particular lifestyle. They say they don't like violence, but there are a lot of other forms of violence around which they've never bothered about before now. Seeing your child slowly starve to death is violence. Rotting in a South African jail is violence. Poverty is violence.

There are some good things coming out of the peace movement though. I think a lot of white women are beginning to wake up. When they get kicked around by the police and check the media's version of events, they begin to see what Black people have to face every day of our lives. And when they get thirty days in Holloway for being assaulted, and find that nearly half the women inside are Black it forces them to confront the realities and to start making the links. That's the point at which any allegiances will be made between Black and white women. Until then, it's all rhetoric.

Despite such scepticism, not all Black women have chosen to reject feminism as a basis upon which to organise. Recognising how sexism and reactionary male attitudes towards women have worked to keep us down, we have set about the task of redefining the term and claiming it for

175

ourselves. This has meant developing a way of organising which not only takes account of our race and our class, but also makes our struggles against women's oppression central to our practice:

Because we were a women's group, we had to question exactly how much of our energy should go into organising in broad-based campaigns because if too much of our time was taken up working in this way, we ran the risk of just becoming like a community group. We wanted to hold on to the idea that we could organise as women, that's why the next issue of *Speak Out* [journal of the Brixton Black Women's Group] was largely devoted to the issue of Black feminism, and how we related that concept to ourselves. The discussion we had formed the basis of the articles. So you see, we didn't want to divorce Black women's oppression from the work being done in our communities. We had to be clear about that, because calling yourself a feminist is not associated in our community with any serious politics. In fact, a lot of Black people use the term in a derogatory way, as a term of abuse. So we felt it was necessary to redefine the word for ourselves and for other Black women. That meant dealing with the practical issue of how we take things up in such a way as to reflect a Black woman's perspective, so that whatever the issue, we can take account of how it affects Black women specifically, we can mobilise other Black women to get involved, and can organise ourselves politically in such a way that we have credibility. Of course, that brings up the whole question of the role women play in campaigns, and the kinds of positions we hold. But being a member of a group of other Black women gives you a measure of strength and confidence which you don't have as an individual, and because of that we felt able to take the men on on equal terms.

Although our differing positions on the relevance of feminism to our struggle are not necessarily mutually exclusive, they nevertheless have serious implications for the ways we can organise as women. It was because of the

176

difficulties of coming to terms with these implications that the rifts in OWAAD began to emerge. They would eventually lead to OWAAD's demise. The organisation could no longer project itself as a united front, nor could it sustain its influence and credibility when Black women within it were so deeply divided. Nevertheless, OWAAD had achieved much of what it had set out to do. It brought Black women out of isolation and turned us into a force to be reckoned with in our own right. It became a forum for us to discuss and articulate our demands. And it represented a period of intense growth and learning for all Black women in this country, the repercussions of which can still be felt today.

When Black political struggles took a new turn in the aftermath of the 1981 Uprisings, we concentrated once again on the task of defending our communties under siege. Black men and women had been in the frontline during the nationwide confrontations between the police and working-class communities which had swept across the country that summer. Their effect was to send a shock-wave of anger through our communities, and the need to channel that anger and disaffection into an organised response had never been more apparant.

In places as far afield as Brixton and Toxteth, Bradford and Birmingham, Black women were instrumental in setting up the defence campaigns and police monitoring committees which emerged in the wake of the Uprisings. Our experiences of organising over the past few years gave us the confidence to do so, and ensured that in many areas we would play a leading role:

> The fact that we initiated the Brixton Defence Campaign, took on a lot of the leadership and, as a group, put in most of the work, shows how strong politically Black women had become and how much support there was in the community for the group. Many of the 'committees' set up by the brothers in the aftermath of the uprisings had failed. In some cases, the first meetings had ended in chaos. There were all kinds of conflicting interests. I

177

remember a Black reporter being present at an early planning meeting. We all thought he was there as a member of the community or because he was interested in setting up an organisation or structure to deal with what had happened, but that wasn't the case at all. When his report came out, it only showed the conflict at the public meeting although hundreds of Black people had attended it. In fact, the conflict was about one of the organisers trying to keep the media out. So we knew how important it was to maintain our own unity because the press was dying to show us all fighting amongst ourselves.

Everybody was really concerned at the time about what had happened. We recognised that the police would step up their operations. We also knew that we had to work quickly to counteract the media's coverage of 'Black Mobs on the Rampage' and 'Black Masses Rioting', so that people could understand what had really happened. Anyhow, after the failure of the initial public meetings, the women's group came together with a few brothers in the community to discuss the brief of the campaign. The first meeting was held at the Black Women's Centre, and after that it became the base of the campaign. We acted very quickly, using the skills we had to start distributing leaflets, organising more public meetings and producing a regular bulletin. We had two objectives really. The first was the practical matter of getting competent legal representation for the hundreds of Black people who'd been arrested. And the other was to publicise the police tactics which had led to the uprisings and to alert the community to particular incidents of brutality. We did this by holding street meetings on Railton Road, bringing the issues to the attention of the people. And we co-ordinated with other campaigns and defence committees in other parts of the country so that we could monitor the police operations in our communities outside London.

The State, however, found a more insidious way of responding to our disaffection. Having witnessed the dire

178

consequences of direct confrontation on the streets of nearly every inner-city in the country, the politicians were anxious to find a more subtle approach to deal with our rebellion. Lord Scarman's much-publicised report on the causes behind the Brixton 'disorders' called for a mass injection of State funds into the deprived areas where Black people were living. Almost overnight, a spate of new ethnic welfare projects, self-help groups, Black women's centres and police monitoring committees appeared on the scene, and because they were often the very provisions we had been demanding for years, our immediate response was to welcome them. Many Black women threw themselves into the task of establishing and maintaining these provisions, and they brought with them the organising skills and political awareness for which Black women were by now well known. But despite the level of our commitment to the work we were now being *paid* to do, our efforts were often frustrated. Increasingly, the effect of state funds on our community has been to neutralise its militancy; political mobilisation has come to be seen as a salaried activity. A whole generation of 'ethnic' workers and race relations experts has been born who are accountable not to the Black community but to the State which pays them. Their brief, however unwitting, is to keep the lid on the cauldron, and their existence is seen as proof of the governments 'concern' to soften the effects of its own institutionalised racism.

Today we are still assessing the effects of these policies of 'subsidised revolution'. Drastic cuts in local government spending and the government's moves towards rate-capping in areas where councils can least afford to deprive people of much-needed resources, have accelerated this process. As always, our communities have felt the pinch first. Despite our growing awareness of the dangers of State-controlled funding, we have nevertheless had to defend our right to these resources – and to intensify our argument that we have a right to control them ourselves:

At present we have two paid workers and a grant from the Greater London Council which we have to reapply for

179

every year. The money we receive is ours. It's our taxes and the gains and profits from our labour. We want to control the way the money's being spent on our community ourselves. The problem really is how to handle the bureaucrats, to negotiate with local authorities so that we get the money in the first place. They give it to us because they want votes – but we don't have any obligation to them, because the money is our right. In Newham particularly, there's a mafia of white voluntary sector organisations who've traditionally got the grants. They're usually right wing or church-based groups which originated in Victorian times and which were set up to correct the morals of London's 'degenerate' poor. Few Black groups have ever received money, so in fact we're owed a lot more!

Newham is a traditionally depressed, working-class area. Housing is one of the worst in the country and there are the largest number of tower blocks of any borough in London. Black women are totally isolated in the top floors of tower blocks. Parents don't let their children out for fear of racist attacks. Some of the women we know have got kids who've had no experience of playing out. The women are afraid to come out at night, the National Front presence is so strong. So those are the things we're dealing with. These Black women need practical help and advice about how to get out. With government cuts and abolition of the GLC they'll need that help even more.

As we move through the eighties, taking stock of our experiences as women and continually seeking our ways of confronting the race, sex and class oppression we face, it is clear that the task ahead is not going to get any easier for us. There are growing pressures for change, both from within and outside our community and the ways we choose to affect these changes will be largely determined by our ability to consolidate the gains of the past four decades of struggle. Black women are well placed to take a lead in this process, for we have learnt some important lessons over the years. We have learnt that our strongest and most secure political

180

traditions are those which have been grounded in the aspirations of our community. We also know our own political capacity as women, and understand the importance of our mobilising role. But above all, we now have the self-assurance to translate our abilities into positive action, secure in the knowledge that whatever the future holds, Black women cannot and will not be intimidated.

5

Self-consciousness: Understanding Our Culture and Identity

Watch her move
Whom centuries have dealt with in
anecdotes
Wrinkles upon her face
The sinewy arms which cradled young
bones
Helped them grow strong
Flabby breasts which dripped
Life's first sustenance
Deep contours upon her taut face
Life's sorrows, pains and joys

Black, solid, granite
Her oxen qualities once moved
mountains
Ensuring our survival

Watch her move
Through us who have not forgotten
And remembering
Will not allow you to forget
                    Angela McNish

Our culture shapes and determines our identity. To convey our sense of self, as Black women, we must first generate a positive understanding of the long cultural tradition which has fashioned our way of life here in Britain.

In describing the Black culture which emanates from the Caribbean, we seek to portray a vital changing phenomenon, created from our lived experiences – something which cannot be separated from the economic realities and political processes which have shaped our history. To us, the only valid definition of our culture is one which recognises that it was and remains our primary means of survival. It represents those rituals, symbols and practices which have given expression to our struggles to triumph over poverty and exploitation.

The unique feature of our culture is that its root and base is Africa. To acknowledge its origins is also to identify the unchanging seam which is common to all Black cultures in the diaspora. Our African origin is the cornerstone of our lifestyle and our perception of the world, the internal dynamic which has enabled us continuously to resist new assaults on our way of life. In responding to these assaults, we have had to create and recreate new definitions of ourselves as a people. As such, our culture has become subversive, for through it we have always had to challenge, combat and find new ways of winning.

Historically, Afro-Caribbean women were in a unique position to sustain our culture whenever it came under attack. When we were captured and herded in chains on to slave ships bound for the Americas, we were already steeped in our national culture. Although the African people had developed a wide variety of cultures over the centuries, most shared a common respect for women, not only because of our role as mothers but also for the role we played in the social, cultural, political and economic life of the community. While the predominant family structure, then as now, was one of kinship relations and communalism, the matrilineal system of property inheritance ensured that African women were held in high esteem. Under this system, family wealth was passed on through its women members, giving women power

183

and status and involving us actively in the decision-making process of our communities.

As African women, we were aware of the value of our labour. It was we who were responsible for the development of many craft and household industries, methods of food preservation, and the extraction of medicines from roots and herbs to treat the sick. At the same time, we held responsibility for the care and education of our children, and participated equally in both trading activities and agricultural production. Even when captured as young girls, we would already have been through our respective tribal initiation ceremonies, marking the transition from girlhood to womanhood. Such ceremonies were designed to impress young girls with a sense of self-worth and importance as the onset of puberty heralded the beginning of our participation in the community as women. They also endowed young women with a sense of individual and collective responsibility towards the community, in the areas of childrearing, production and the preservation of family and tribal honour.

These were the qualities and attributes which enabled African women to survive and resist the horrors of the Middle Passage. Transported in shackles alongside the men, and packed into a space no greater than six by sixteen feet, we were afforded no special status or concessions because of our sex. Black women suffered rape, pregnancy, childbirth, and the hollow, lasting grief of forcible separation from our children as we made that journey of no return to the Americas. We survived the filth, the disease, the malnutrition and the unfeeling brutality of the European sailors, and we clung on to our human dignity although we were being transported like cattle. The purpose of this brutal treatment was to break our spirit, in preparation for the life of slavery which awaited us. But it did not succeed. Many defiant and desperate women jumped overboard and drowned rather than accept the indignity of this dehumanising experience. Others planned and took part in slaveship insurrections. Their bones litter the bottom of the ocean, but their spirit of resistance lived on in the women who, miraculously, survived to establish our culture anew in the Americas.

184

The West Indian islands were often the first point of arrival for transported slaves, many of whom were subsequently taken to be sold to the Portuguese and Spanish colonists or to slavers in the southern states of America. It was in the Caribbean that the first, bitter lessons about slavery were often learnt. Any attempts we made to re-establish community and family life were under constant threat of disruption, and compounded by the arbitrary sale of our children and loved ones. The task of preserving and perpetuating African cultural values and traditions – knowledge about food preparation, hair care, traditional songs and dances, family customs and religious practices – became a daily struggle. This struggle succeeded due mainly to the efforts of women.

Our role as mothers and workers ensured that Black women were instrumental in perpetuating those aspects of our culture which re-affirmed our people's capacity to celebrate life. Clothed and fed simply so that we could continue to work and breed, we turned the clothes we wore and the food we ate into lasting evidence of our African heritage. We entered the plantations armed only with the tools of our earlier tribal socialisation. Every shred of knowledge we had acquired – of human behaviour, of our environment, of life itself – was pooled and adapted, enabling us to resist the ongoing process of racist dehumanisation, and so to survive. Our foremothers, drawing on their recent African history of female creativity and resourcefulness, were thus able to find the strength and the will to live through the years of slavery. And their struggle was not merely for the right to live, but for the right to celebrate life by giving expression to that experience in such a way as to give it meaning and validity for us, their descendants.

Language

Through our language we express and define our collective consciousness as a people. Its development has been central to our history and our political experience, for it is through our language that we articulate our reality.

Creole, in all its variations, is uniquely our creation. Brutal necessity prescribed the means by which it was born. It came out of the bitter experience of the Middle Passage and the urgent need to forge links of community and communication with peoples of differing cultures and languages. The circumstances compelled us to recreate an autonomous language, a means of collective self-expression which would defy intimidation. We took the diversity of African languages we had brought with us to the Caribbean, and formed them into a complex system which had its root in Kwa but included such languages as Ewe, Twi, Fante and Hausa.

For the slavemasters, the first priority was to eradicate these languages, for they articulated our hopes of freedom and our plans for rebellion. This is why slaves arriving from different African ports were deliberately mixed together, in an attempt to make communication difficult and to inhibit revolt. Our families were split up and African 'tongues' were forbidden under threat of brutal punishment. It was our urgent need to communicate with each other and to make sense of our new and hostile environment which ensured that a collective means of expression would quickly take root. Within a few generations we had developed a new and self-sufficient language, retaining our African syntax and structures as the baseline and adding a vocabulary which drew on a variety of sources, including the languages of the indigenous Caribbean Indian peoples. It would have small beginnings, but as we came to use it increasingly in our daily lives – between mothers and children, siblings and friends – it would expand to become the dominant and common form of language among all Black slaves. It became a vehicle for expressing all our desires for freedom, our secret subversive comments and our rejection of those who held sway over us. Above all, it was a language our oppressors could not understand. Black women were instrumental in ensuring that this language was preserved and handed down to future generations. The mothers who admonished or soothed their children; the grandmothers who recounted stories and passed on the wisdoms of our African past – these women were playing a vital role, as they moulded the oral tradition which would perpetuate our language and our culture. But language was preserved not only through oral traditions, but also through music and musical forms. Songs, dances, the drum, the African flute – each contributed to the self-expression of a people whose right to be was constantly under threat.

Centuries later, Louise Bennett, a Jamaican woman whose roots are grounded in this history of oral resistance, would play such a vital part in reclaiming the language for us. Through her poetry, which spans more than forty years, she has made the single most important contribution to the popularisation of Jamaican Creole in oral and written form, and it is Louise Bennett, above all others, who has paved the way for the 'dub' poets we know today. However, her writings have done more than reclaim the language for future generations. By conveying its use in an everyday context, she has succeeded through her poetry in expressing the essential qualities of humour, vitality, insight and resistance which have sustained Afro-Caribbean women through centuries of toil.

Jamaica 'Oman

But Black 'oman cunni' sah!
Is how dem ginal soh!
Look how long dem liberated
And de man dem never know!

Look how long Black 'oman
Mada, sista, wife, sweetheart,
Outa road an enna yard deh pon
A dominate her part!

From maroon Nanny teck her body
Bounce bullet back pon man,
To wen nowadays gal-pickney tun
Spelling-Bee champion.

From de grass-root to de hill-top

In Profession, Skill an' Trade,
D' Black 'oman dem teck her time
Dah mount an meck de grade.

Some backa man a push, some side a
Man a hole him han',
Some a lick sense ina man head
Some a guide him pon him plan!

Neck an neck an foot an foot wid man
She buckle hole her own,
Wile man a call her 'so-so rib'
'Oman a tun backbone!

An long before 'oman Lib, bruck out
Over foreign lan'
Black female wasa work out
Her Liberated plan!

Black 'oman *know* she strong
She *know* she tallawa,
But she no want her pickney dem
Fe start call her 'Pupa'

So de cunni' Black 'oman,
Gwan like pants-suit is a style,
An Black man no know that she wear
De trousiz *all de wile!*

So Black 'oman coaxin
Fambly Budget from explode,
A so Black man a sing
'Oman a heaby load!'

But de cunni Black 'oman
Ban' her belly, bite her tongue,
Ketch water, put pot pon fire
An jus' dig her toe a grung.

For ''oman luck deh a dungle'
Some rooted more dan some,
But as long as fowl a scratch dungle heap
'Oman luck mus' come!

188

Lickle by lickle man start praise her
Day by day de praise a grow,
So him praise her, so it sweet her,
For she wonder if him know.

Religion as a Liberating Force

Religious ceremonies and rituals were central to life and culture in the slave communities. They served as a creative and sustaining force, a means of articulating our joy at our continuing survival and our hope that salvation would come. Religion provided a means for our liberation. It was at religious gatherings that specific codes of communication were developed, and where sacred rites brought from Africa were performed. In those meetings, we not only determined the specific means to organise rebellions and escapes, but we also developed a collective strategy to sustain us in our day-to-day existence.

Black women, in particular, continued to play the important roles we had always performed in West African religion. Miss Queenie, the Kumina Priestess, survives today in Jamaica as living evidence of the strength and power of African religious traditions, and of women's role within them. Miss Queenie received her calling as a young girl to be a 'diviner', a mediator between human and divine forms, assuming a role which is mostly conferred on women. Her Kumina 'bands' attempt to preserve a sense of historical continuity through spiritual and cultural means. One of the religion's focuses is the role of Miss Queenie herself: she serves the spiritual world by observing duties on behalf of the ancestral spirits, interpreting the messages of the other world for those without her psychic powers, and releasing others from their physical and spiritual illnesses. The spirits are kept alive through the offering of gifts of food, thus maintaining a continuity between the worlds of the living and the dead. In African religions, the art of 'feeding' the dead demonstrates the need for us to remember and revere our dead, and increases their life force. An act of offering is a call, an invitation to our ancestral spirits to manifest their

189

presence and intervene in our lives.

It is a miracle of positive survival that the Kumina religion, with its African forms, has lived on in a society which has treated all evidence of African culture with hostility and scorn. Once again an important factor in its preservation has been our language. It represents a bridge of communication between Africa and the Caribbean, and Kumina believers have jealously maintained the Kongo language within their circles. When Miss Queenie sings now in rituals which have only recently become accessible to non-Kumina believers, she retains the original Kongo words and phrases, and recreates the traditional African falsetto tones, in a way that has been done for centuries.

Many other African traditions which we retained as women during the violent Middle Passage had their origins in African religions, particularly those traditions which were healing and binding to us as a community. Aspects of our culture, such as celebrations of birth and death, naming ceremonies, burying the navel string of a new-born child to safeguard its spirit and the nine nights' wake for our dead – these rituals were preserved to give meaning and structure to our lives in a destructive and distorted environment. As women, we strengthened our people by continuing to practice herbal medicine. Many of the herbs and barks such as pimpe, mapimpe and pem-pem have retained their Ashanti names to this day, evidence of how we succeeded in containing the practice completely within our own communities. The best known herbal practitioner in the West Indies was Roxanne Forbes who, in the late nineteenth century, set up a herbal centre in Lacovoa. She passed on her wisdom and healing powers to her daughter, Rita, and eventually to other women, who still run the centre today.

The culture which defined and ordered our lives in Africa was born of thousands of years of experience and change. The uprooting of the African people made it necessary for us to adapt our customs, traditions and practices, so that we could survive that critical period of our history. The fact that we have survived to rebuild our culture in Britain, four

190

hundred years later, is a testimony to its worth and durability, to its power to transform all our experiences into a positive statement of being.

Racism and Culture

The mainstay of British culture has been the assertion of its superiority over others, its total negation of non-European cultures in general and Black people's cultures in particular. The message that European culture and whiteness itself represented 'civilisation', while African culture and blackness represented the primitive and the barbaric, was transmitted around the world through the white man's religion, literature, music and art. The myth served to detract attention from the decadence of his own culture, an extension of which was the savage and barbaric way he asserted his superiority over the 'inferior' races. White men have always known the value and richness of the peoples and cultures they have sought to dominate. This is clear from the way in which the material forms of those cultures have been stolen, sometimes to be recreated and passed off as part of the British heritage, sometimes to be hoarded in their national museums. Continuous attempts to negate and undermine Black culture are, in themselves, a recognition of the threat we pose as a people to the legitimacy of the system.

But Black women have always had to contend with more than racist definitions. As slaves, we were confronted daily with an image of womanhood which sought to negate our very existence outside the role of breeders of human livestock. For colonial societies in the nineteenth century, the 'ideal' women was European and white. Black women had to resist negation by a culture which valued only a woman's physical appearance, a culture which debased in women those very attributes which we found it necessary to cultivate, such as self-reliance, courage, strength and physical endurance. In a culture which was obsessed with creating and recreating the ideal through fashion, art, poetry and other forms of European self-expression, there was no

191

room for any appreciation of African beauty. The very term implied a contradiction. The only images of women we were exposed to, outside our immediate communities, were those depicting white, female perfection, from the Virgin Mary to the slavemaster's wife. Self-denigration and self-denial would have been unavoidable, had it not been for the strength we were able to draw as women from within ourselves, our culture and our communities.

Entrenching the Stereotypes

As the dominant culture developed a more advanced technology, and a mass media with which to confirm and perpetuate itself, cinema assumed the role formerly played by books, sermons and the lectures of eminent speakers. The religious, scientific and philosophical arrogance of European racism transported itself onto the big screen. The negative images and insulting stereotypes which had been developed as a justification of slavery were thus carried forward, unchallenged, into the twentieth century. So it was that the same cultural tools which had become, for us, a means of self-assertion and self-defence became a source of ridicule and vulgar exaggeration for the entertainment of white audiences in Europe and America.

Although, to begin with, few Black women were ever shown on the screen, those who were invariably portrayed characters who were obese, ugly, clumsy, stupid and above all, servile. According to American cinema's romantic depiction of slavery in the South, Black women had no other role than to serve loyally their white masters and mistresses. To care for a white family was the only valid aspiration for us, and the screen mammys treated it as such, appearing to love their white charges more than their own 'picanninies' (for children, too, came only in one colour). Such sentiments were seen as inevitable, of course, particularly by the white audiences which flocked to see films such as *Gone With The Wind* and *Birth of a Nation*. In the absence of any of the popularly cherished physical characteristics in oneself, one's children or one's race, what could be more gratifying than to

192

serve perfection in others? For the isolated Black women who appeared on the screen in roles other than the devoted mammy or the invisible maid, the only other options were to play the tragic mulatto, caught between two cultures yet belonging to neither, or the Black whore and seductress, exotic, amoral and invariably fair-skinned. In both roles, our 'rampant' sexuality became our dominant 'attribute', the factor which explained why men were driven to desperation and women to jealous distraction. By labelling Black women as sexually promiscuous in this way, white men were thus exonerated for their sexual excesses under slavery. The function of this stereotype, even today, is neither to flatter nor to bestow us with an identity as sexual beings. It is simply a justification for the centuries of sexual abuse of Black womanhood.

Even the first, and for a long time the only all-Black cinema production, *Carmen Jones*, tells the story of a clean, conventional, noble Black hero, driven to distraction and eventual death by the wild, faithless, emasculating (and fair-skinned) Black woman. The power of such media stereotypes is constantly being challenged by Black women who reject them as irrelevant and sterile. Yet even without this historical perspective, a casual glance at the porn magazines and sex shows in London's Soho reveals the extent to which white men have debased our sexual identity for their own self-gratification. Our sexuality is neither uncontrollable nor indiscriminate, yet the myth survives.

British Television and the New 'Ethnic' Awareness

Many of the stereotypes which continue to pass for real Black women have survived because of, rather than in spite of, the new ethnic awareness which we have witnessed recently on British television. Mirroring the American experience of a decade or so ago, the token presence of a few Black faces is gradually beginning to make way in the eighties for an entire Black media ghetto, characterised by a general lack of resources and technical expertise. Its success depends on how closely it can emulate the ethics and values

193

of the existing media industry, and its control remains firmly in the hands of middle-class white men who also determine when, in what form and how often programmes are broadcast. Nevertheless, this apparent liberalisation has meant that we no longer have to make do with a limited number of standard stereotypes. Instead, we are confronted with a full range of them, which may well appear on first sight to be less obviously objectionable, but are frequently more insidious.

For Black women, this has meant an increasing repertoire of roles which are mere variations on the original themes – the domestic, the night-club singer, the hooker, the prolific breeder and the State scrounger. Recently, Black women singers, dancers and athletes have appeared in growing numbers, too. Yet the absence of 'successful' Black women in any other roles has tended to confirm the notion that sport and entertainment are the only areas in which we can excel. To succeed in any other profession, a Black woman must dress, think, talk and act white. In other words, she must first lose all sense of her Black cultural identity if she wishes to find acceptance from the mainly white audiences which determine TV ratings in this country. Where attempts have been made on either of the channels to portray Black women outside the usual stereotypes, we have invariably been treated as a 'social problem', whose lifestyle and culture are responsible for any disadvantage we encounter.

The advent of Channel 4 in 1982 held the promise of a real alternative, one which would stop regarding us voyeur-istically and cease treating our lives as a 'sub-culture' based on crime, weed and reggae. However, in an apparent attempt to look beyond the stereotypes, liberal/left television productions have, for the most part, only succeeded in projecting Black women in the role of 'oppressed victims', dependent on State benefits, council housing and the intervention of social workers. Thus Channel 4 has failed so far to meet the expectations of the Black community as a whole and in particular, those of Black women. And this is despite the appointment of a Black woman, Sue Woodford, as commissioning editor at Channel 4 from 1982–84, crucial of

194

course for Channel 4's image as the 'alternative' channel. This in itself has not given Black women a voice, and the few Black women who work in the television industry are still concentrated in the jobs which offer the lowest pay and the least decision-making power.

Arguments about TV ratings have been used to divert the public's attention from the real causes behind the suppression and distortion of our culture by the media – namely, the longstanding recognition that Black people represent a subversive and potentially radical influence on the indigenous population. Every effort has been made to ensure that programmes which are for or about Black people have kept well within the limits of what is 'acceptable', despite the newly awakened 'ethnic' consciousness of television producers and playwrights. How much easier it is to concentrate on multi-culturalism, feeding viewers with a diet of 'Reggae Sunsplash', 'No Problem' and 'Frontline' than seriously to attempt to challenge racism by debunking the stereotypes and historical distortions which perpetuate it? Perhaps the clearest example of this failure can be seen in the ethnic current affairs programmes such as 'Black on Black' (Ch4) and 'Ebony' (BBC2). The brief of all such programmes has been to stay 'balanced' and uncritical at all costs within a light-hearted, chat-show formula. The result has been a general trivialisation of the real issues which face the Black community, and an untimely easing of the pressure from the Black and anti-racist lobby for better representation of Black people on TV.

But our community has sought out ways of challenging these media distortions. We have looked for alternative ways of communicating the realities of our lives and our history, and because we have no power within the white-controlled media, we have had to find ways of turning the technology of mass communication into a weapon which we can use for ourselves:

Our group started with myself and another Black woman having a discussion while we were waiting for a meeting to start. We got talking about the need for us to redress the

195

fact that we're not taught anything in the mainstream education system. White people still ask us how long we've been here, even when so many of us were born here, and that's a real indication that white society is trying to deny our existence. No one ever records our achievements, we only get coverage in the media when we riot. The meeting started late, and we had a really long talk about the importance of recording our own histories, the kinds of things our mothers used to tell us, the songs they used to sing, and so on. What we were really talking about was the need to pass this down to our children. The woman I came with had a daughter and she was concerned about the years of mis-education she faced. It was that discussion which made us decide to form the Black Women's Radio Workshop.

In the group, we feel that our informal culture centres around our mothers. In Black families, our mothers are the lynch-pins. Our traditions around food, clothes and ways of working come from our mothers. They're the ones who really organise family life and we're always more conscious of their presence than our fathers' (which isn't to deny the influence of our fathers, of course).

Traditionally, things considered 'technical' are seen to be out of the reach of women. A lot of Black women live in houses with stereos, for example, but they've never touched them except to put a record on. Girls never receive encouragement to get into these areas which are traditionally considered male domains. We try to show them how to edit tapes, and to familiarise them with the technology. Although Black women are our priority, we work with mixed groups because we recognise that both Black women and Black men face oppression in this society through the media. We go into youth clubs, for example, and use the things we discuss on the tapes as a basis for discussion with the youths. We try to explore things like roles and stereotypes of Black men and women. We use different techniques like separating the boys from the girls and having the same discussion with each group, and then playing the discussions back to the other group.

196

Although our group is aimed at both men and women, our main aim is to deal with the things which specifically affect Black women. At the moment, we're doing a project on hair care, and looking at the ways in which Black women have been exploited by the multi-nationals. We don't need to challenge the allegation that hair care is traditionally a woman's issue, because the purpose of what we're doing is to examine the politics of the subject. Our hair is an important thing to the majority of Black women, and using a subject like this enables us to arouse their interest and prompt them to listen to a discussion about the wider implications of the way we care for our hair. Radio is about communicating, and we want to reach Black women who aren't organised in formal groups. To grab people's interest, though, you have to be entertaining and flexible – we can't just focus on the issues we think are important and get bogged down in middle-class feminist preoccupations. In other words, we don't have a hardline dogma about what constitutes a woman's issue.

One of the things we'd like to do is a series on mother and daughter relationships and all their complexities. We also want to include records of the early experiences of older Black people in the community, which is like living history and is in danger of never being recorded. We'd like to do music projects, too, listening to Black women DJ's and talking about the differences between the styles – the different raps. Music is political, and music can be used very effectively in this way.

Another plan we have is to get Black women's groups into the station, to explain what they are doing and the political positions they hold. Women in the community could be encouraged to come into the station to discuss these politics and if necessary to challenge the women who are organising in a particular way. I think that community radio would be a good way of publicising the work that Black women's groups are involved in.

Ultimately, we want a Black radio station so that we can have control over the way we are represented. Radio is still a popular means of communication, even though it may

197

seem to have been eclipsed by screen technology. People still play a lot of radio during the day, in the home and in stores, and DJ's often make derogatory comments, interspersed among the music, using racist and sexist stereotypes to make jokes, things like that. The group is busy working out the kind of radio station we want. We're not just looking for a Black version of 'Capital'. At the moment there are very few Black radio programmes, and many of them are on at a time when few people listen to the radio anyway. The content of present programmes is fairly static, and we think that a lot of Black people aren't bothering to listen to these programmes any more. So one of the most important objectives of a Black radio station is that it should be accountable to the Black community. Our approach to the subject of interviews would reflect this aim. Now, when we work, we don't just go out there and say to somebody, 'Give me an interview.' We want them to have an equal say in how the material is produced, so that the people who participate by giving interviews can also learn something from making the programme.

We also have to work out the way we want to communicate, which means incorporating the wide variety of accents and expressions Black people use. Many of the Black presenters can't disguise the strain of trying to communicate in orthodox media English. When they talk, their faces are twisted with anxiety. We all experience a certain amount of schizophrenia when we communicate in day-to-day situations. It's not just our accent, either – it's our language, phrases and tone of voice. When Black people present anything in the media nowadays, they feel they have to narrow themselves down to fit a certain model or type. But we'd really like to widen that, and present Black people talking and behaving naturally.

We're actually in the process of taking on the projects I've mentioned, and we're encouraged by the fact that we're supported by other groups, such as the Black Women's Film and Video Group and the Black women who are involved at the moment in setting up the Black film company. Black women are right at the forefront in

198

the struggles to combat racism in the media, and as a group, we draw a lot of strength from that fact.

Re-affirming our Culture

Cultural imperialism takes many forms, and undermining our positive sense of self and social identity is its most insidious: there is no single aspect of our culture which has not, at some time or other, been subjected to this assault, either to be taken over or trivilised. The media has played a central role in this process, not only through its use of stereotypes but also through the way it portrays Black art and culture. Our music and dances, our art, literature and poetry have been either ignored or patronised. But despite this, Black people have always found ways of re-affirming our creativity and ensuring that our culture survives. For example, although the drum was banned under slavery, we have preserved not only the skill but also the significance of drumming, which was part of our African heritage. Claiming that they would help us to work harder, we brought our Buru drummers with us into the fields. After slavery, they were used by the community to expose and deride wrong-doers, as they went from village to village, performing the same function as traditional African praise-singers. Today, Buru drumming has not only survived in its original form in the Maroon communities of Jamaica, but also forms the basis of the Rastafarian 'Nyabingi' drumming.

Songs, which are an integral part of our oral culture, were and still are a means of preserving the language, communicating news and relating our history. The lyrics which accompany Caribbean Calypso, Soca and, more recently, Reggae, still provide evidence of the mood of the people, not only at particular points in our history, but also in the present. Our songs have depicted the violence and terror of life in the urban ghetto, and DJ lyrics both here and in the Caribbean have decried police brutality, corrupt electioneering and other forms of suffering. Black women have made a particular contribution to this process, giving voice to our experiences as women and exposing the abuses

199

which we have had to tolerate from men and society. Today, growing numbers of Black women singers and DJs are launching a counter-attack against the sexism which has characterised male lyrics over the years. Despite the pressure from record companies to commercialise and depoliticise Black music, we have used these same forms of musical expression to validate our experiences here in Britain:

Our lyrics reflect our experiences in life, how we feel as women, our family life, our day to day living. When I say 'how we feel as women', I mean that we are describing life from a woman's point of view, her relationship with her children, school life, etc. all from her eye view. (I should say that some of our songs are written by men, but the majority are by women.) Abacush's lyrics and our DJ lyrics come from the same source. We are dealing with reality. We're like a newspaper, showing people what is happening now and providing information for people. We sing about our experiences as Black people, and about our belief in God. That belief, which we all share as Rastas, gives us a certain discipline and understanding about ourselves. That helps us to be strong and not to let our bridge down and not to let other people get us down.

A lot of people see us perform and label us as feminists, but we are just ordinary Black women living in Britain and we reject attempts like that to classify us. Our understanding of ourselves as women and as musicians is firstly that we *know* that Black women are strong, and we know that Black people, especially women, take part in their culture and add to it. We know this by looking at our own families, because in there it's the women who hold us together as a family. Going back in our history, we can see that women have taken an active part in things. Because of our history, though, people tend to look at Black people and think that we're weak. In fact, they try to break our confidence in ourselves, as you can see by the way we're treated in schools and all kinds of other institutions. It's like treading on your confidence.

There really is a big brainwash thing going on in this

country. It stems from an early age at school and at home. I was fortunate because my parents brought the Jamaican culture with them here, and always upheld it. They took me back to see my family, so I was aware of it. Some Black people forget about their culture and bring up their children with this society's values, so that they know nothing about their history. But as Black people, we have to seek these things out for ourselves. No one else is going to do it for us. If the understanding is not in the home, then you have to go and seek it out and that's more difficult. That's why it's harder for this generation. Black people need to be more positive and more together. If we're not together here in this culture, then there's no future for us. Black people are getting wiped out, physically and mentally. We've been downtrodden, sent to the mad-house. The system is getting to everyone's head. But the white man *has* to give us respect. We're here without anything, but Europe was built with Black people's strength and blood. Our positive force and energy will *make* them respect us. The Black community can organise and come out in numbers – look at the New Cross march. Anything affects us and we come together.

In terms of music, I see this slackness trend as a negative thing. It's culturally backward because it doesn't do anything to enlighten us as a people. It's a gimmick, that's why it's so popular. There are a lot of serious people in the music business who aren't getting promoted. When I see things like the white dreadlocks, using our locks as a fashion, it really hurts me. I just think that it's making fun of our culture. Things like that are important to us and they're just using them to mock us. It's as if white people know the history of how Europe raped the gold out of Africa and they're prepared to take that on. But now they're oppressing us in a different way, by infiltrating us and our culture. They know that what they did in history was bad, but they're still prepared to re-do the same thing in a different way. The white dreadlocks thing really sums that up. How can a white man say he's going back to Africa?

I believe that Black people have to organise themselves.

201

Music is the platform I use to express that and in that way we can break down barriers that in ordinary situations might prevent communication. I deal with positive people, like the women in the Black women's movement and any other group that's organised, as long as their views don't conflict with mine.

As a singer, I would like people to see us and take inspiration from us. When we're on stage, I'd like to be saying to other Black women, 'Look, you can do anything with confidence in yourself. It's not easy, but it can be done. We've come through that domination and oppression and we've done it.' There's a new era coming up for Black women singers. Before in music we were confined to 'lovers' but now there's a new force of women, whose works are positive. And people respect them. We don't want people to say that the band is 'great', just to respect us as musicians and as women.

I know that Black women have been doin' since whenever, but the past can only help in terms of enlightenment. We have to take action on the present and the future. When we go on stage, we want to say that you *can* do something if you put your mind to it. We never had no superstar childhood.

Alongside music, dance has been our most important form of cultural expression. It has been used to give importance to all vital activities, from cooking and love-making to birth and death. In Jamaica, the Myal and Puk Kumina dances still accompany religious ceremonies, and although they are retained in fairly isolated rural areas, the tradition of religious dancing has also permeated Black Christian churches. This is particularly true of the Revival churches. One of the most popular and long-lasting traditional dances is the Jonkonno, a parade and dance, usually performed at Christmas, representing about seventy traditional 'masked' characters. Perhaps one reason for its survival lies in the fact that it was encouraged by white slavers, who found its colour and vivacity confirmed their stereotyped impressions of Black culture. Originally, the dance was a religious one – the

202

'masque' in African culture being a symbol and manifestation of the spirit world. Many of the masks today still represent features of African culture. The dancers who masquerade in elaborate skirts at Carnival, for example, originate with the Oba of Benin.

Many of the meanings behind popular Black dance today have been lost even though the form has been retained. Central to many African dances, for example, is the celebration of fertility and procreation – hence the sexual hip movements. This lives on, more often in parodied form, but its meaning has been lost. Instead, our dances are seen as a source of entertainment, performed for effect and sensation.

Always conscious of the threat from an increasingly sophisticated media industry, Black women have been central to the process of reclaiming and recreating traditional cultural forms, and grounding new forms in that tradition. Black artists today are not merely involved in 'instinctive' creativity. We are constantly seeking out our African heritage, researching the meanings and history behind the forms which have survived and ensuring that they are passed on.

Historically dance has always been integral to Black culture. There is literally a dance for everything, back in the land of our ancestors – a dance for death, for birth, for weddings, for social occasions, for everything you can imagine. So dance rotated around our entire working life and there was no distinction between the performer and the dancer, everyone danced, everyone performed. When we were taken away from our Mother Country to the Caribbean and America, Black people danced because it was a link with our mother culture. But what you found was that there were different tribes, each one with a slightly different culture – different customs, different languages and so on. And they mixed the tribes up as a way of quelling rebellion, because if you don't have a common mother tongue, of course you don't have a unified group of people.

The way they suppressed dance was by banning the drum. The drum incited people to dance and it also incited people to come together and organise, so it was banned. And later, of course, Black people were converted to Christianity, so dancing came to be frowned upon, especially Black dance. When it came to dances like the quadrille and the more regimental English and Scottish dances, those were allowed, because they were considered by the Europeans to express the finer qualities. So drumming was banned. But the fiddle wasn't, and we found that we could still dance to the fiddle. And an interesting thing developed then, because we began to stomp our feet and clap our hands and even when we were converted to Christianity, we continued to do that. We'd clap our hands and use our tambourines and we'd sit and rock our bodies when we sang – and that's dance! I think that the Black woman played an enormously important role in all this. She helped the child to develop a rhythm for dance probably more than anyone else. Don't forget that when she walked, or when she rocked herself while she was pregnant or when she rocked the baby to sleep, she was imparting a rhythm to her child.

Dance has always had a therapeutic value for us in that you can escape into it. Whilst you're dancing, you can forget about your problems. Also, it is a link with your culture. When you are taken away from your roots, don't forget, you're uprooted and the only thing you can take with you is your culture and your will to survive. With our Black culture, everything has had to be passed down either orally or through dance. You see, with the Europeans their culture is in their buildings and their artifacts, their paintings and books and so on and this is why they say that Black people have no culture. But our culture has been passed on in a different way, in an oral form and through dance. In any culture at all, dance is important – no matter where you go, you'll find people dancing, but I think that within the Black culture, dance is particularly important because it revolves around everything. You won't find that in most other cultures,

204

they only having dancing for specific purposes.

It wasn't just a case of the dances we brought with us from Africa. Those dances were modified and developed and that process has continued right up to the present day. For instance, you'll find that the Brazilians dance the Bongo and the Cha-cha-cha, and if you watch the rhythm and the steps you'll see that all those dances come from Africa. But a lot of our dance has been stylised and integrated into western culture. For example, in the 1920s there was this dance the Charleston. Now that was developed by Black people in America, but no credit was ever given to them. It was said that no Black could possibly have created a dance like that, we haven't got the mentality for it. And you'll find that a lot of our dances today are dances which our forefathers and mothers have been doing for centuries, but they've been taken over and refined – even calypso or soccah, which are based on African highlife. And what they call disco dancing – it's all basically Black dances that people are doing.

In many ways, we still don't recognise the importance of our dances. But one of the reasons for this is that historically Black people have been conditioned to regard dance as something crude and primitive. It's only recently that Black dance has begun to take its rightful place within this society, and even now some sections of the society still frown upon Black dance and Black music. But in another sense, we do recognise the importance of these things. If you go back and look at reggae music, for example, you'll find that it has always been regarded by us as a form of protest. If you listen to the words of the early reggae songs, they were nearly always protesting about something. The first reggae records to come out of Jamaica were mostly protesting about the political situation in the country. And when we dance to the music, we also relate to its message.

Blues dances also have their history in our struggle. When we came here from the Caribbean, we found that we were social outcasts and the only way we could socialise and come together was at the Blues dance or the

Saturday night parties at people's homes. And those things didn't just happen when we came to England, people had to organise them. Looking back into history, you'll also find that Saturday night was usually the only time that the slaves had as free time, it was then that we could socialise and find out what was going on in our communities. So when we came here we were just carrying on a centuries-old tradition, and because we were dispersed, those dances and Blues were tremendously important to our new communities, they were the only times when we could really come together. But despite all this, Black people often fail to recognise dancing as a part of our culture, part of something which has enabled us to survive. Black people can reclaim dance, but we have to start young. We have to teach our kids what dance means to us and our culture. And it's for us who know and recognise these things to point the way. We have to redefine the dances that we do so that they take their rightful place in history. And we have to stop accepting the derogatory labels which white people have given them. For example, a lot of people look at limbo dancing and think that it's really crude. But it is *not* crude, it's part of our culture. In fact, limbo is one of the funery dances, a dance which used to be performed when someone died. It was usually performed by the young men, who used it to show off their agility. When an adult died, there was no mourning, that only happened when there was the death of a child. The limbo dance represents the soul in suspended animation, half way between hell and heaven. When we danced the limbo, we were helping the passing soul to wing its way to a resting place. You can see this even more clearly with the fire limbo – the soul suspended between heaven and hell. There is a meaning like this in the origins of all Black dances, but a lot of Black people don't know this, they've been brought up to believe that dance is just a form of entertainment. But it's far more than that to us. It's a unique body language, one which we ourselves have developed to express our unique experience in history.

206

Our long record of self-preservation and cultural self-determination has also relied on oral traditions, such as poetry and story-telling. In particular, our acute awareness of our position as Black women in a white society has compelled us to make our way past the stereotypes and the gimmickry, and the structures which produce them, forming from ourselves and from within our community definitions of self and culture which confirm our inventiveness and our will to survive. Part of this process of re-definition has been the expression, by Black women, of a distinct identity within the Black cultural experience. This identity is only new in that it has been developed out of our experiences here in Britain, and out of our need to find new ways of expressing our responses to racism and sexism in the British context.

I found myself as a single parent being frustrated and having a lot of things inside to get out. The easiest way was to just put it down on paper, and it just came out because I felt so bitter about my life, particularly about not having the support of my child's father. I started writing at school, but because my teachers said I wasn't very good at English I wrote things down on small bits of paper and hid them underneath cupboards and things. I didn't think anyone would be interested in them.

I used to write in standard English, but later on, when I met people like Linton Kwesi Johnson I liked the way he was using the language and decided that if he was using it that way then I could too. I found that when he wrote about 'the youth', he was basically talking about young men. I realised that he wasn't necessarily dealing with Black people as a whole, he was just dealing with Black boys and Black men. I wanted to write about Black women's issues.

When I went to the OWAAD conference in 1980 and read some of my poems, I had a really great sense of people wanting me, and wanting to hear me. I felt nervous at first, but in a way I also felt safe, because I knew I was around sisters and had nothing to worry about. For the first time in my life – and no one had ever said this before

– people started telling me, 'You're a writer'. That's when my writing really began to develop. One of the first poems I wrote in Creole was 'Sally and Harry'. It describes Sally as being a 'virago' – that's basically someone who's bad, but there's also a lot of strength implied in the word – it means rebel and fighter. That's how I see myself, and it's also how I see my mother and my grandmother – as women with a fighting spirit. The poem was actually written for a woman who'd been in prison and had a bad experience with a man she thought she trusted. But she dealt with it. I liked the word 'virago' so much that I just matched it with the story she was telling me and that's how 'Sally an' Harry' came to be written.

Sally an' Harry

Sally was a virago gal
And Harry was the gorgan
Sally do six year bird
Harry 'im stay outside an' work
Work get car, get some gold, get some chicks
Bwoy, 'im rich!

Sally do cheques fe give Harry
'Is t'rough dat 'im an' 'er marry
But remember – Sally a virago gal.

Sally finish do bird
Harry t'ree piece suit an' ting
House, car, chick
Sally a look fe Harry
She get a tip from brudder Barry

She tred down a Finsbury Park
Pass all the bwoys in chambers
Out a de bookie shop
'Sally, wey Harry?'
Sally jus' cut her eye
An' jus' bop.

She stride pass Roy Barber Shop

'Wa'apen, gal?
Me jus' cut you hair las' week.
Wa-ya-a do walk street?'
Sally jus' cut her eye
An' jus' bop.

When she reach wey she have fe reach
She tan up still
Bwoy, boccal a go mash!
De sister come out

Harry bawl out
'Sally, de sister a carry!'
Sally pull.
Harry fall.
Sister bawl.
End of all.

A lot of young Black women now are very strong. They are choosing what they want in a relationship and if they're on their own with kids, it's often out of choice. They're not going to stand for some man just coming into their house, saying he wants to stay and making a nuisance of himself. They're demanding something from the relationship.

About two years ago, I changed my name to Nefertiti. A sister had introduced me to a tape-recording of Queen Mother Moore, and I listened to this woman talking about all the fighting she had done and it just made me really want to meet her. You know she taught in the Garvey Movement in 1913 and she was around at the time when the Ku Klux Klan were lynching Black people every day. So when I went to the States, I went to visit her. I introduced myself as Rosemary and she said, 'No, you're not Rosemary, you're Nefertiti.' She was eighty-three, and I just loved that woman like my mother, so I felt honoured by that name she'd given me. Nefertiti was an Egyptian Queen, but she was also a poet and very musical as well. During her reign, they encouraged a lot of music and poetry. When I got back, I talked it over with some close sisters, and they said I should change my name. You can't just take on a name like that. You've got to know why you're going to carry that name. You've got to look at yourself and at what you're dealing with and where you're coming from, so that when people ask you about it, you've got a positive answer. I've learnt a lot from changing my name. A lot of people think it's a kind of joke, and they try to shorten it or make fun of it. So you've got to be able to stand firm.

When I went to Jamaica earlier this year, I went to the archives in Spanish Town where they keep all the records of births and deaths from slavery times. Under the names of plantation owners like 'Brown' and 'Williams', they had their slaves listed with names like 'Mulatto' or 'Sambo', next to the cattle. Although I know our history, that's when the full meaning of our names dawned on me and I became very emotional. Because I see things this way, I've felt strengthened and I've been able to reject my slave name.

I think Black people need the culture, because it gives them the strength and the awareness to deal with racism and the political situation we're in. The culture on its own is not enough, of course. Although I'm writing about women, I'm still involved in thinking and writing about the general political situation. I've been to Jamaica, and I've looked at the political situation there. I've checked what it's like to live in the ghettos and the American influence on life in the Caribbean. I've also looked at the different Black people here in this country – the bourgeois Black people, the people who are exploiting Rasta, the people who are intellectualising about the multi-ethnic-this and the multi-ethnic-that. And my poems are about all that, as well.

One of the last poems I wrote was based on an old song called 'Every time me 'memba Liza …' I changed that into 'Every time me 'memba Elaine (Elaine Clair)', 'Every time me 'memba Colin' (Colin Roach) …' and I talk about the youths in Soweto and Atlanta, Georgia, all the young Black people who are being killed. And what I'm saying in that poem is that they're killing Black children because

210

they are trying to wipe out the part of the race which is militant. And although it's not stated openly, I'm also saying that the youths are coming up militant, thanks to the Black women who raised them.

Every Time Me 'memba

Every time me 'memba New Cross
Water come a mi eye
Every time me 'memba Elaine
Water dry ina me eye
Every time me 'memba Colin
Water come a mi eye
Every time me 'memba Georgia
Mi wan get up and fight
Every time me 'memba Soweto
It's time to organise.

You can't leave it up to peace anitiative
Peace anitiative
Peace anitiative.
You can't leave it up to peace anitiative
While African yout's a die
An' you can't wear a disguise
While time a fly by
We have to organise.

'Cause de killin of de yout's
An' de killin of our race
Is happenin right in front of our face
An' we haf fe realise
Dat dere's no disguise
When dem killin and shootin
An' covering up lies.

(See note at the end of this chapter about Nefertiti's poem.)

As our lives here have taken shape and form, we have had many rich sources to draw on, a long tradition of creativity and inventiveness. It is these solid foundations, laid by our African foremothers which have aided, inspired and

211

sustained us in this process. It is therefore to them that we owe our militant heritage.

Any expression by a Black woman of her cultural and political identity must be seen to represent centuries of struggle. Whatever we present and however we define ourselves comes directly from that history. Our sense of self cannot be divorced from our collective consciousness because every statement underscores the reality of a poor and oppressed people struggling to be free. Whether our statement is conscious or instinctive, whether it is expressed superficially, through outward appearance, or through fundamental changes in outlook and lifestyle, it will serve to reaffirm our rejection of the dominant culture and its attempted negation of our way of life. So any act of cultural defiance or ideological independence – whether it be through song, dance, our use of language, the way we style our hair, our dress, our view of the world, a painting or a poem – testifies to our existence *outside* the roles in which British society has cast us.

Black Woman and Sexism: Challenging the Norm

It is the fact that we are women which has distinguished our experience of life and culture from that of Black men. Our relationship with men – both Black and white – has meant that in addition to racism, Black women have had to confront a form of sexism and sexual abuse which is unique to us. But it is impossible to separate our understanding of sexism in our community from its context in a racist society because popular acceptance of racist stereotypes of Black women, Black men and Black families not only compound our sexual oppression but have also become internalised.

Under slavery, Black women were routinely abused by white men. Sexual violence against us was used as a form of control and served to disrupt any attempts we made to live as families. It was white men as slaveowners and later as employers (especially where we were employed as domestic servants) who violated our bodies in rape and sexual servitude. The myth of our 'animal-like promiscuity' was

212

used to justify these acts, and to exonerate white men of any blame. Similarly, the myth that Black men could not control their lust for white women was used as a means of terrorising our menfolk, and gave rise to the notion that our culture condones acts of violence against women. These stereotypes have survived today, and live on in countless media images depicting the Black women as 'exotic whore' and the Black man as 'sexual brute'. Meanwhile, our failure to conform to western notions of the (nuclear) family is not seen as a legacy of slavery, when marriage was actively discouraged, or even as a remnant of our African past when polygamy, the extended family and other alternative models of marriage and family life were prevalent; instead it is blamed on our promiscuity, our irresponsibility and our general lack of 'moral fibre' as a people.

In seeking to explain why many Black women today raise their families alone – and often successfully – Black male sociologists and psychologists such as Orlando Patterson, and white historians like Edith Clarke, have frequently chosen to apply the stereotype of the powerful Black matriarch, responsible both for the emasculation of the Black man and for the fragmentation of the family. Slavery, they say, brutalised the Black man and negated his role within the family. Black women are described as having taken over the more powerful role of 'head of the family', rendering Black men powerless and insignificant. This interpretation, however, is a sexist one and does not take account of where the real power lay during slavery. It is true that Black women played an active and positive role in the family, under both slavery and colonialism. But administering to the needs of our children and kinfolk was the only work which we could perform which was not under the direct control of the slavemasters. It also extended the role we were able to play within our communities. Black women were 'equal under the whip' where our labour and physical punishment were concerned, but this equality only applied to the means used to oppress us. The work we shared with Black men vested us with no more power or status than they had. Within the family structure, there is no evidence to show that we

213

dominated Black men, or even that most families were 'headed' by Black women. The burdensome responsibilities we shouldered under slavery cannot, by any stretch of the imagination, be described as 'matriarchal'. Nevertheless, the image of the Black matriarch survives, and has had a profound influence on our relationship with Black men today.

Black men in this society are as much the victims of race and class oppression as we are. The resulting projection of worthlessness cannot help but have a negative and damaging effect on how social and personal relations are perceived by both parties. The domestic arena has become the only area in which Black men are able to conform to the dominant male role. Thus their attempts to subjugate Black women who are in a position of even less power must be seen as the evidence of their alienation. This is not to make apologies for their oppression of Black women, for it is clear, from where we stand, that their abuse of us only serves to increase *our* alienation as women both from Black men and society at large. But it *is* to recognise that Black men's oppression of us is merely a façade of power.

Because Black women are conscious of the way racism operates against us as a people, much of the sexual abuse to which we are subjected goes unreported. We are aware of the prevailing stereotype of Black women as sexual predators, and know that we stand little or no chance of being taken seriously if we report incidents of abuse to the police. We are also highly sensitive to the way in which this society has criminalised Black men, which means that once arrested, they are often victims of police brutality and are left at the mercy of a racist judicial system. It is because Black women recognise such injustices, rather than because our culture condones violence against women, that so many Black women are reluctant to report Black men when we become the victims of domestic or sexual violence. Consequently, we have had to find ways of dealing with such violence from within ourselves and our communities. This often involves drawing on the support of our mothers or other women members of our family, relying on them rather than the State

214

physically to confront the men who perpetrate such acts. Far from accepting or condoning male violence, many Black women have traditionally resisted and fought back against sexual attack, recognising that no other form of redress exists for us than self-defence and female retaliation.

I got married when I was seventeen. At the time I suppose I believed all those things girls are brought up on about the only thing in life for a woman is to find a husband and have children. But I don't think I ever thought about it that way – it was just the thing to do when you thought you'd found the right man. My parents were dead against the marriage. Not because they didn't like him, they just thought we were too young. And they were right. By the time I had my first child, we'd split up. We started arguing a lot, mainly because he wanted to carry on exactly as he had before we were married – you know, going to Blues every Saturday, chatting up other women, that sort of thing. When I fell pregnant, it just wasn't part of the plan, especially since he wasn't working. Things just came to a head, being stuck in the house together all day. When he did go, finally, he just got up and left one day. He didn't even stay around for the baby to be born. I heard later he'd moved in with some women he'd been seeing, but I thought good luck to her, rather her than me. My friends used to tell me I should go round and mash her up, but I could never be bothered with all that; as far as I was concerned what had happened was his fault, not hers.

When my daughter was born, that's when I really started to find out what it was all about. You know, you see all these ads on TV of women smiling down at happy babies, but they don't tell you nothing about what it's like to cart all those dirty nappies round to the launderette every day, or when they get sick and you can't even go round the corner to phone for an ambulance because you've got no one to leave them with. If it hadn't been for my mum, I'd definitely have cracked up. She helped me out a lot at that time, and I really appreciated it because she never said, 'I told you so'. I know she was upset by

215

what happened, especially since she had all these ideas about me going to college and getting a good job before I settled down. But I suppose in a way she was just glad I'd got off as lightly as I did, because if we'd stayed together and carried on fighting like that, one of us would probably have ended up dead.

I lived on my own for about two years after that. I just felt really disillusioned about men, it's all a big con that stuff about 'to love, honour and cherish', or whatever it is they make you say. When I met my second child's father, I was determined not to make the same mistake twice. I had this idea that you could just let them come around when you wanted – you know, 'You can stay the night, guy, but don't expect no breakfast if you do.' But it didn't work out that way. They stay one night, then two, and before you know it you're ironing his shirts and cooking his dinner for him every night. Anyway, that relationship lasted a bit longer than the first one. By the time I fell pregnant again, I really believed it was going to last, that's why I went ahead and had the baby. Plus he kept on about 'have a baby for me', like it was something I would be doing for him. Don't get me wrong, I wanted the baby too. My eldest daughter was about three by then, and I didn't want an only child, I don't believe in it. He changed after the baby was born, though. He started going out with his spars, then he'd stay out all night and come in in the morning as if nothing had happened. And he started getting violent over any little thing, like if I said something he didn't happen to agree with, he'd just lay into me and knock me about. I don't know what happened to him, really, because when I first met him he was a really nice bloke, really kind and considerate. A lot of blokes are like that, though. They just change.

Anyway, it reached the point where I couldn't take it any more, so I asked him to leave. But he wouldn't go, he was on to too much of a good thing living with me. He used to say things like, 'I'm not leaving you bring up *my* child', that sort of rubbish. *His* kid – the cheek of it! I was the one who fed her and made sure she had shoes on her

216

feet, he never gave me a penny to support that child. So I never saw it that way, as far as I was concerned, they're my kids and it's for me to bring them up. Anyway, he wouldn't go and things just got worse and worse. My mum found out what was going on and she got really angry. She kept telling me I should kick him out, but it's not that easy. What can you do? I mean, okay, if he gets really violent you can call the police, but what are they going to do? They just put it down to a domestic tiff, tell you both to calm down and leave you to it. I know, because that happened to a girlfriend of mine, they just left the man to carry on beating her up. Anyway, I don't think they are allowed to arrest a bloke just for slapping a woman about – you have to wait until he does something really out of order, like pulling a knife on you before you can go to court and get an injunction.

Anyway, he knew I wouldn't call the police on him, no Black woman's going to grass up a Black man to the police, don't matter how bad things are. It got to the point where he was just using me like a punching bag. Whenever anything got him down, he just took it out on me. Once he punched me in the head so hard, I got a perforated ear-drum; another time, I had to wear shades for two weeks because I had two Black eyes and a fractured nose. In the end, it was my mum who got him to go. She came round one night after he'd been laying into me, and she was so mad, I've never seen her so angry. I was crying, the kids were crying, it was a really bad scene. She just stood there and told him that if he didn't leave right that minute, she'd kill him, and she meant it, too. My mum's a big woman, and there's no way he was going to mess with her. After he'd gone, it was like I'd just woken up from a bad dream. I'd let that man tread all over me for nearly two years. Looking back, I can't see how I stuck it for so long, but at the time I was just scared. Never again, though. I'd rather just live on my own and bring up my two kids in peace. Any man who starts looking as if he's getting ready to move in here, I just tell him straight, 'No way, brother, this woman's quite happy living alone, and that's how it's going to stay!'

217

We cannot – and would not wish to – deny that sexism is rampant in our culture. This clearly reflects the sexism pervading the society we live in, which has nurtured and perpetuated derogatory male attitudes towards all women. Such attitudes are apparent at every level within our community, both in our family relations and structures, and in our social institutions. Dominoes clubs, Blues parties, reggae clubs and youth clubs are all male-oriented, for example, and women are expected to conform to certain roles within them. But young Black women in particular are finding new responses to this situation, and are refusing to go along with the notion that we are merely sexual prey.

Sexism at de Club

Mi guh inna de club
dress up inna mi track-suit an' ting.
see de yout-man dem 'tan up,
dem jus 'tan up an' stare
pan de clothes I wear.
Den mi hear one ah dem seh
'What a way de gal tink seh she fit.'
But let I tell dem som'ting.
I don't wear dem clothes yah fi look fit
or even hip
I wear dem cause dem comfortable
when I ride my bicycle.

Mean-while still in de club
a table-tennis game in session,
mi show de bruddas fi hold I
a game when dem done.
Yuh should a si de way
dem watch mi up an down.
Like fi seh
Gal why yuh don't shut up
and sit down.
De tall one beat de short one,
now is me turn fi come on.
Him seh something to me dat I didn't

218

understand, an just hold up him trousers
front; like me a tretten him manhood
in more ways dan one.
I beat him three straight games for
de set, him fren', yes de same short one,
call him saaf.
fi mek a gal teck him off
    sistas don't be put off,
by the brothers showing off,
when yuh go into any club.
'Cause how will yuh ever learn.
by shying away, and leaving it for
another day, when only other sistas
will be there, and who, like you, jus'
sit around.

Donna Moore

Despite such challenges, Black women still have much to
contend with. The music played in Black clubs and homes
frequently contributes to the sexist ethos. Male contempt for
women, which defines us as sexual prey, is reflected
particularly in the DJ style of reggae music, which
perpetuates the notion that Black people are defined and
obsessed by our own sexuality:

I need a fat girl tonight
(fat girl tonight)
I'm in the mood
I'm feeling so rude
When you feeling it girl
You gotta say it so nice
see it deh, fatty
(see it deh)
In deh, fatty
(in deh)

You think I love you for just one thing
Aint that lovin' you girl ...?

The Heptones

219

Much of the soul music emanating from America emphasises the sexual prowess of Black men and the sexual debasement of Black women, in a similar fashion. Lyrics abound which portray Black men 'taking' women and 'needing' to be satisfied by us. And when Millie Jackson croons that she needs 'sexercise', she demonstrates the extent to which Black women have internalised prevalent notions about our sexuality.

Because music plays such an important role in our culture, messages such as these have a major influence on Black women's self-image. By perpetuating the myth that many simultaneous sexual relationships are proof of male power and sexual prowess, they are largely (though by no means wholly) responsible for the way in which Black men have internalised the sexism which pervades this society. While no culture, however progressive, can be said to have rid itself of its sexism, it is nevertheless true that Black men are particularly guilty of taking on the role of sexual predator in a way which oppresses women. An example of this is the way in which women, and young women in particular, are pressured into having children, or 'breeding' (the term used by our slavemasters has unfortunately survived in our vocabulary). Women who do not have children are labelled 'mules' (i.e. unnatural). Rasta women in particular are encouraged by their men to reject all contraception and to regard it either as a form of genocide, or as an unacceptable facet of Western culture. Childbirth is seen to confirm womanhood, and it is taken for granted that Black women should be able to raise and organise a family, if necessary without support, thus leaving the Black man free to move on to his next sexual conquest. If some Black women's response to this is to reject relationships with all men, Black or white, it can only be seen as the legitimate response of women who are refusing to accept such roles.

The reality today is that many Black women do bring up their children, and the children of other relatives, on their own. It is our mothers and other women who provide the support which the men so often fail to give us, reflecting a long tradition whereby responsibility for our children has

220

been shared. Recognising this reality does not, however, mean that we would wish to romanticise the role played by Black women who raise their children without the support of a man. We do not raise our families in this way because we are superwomen, or 'sturdy Black bridges', but because we have been compelled to accept this responsibility both historically and as a result of the internalised sexism of many Black men today. There is no power or respect to be gained from performing such a task, particularly in a society which invalidates any family structure which does not conform to the nuclear model, with men as the providers and decision-makers. The fact that Black women are often prepared to raise a family without a male figure around does, however, attest to a different kind of strength, and an independence which the pervading oppressive sexual stereotypes have not undermined.

TO A DEAR FRIEND

The men may come and go
but the women in your life are always constant –
always –
the mothers, sisters, friends,
most of all the friends, who
because they can be in a way that mothers and sisters can't
    always
are sometimes the only lifeline.
Friend –
I think if I were a man
i would see in you
the calm at the edge of a whirlpool and would stay by you,
a live, burning torch in a dark open space,
i'd want to cradle you from the ill-winds that may disturb
    your brilliance.
For you are at once calm, gentle, sensitive, knowing, giving,
    sustaining,
you are all these things and yet un-definable –
for how often haven't you forgiven me
when I couldn't forgive myself for having been 'foolish
    with a man'

221

and comforted me with insights so gentle, they did
not need to declare themselves or to deny others their
    dreams or shout down their folly.
If I were a man
i would have the ultimate respect for your 'Black-woman'
    self
and your 'Black-woman' body
i would not sully you with my own shortcomings,
and though I don't know if I even believe in god
I pray that he holds you as dear as I do,
and that whatever happens you never waste any part of
    yourself.

Iyamide Hazeley

Rootedness: The Quest for Self-knowledge

Just as we have had to find ways of challenging and redefining our relationship with men, Black women have also taken part in the struggle to redefine what it means to be Black. This struggle began to take shape and form in the late sixties, when, thanks to the influence of the Black Power movement, we began to enter a new era of Black consciousness. This influence was both political and cultural. As an ideology which expounded pride in our African heritage, Black Power gave rise to one of the earliest conscious and collective expressions by Black women of cultural self-respect. After decades of bombardment with the message that 'white is right', of seeing ourselves through a mirror of racist distortion, the new movement signalled a fundamental reawakening – a rediscovery of the cultural values which Black women have played such a major, though anonymous, part in maintaining over the centuries.

The cultural nationalism which characterised Black Power politics resulted in a complete radicalisation of Black women's self-image. Songs and posters proclaimed that 'Black is beautiful' and that 'to be young, gifted and Black is where it's at'. Black women seized the revolutionary implications of this message, giving expression to our reawakened cultural pride in every sphere of our lives over

222

which we exerted control. We began to wear flowing African robes, turbans and jewellery; we began to give our children African names like Ife and Kwame. Above all, we stopped straightening our hair, demonstrating that, as women, we had succeeded in resisting the social, cultural and commercial pressures to strive to imitate the white ideal of womanhood. We learnt to reject those products which merely embodied the potential to rub away some of our Blackness. We started to emphasise, rather than minimise the physical characteristics which set us apart from white women. We learnt to 'Say it loud, I'm Black and I'm proud!'

That was a very important and exciting time for me. It showed that we had to fight for our rights. Joining an organisation was a natural thing to do. It was a way of making a public statement about the way forward for Black people. On a personal level, too, it changed my life. I had been through all the ugly things that Black women do to deny themselves and their culture. I had bought bleaching cream, telling myself it was to improve my uneven colouring. (But the thought of how it might work frightened me, so I didn't even finish the tube.) I had stitched horsehair into my own hair – the 'weave-on', they called it. After that, I had cold-straightened it, but only once because it fell out. Apart from that, I was used to pressing it almost every night. My mother used to run me out of the kitchen late at night, saying, 'Yu marva gwine ratten'. I'd abused my hair so much, and all because the white ideal was the one we had to aspire to. The magazines told us that to have straightened hair and fair skin was to be beautiful and feminine, that to be Black and female was to be poor and ugly.

The changes I went through with Black Power were changes in how I saw myself. I remember consciously chucking out my hot combs, bleaching creams and all those things that spoke of my rejection of who I was. No more fried hair, no more mottled skin. For me, the Afro symbolised pride in my blackness, an acceptance – no, even more than that, a celebration – of our African-ness, not only African features and dress but African militancy, defending our rights. Angela Davis was a powerful influence at that time – I saw her as a proud, Black woman, imprisoned because she was fighting against the State. Her image inspired a lot of Black women in Britain.

But the kind of positive and liberating statements we were making about ourselves began to be compromised. Some of the multi-national drug companies were able to reap huge profits from the Black cultural revolution. They started marketing a whole new range of Afro products for the 'Natural Look', for example. Once you get hooked on that packaged concept, of course, you easily succumb to other forms of so-called 'Black' advertisements – and to the idea that there's a need to change the package regularly. So when companies in America started to say that the Afro had had its day, implying that it was just a fashion to us, what they were really doing was trying to take control of us again, trying to move us on to a style which they could influence. Added to this, they had got white women to take over the Afro, as a way of sending it up. Theirs came in red, green, pink – all colours of the rainbow. They were trying to make what Black women were saying through the Afro seem meaningless.

But we just found other ways of asserting ourselves and our separate identity. A lot of sisters began to braid, bead and cane-row their hair again, which was just another expression of our African heritage. It was amazing, really, because some of these creative skills we didn't even know we had it in ourselves to do. They'd been passed on by mothers and grandmothers and had survived for centuries, under cover. When we were busy frying our hair, cane-row hadn't been fashionable or stylish. Most of us plaited our hair out of convenience rather than choice. But as we got more conscious, it became a proud way to carry yourself. It signified so many cultural bonds for us, especially when we saw Black American women wearing the same styles. This was something which was firmly under our control!

Before long, of course, they came out with the 'Bo

Dereck' look, which was another attempt by whites to appropriate something which was ours. It was outrageous. Nowadays, you've got top hairdressing salons offering a 'hair-locksing' service, as if Rastafari is some kind of fashionable 'cult' to be followed. As far as I'm concerned, these are just some of the more subtle forms of cultural control which they have tried to exert on Black women. It might seem a lot to attribute to hair, but what it shows is the way aspects of our culture have been undermined. Black culture isn't a craze or a style that's up for grabs. When whites try to take it over, they just demean and degrade it. To me, the Bo Dereck–Boy George scenario with the multi-coloured locks, the beads, the bows and so on, is a symptom of the general decay in Western society. It bears no relation to solid and enduring African traditions, the things which have given us strength over the centuries. So I feel that Black women have got to continue to find new ways of expressing ourselves, until we reclaim everything that belongs to us. And that's what's happening now, even if you look at the way Black women have gone back to using string and twists. I suppose in the end, our roots will always sustain us.

Because of our history, this process of redefinition has always been a complex task. There can be no automatic assumption that the image we see reflected in our mirror tells us all we need to know about ourselves. The recognition of blackness, even when confined to the physical, can be a gradual and sometimes painful process of self-realisation. For Black women who were born outside Britain, in the Caribbean or in a country where Black culture is the dominant force in everyday life, this process is more likely to be a positive one, bolstered by the security of knowing that one is part of a people and a culture which is valid in its own right. Even the myths of a colonial education cannot fully detract from that instinctive sense of self-worth and from the understanding that our heritage is neither determined nor negated by European civilisation and culture. But for those of us who were born or raised in Britain, the process often involves a long struggle with definitions of Self, Culture and Identity.

As a consequence of the Black cultural revolution of the past two decades, an increasingly positive sense of self and blackness has come to dominate the consciousness of Black women not only in Britin but throughout the diaspora. As more and more Black women are able to sing, write and speak out about the realities of being Black and female, rejecting the myths and stereotypes and reasserting those aspects of our lives which *we* have determined to be valid, the knowledge that Black womanhood is a positive, vibrant force is re-entering the consciousness of our community.

That consciousness has not always been there. Slavery took on many different forms, and our rejection of mental slavery – the notion of white (male) superiority – has been an inevitable phase in the lengthy process of self-liberation as a people. If Black women have been guilty of wearing straightened wigs or applying bleaching creams to our skins, it was because of the power of the message that fair skin can be a passport out of poverty and exploitation.

It has always been central to cultural imperialism to promote self-hatred among those it oppresses. It provides a means of legitimising the actions of the white ruling class against 'inferior' races, and also facilitates the process of 'divide and rule' which has been so essential to colonial and neo-colonial practices. Part of the process has involved the elevation of fair-skinned Blacks to the ranks of the petty-bourgeoisie. This was a particularly well-worn strategy during British colonialism, when a small class of Black administrators with vested interests in the system was needed. When Black people have emulated whites, it has usually been out of the misguided belief that self-denial would promote their social mobility and integration into a particular class of white society.

Our experience of Britain has often served to compound this notion that whiteness and success are synonymous, leading us to a confused sense of self and culture. Although our mothers have been instrumental in perpetuating our culture through us, the experience of living here made some of them seek out ways of protecting us from racism, by

226

encouraging us to assume the trappings of the dominant culture, or to 'act white'. But we have invariably learnt that the best way to protect ourselves from racism is to equip ourselves with our culture, and use it as a buffer against the society's assaults on our identity.

My parents, although both Black, were from very different backgrounds. My father was Nigerian and my mother Jamaican. Even now their marriage can be difficult but at the time it was disastrous. They faced opposition on all sides. My father's family accused him of going to Britain and marrying the descendant of slaves. My mother's family didn't want anything to do with her marrying a Black African. She had 'spoiled' herself. It was all to do with status. A beautiful brown-skin girl wasted.

With that kind of confused, culturally insecure background it was understandable that I took on white ways. My father schooled me to 'speak properly' so I sounded white because he was keen on education so even when looking at my Black face, people used to ask if I was mixed because of my accent. I did come over to others, especially other Black girls, as though I was trying to act white. They felt that I was just being snobbish. The white girls tolerated me. When they made their racist comments, it was a case of 'Not you, you're different'. That was what I had to live with.

Fortunately, it didn't last and as I came through my mid-teens I did begin to change. From there I made a conscious effort to take on my mother's culture. Why my mother's? Only with Black Power did Africa become fashionable. Before that, when I was just into an understanding, I thought that to be accepted meant to be West Indian. So I taught myself to speak Jamaican and learnt how to cook – not as a programme, but I'd go to the kitchen and watch my mother. I'd go and watch a domino match, go to a shabeen, picking up bits of Black life all the time. It was the only way I could learn to feel part of my people.

That was the beginning, but I've been through enough

227

to know myself now and how to handle what this society can deal out. I hope to equip my kids with a total education so that they will understand how to deal with it, too.

For those of us who have been brought up in isolation from our communities, without the security and instinctive support that comes from having other Black people around, the experience of cultural isolation can be equally confusing:

My parents were born in Trinidad, but I went to school in Newcastle. I can remember going to St Josephs, but I can't remember if it was a nursery school or some other kind of school. I felt white growing up with white people. The only Black people I came into contact with was my family. The area we used to live in when I was small was very rough. People didn't call me names, though. It was only when I got older that I felt it. My first experience was when I was in primary school. I used to be very good at sports. My favourite game was netball. I was literally the only Black girl in the school, apart from my sister, and I think the other kids were jealous that I played so well, because I would hear them making remarks about 'Black' this or 'Black' that, and it really hurt me, although I was still quite young at the time.

I hated school because I was on my own and I couldn't handle it. I was too young, at the age of nine, to do anything about it. I couldn't call them any names back, because I didn't know any. I hated being Black because they called me names, and I wished all the time that I was white.

I have been to the West Indies, and I loved it. But even when I came back things were still the same, and I still felt that way. I was never proud to be Black. I felt ashamed of it, because there was only one of me and thousands of them, and I felt useless because I couldn't do anything about it. I didn't tell my parents. They used to tell me, 'You've got to work harder because you're coloured.' When I used to go into town, I didn't like going because I felt alien.

When I went to secondary school, it was a kind of convent school which was very strict and I didn't get called names very much there. Sometimes boys used to wait outside the gate and I used to hate passing them, because I knew they would make remarks. There was one other Black girl who went to my secondary school, and my cousin. This girl got on with the white girls very well. She was a punk, and she was more accepted than I was. I think she got on better because she cut her hair like theirs and did what they did, but I wasn't into that kind of thing.

I don't talk about it so much to my two brothers, but my sister and I talk about it a lot. She's two years younger than me, and she used to feel the same way. I remember her telling me that when she went to school, people would touch her hair to see what it felt like. One day she went to school without combing her hair, and when she took off her hat the other children stared so much that she ran out of the classroom to the toilet. When we went swimming, white people were always asking why our hair was like that.

The first thing I noticed when I came down to London was that there was so many Black people. I felt better, more at home. That's why I don't want to go back to Newcastle. Now that I know something different, I feel that I can walk out of the house and people won't stare at me. I don't feel ashamed of being Black anymore.

The reality of racism in Britain has debunked the idea that we can escape this feeling of alienation and 'otherness' for all but a few. Whether born or bred here, our experiences at the hands of employers, police, teachers and white society at large have forced us to acknowledge that we are something other than 'British', sharpening our collective awareness of our differences. The fact that this awareness is widespread, particularly among young Black people, most of whom know no other country than Britain, confirms the fact that, as a people, we have firmly rejected the notion of assimilation.

For many Black women, particularly younger Black women who may not have been directly exposed to the powerful cultural influence of the Black Power era, Rastafari has provided us with the cultural security we need to carry through our rejection of dominant cultural values and replace them with a sense of blackness and rootedness:

The first time I was aware of the fact that I'm Black was at infants school, and we had to draw pictures of each other. Everyone was drawing matchstick figures with long hair, and I copied them. The girl I was sitting next to turned to me and said, 'That isn't you, you haven't got hair like that, you're Black.' When I look back on it, I don't think children really see themselves as being a particular colour, because the visual aids and textbooks we get at school don't recognise that we exist. I think it all boils down to culture. Black children need to see themselves as they are, and to identify themselves. Obviously, young children are at a very impressionable age, and they identify with what they see around them. They see the world as it is portrayed in picture books like *Little Red Riding Hood* and *Cinderella* and *Peter and Jane*. That's why Black kids end up thinking they want to be white. Another thing about that which I remember – although I don't think I did it myself – was when we used to go to my sister's friend's house. Some of the little Black girls used to put cardigans around their heads to pretend to have long hair. I may have done it too, I don't remember. I think this is how the books tend to reflect those ideas, that it's better to have long straight hair. You just don't see ordinary Black children in the pictures, so you end up trying to be something else. Now things are changing a bit, but we've still got a long way to go.

I hope I don't have children in this society, but if I do I'll bring them up in the Rastafarian faith. As this is a capitalist society, I would try to teach them that they need a future. I would also teach them about Africa, because at the moment I see Africa as my future. I'd teach them to make good use of school, and I'd want to know everything that was going on in their classroom. I feel that the more you make yourself known around the school, as a parent, the more they are going to watch what they do to your children. When you're Black in this country, you have to do three times better than the white person. Some of the freelance dreads say that they're not going to send their kids to school here, but who is going to lose out in the end if they don't?

You don't know about the system unless you've been through it, and I feel that my generation will make it better for the next. No one will tell me that my child was misbehaving at school, because I will not believe them like some Black mothers do. I would bring them up to have self-respect, because as long as you have respect for yourself, no one can touch you. We have to know our culture.

'Knowing our culture', however, has never been an automatic process, particularly where the dominant influences on our lives are both controlled and determined by white cultural values. Increasingly, Britain's multi-racial society is producing Black people with one white parent, or Black children who've been raised in white families or institutions, in isolation from any sense of Black community or culture. Largely because of the efforts of Black people themselves, welfare and adoption services are at last beginning to acknowledge that this kind of cultural isolation should be avoided. Slowly, and not before time, the traumas of having to deal with racism with no Black cultural terms of reference for guidance appear to be sinking into the society's consciousness.

Short of apartheid or total repatriation, nothing can prevent the increase of Black/white relationships which result in children of mixed race. These children, in order to survive the racism they will inevitably face, will need to go through the same struggles consciously to seek out a sense of self, culture and identity as other Black people who have grown up here over the past thirty years.

Growing up as a half-caste in Liverpool was difficult. You had your father's Black culture on the one hand, and your mother's on the other. Until my mother died, they were

231

very happy. They had gone through a lot of shit. I remember when I was eleven, my mother asked me to whiten the steps in front of our house. I heard her shouting and screaming at the front door, and when I went out to see what was wrong, somebody had smeared excrement all over the steps I'd been cleaning and written 'Nigger Lover', 'Go back to Bananaland' and 'White women who live with niggers are trash' all over the door. I don't know how they coped with it all. My mother's parents had disowned her, and their only other contact with her family was through a girl she had had from a previous marriage. The grandparents had kept her, so we didn't see much of her, but she used to come back for holidays. I can remember going to them at the age of eleven or twelve for the summer holidays. They lived in Manchester. Someone in the family died, and all my mother's brothers and sisters got together, all the members of the white side of the family were there. All they could say was, 'What's she doing here?' and 'How can you allow a Black child in the house?' Although I was due to stay there for six weeks, I told my grandfather that I didn't want to stay there any longer. I have not spoken to them or forgiven them to this day for that. They all came to my mother's funeral, but I still didn't speak to them. What can you do when half your family's white, and none of them wants to know you? I also felt isolated from the West Indians who were living around us in Liverpool. They called me what they considered me to be – a 'half-breed' – even people who became close friends. I resented that, because I had it tough enough from the white people. It was a very confusing time. I went through a phase where I joined the Black Power movement. We used to go to meetings about Angela Davis, police brutality – all the things that were happening to Black people – and I became very active politically, at that time.

All my family was deeply affected by being mixed. My sister, for instance, would go from one extreme to the other. At sixteen she came to London and became very Black. She wouldn't speak to anyone white, but whenever

232

Black friends were around, the conversation would flow. Can you imagine it? She's mixed, and took this line?

The colour thing stands out even more now, because my kids look white. I really wanted them to be darker. When my daughter was born, I was sure they'd made a mistake, because she was blue-eyed, fair-haired and fair-skinned. Even so, she still has to deal with racialism. She went to a party the other day, and when I asked one of the other women if she'd enjoyed herself, she said, 'She gets on well with the boys – like mother, like daughter.' I looked at her and asked her what she meant. She said, 'Nothing,' but I know exactly what she was getting at – in other words, Black and flighty and promiscuous. So I still have to protect her from racism.

Today, growing numbers of mixed-race children are being raised in this country who will have to confront this kind of racism and question who they really are. And they will learn that their experiences are not unique. Our struggles today and in the past to define ourselves and to seek out our roots will serve them in good stead. And because we know how racism works, both on us and our children, Black women will be a major influence in helping to shape this growing quest among young Black people for self-knowledge. Already we have begun to demand redefinitions of our understanding of blackness, rejecting divisive terms like 'half-caste' and challenging the confusions which still survive in our community about mixed race.

For someone like me who's been brought up by a white mother, I think the whole question of identity can be fraught with contradictions. You've got the racist attitudes of your so-called family – in my case, my mother's own unacknowledged racism – and all the self-hatred that can lead to. Then there's the attitudes of your teachers and school friends and everyone else around you who's white, which makes it impossible for you to keep up any delusions that you're *not* Black, as you grow older. And if you're around Black people, there's the labels like 'half-breed' and 'half-caste' which single you out as

233

someone who doesn't really belong there either, even if you've got all the physical credentials.

For me, being Black is not just about skin colour. I can understand why some people see it that way, especially in Africa or the West Indies, where fair-skinned Blacks have been used as a kind of buffer by the whites and allowed to move up in the society. But in Britain, it's not about that at all. It's about understanding racism because you've *lived* it; it's about the fact that if you're not white in this society, no matter how fair you may be, you are going to have to deal with racism. So whatever you may have been brought up to think, there's no escaping it, in the eyes of this society you're just another wog who should 'go home'. The way I see it, that skinhead isn't going to tap me on the shoulder and say, 'Oh, excuse me, I didn't realise your mother was white,' before he puts the boot in. And the same goes for employers, teachers, and the police.

I think that in Africa, people probably have a better way of dealing with children who are fair. I've met cousins on my father's side of the family who range from high-yellow to blue-black and they all have the same mother. They are just seen as a product of history, as proof that somewhere, at some time, a white man got in there – probably a trader or a sailor or some colonial or other. If you're brought up within a Black culture like that, you're going to feel more secure. That's why people say that if your father's white and your mother's Black, you're less likely to have problems coming to terms with who you are, because it's your mother who passes on the culture. But here in Britain, because of racism, Black people are very aware of colour politics. And what that means for people who are mixed race is that you often have to 'prove' your blackness because I suppose other Black people suspect you of having mixed loyalties. As far as I'm concerned, that kind of thinking comes out of a faulty understanding of what's been happening to Black people through history. There are hundreds of examples of Black people who've been bought off by whites, just as there are hundreds of examples of Black people of mixed

234

race who've been on the right side of history. For instance, Mary Seacole's father was a Scot, and Malcolm X had ginger hair and freckles!

The first time I came up against this kind of suspicion was when I started going to Black meetings. All of a sudden, you'd hear people talk about you as if you posed some kind of a threat to security, simply because they knew your mother was white. The joke is, if some of them had gone back a few generations, they'd probably have discovered that they had exactly the same kind of background, it's just that it wasn't so obvious in their case. I think this is partly why you get so many fair-skinned Blacks trying to act 'blacker than Black', because they find it's easier to just not admit that their mother is white or whatever. But they only end up living a lie. You can't go around believing that white people are the 'enemy' when part of you is white, it's just another kind of self-hatred. White society and racism, yes, but not individuals. It's the system we've got to check. Or to put it another way, racism isn't about bigoted attitudes which this person or that person may hold, it's about institutionalised policies which are laid on a given race of people because of economic reasons. So if Black people are going to fight it, that's where we're going to have to start.

I think Black people are going to have to work this one out sooner rather than later, anyway. There are a lot of Black kids growing up in Britain today who have white mothers or white fathers or live in white foster homes – and one thing's for sure, the problem isn't going to go away. A lot of these kids are growing up totally confused about who they are, and it's for the Black community to *tell* them. Black people are still working this out and there's still a lot of confusion about mixed race. But no one's going to tell me that Mary Seacole who was half Scottish was Black, and she's okay because she's dead anyway, when here's me, a living, breathing product of British racism, I don't count. That kind of analysis just doesn't hold up when you get into a serious discussion.

I think the time will soon come when terms like

235

'half-caste' will die a natural death, just like 'negro' did. It's negative, it's meaningless where racism is concerned, and in any case, it's not self-defined. I went to a Black women's conference a few months back, where there was a discussion on mixed race in one of the workshops. A lot of the women there were angry about terms like 'half-caste' and 'coloured' because they saw them as being divisive. When you think about it, even the word sounds like a put-down, like 'half-done' – and there's a whole range of them, like 'mulatto', which is a mixture between a mule and an ass or something. As far as I'm concerned, I'm a *Black* woman, because I live that reality. That kind of detail about me just isn't up for discussion any more. If anyone wants to check my credentials, all they have to do is go study some history!

To resist cultural suicide in this way, when for many of us there is little doubt that we are here to stay, cannot be seen as a simple act of preference. Whether we express our rejection of dominant cultural values as a desire to return to Africa or by simply insisting on our right to dress, think and act 'Black', we are demonstrating our adherence to the culture *we* have determined autonomously, our quest for a form of self-knowledge which transcends the stereotypes. We are affirming that we have a life and a purpose outside the roles which British society has tried to force upon us.

It was a shock to my system when I came to Britain and confronted racism for the first time. It was difficult to cope with, and for several years I fought back in the only way I knew how to. I had lots of physical clashes with other kids at school. Boxing a few of them seemed to be the only way of responding to their taunts of 'jungle bunny' and 'wog'. I became wild for a while. But this rebellion was beaten out of me and almost without noticing it, I was changing. For one thing, I lost my accent and the whole Creole way of speaking. After a few years, I was the real English 'Miss' – at least, in speech. As well as this, I was being singled out with one other Black girl for favoured treatment by some

236

of the teachers at school. We were the only Black 'A' level candidates, so we were the ones on show, the ambassadors, so to speak. So mine was a classic integration case. Yet I didn't really accept the English way of life, nor did I really see myself as English. How could you when you were so abused as well? I didn't feel part of this country, and I knew I had another home which was still vivid in my memory, a place where there was still family. I didn't want to turn my back on that.

What made the school situation more awful, though, was that I was being ostracised by the other Black girls in the fifth and sixth forms, who were just being kept on but denied the opportunities to do exams. Mixing more and more with these girls who were critical meant that I had to consider what I could allow to happen to myself. Black Power consciousness was crucial, not just for me but for everyone in our age group. People who had teased me for looking like an African, because I was dark, or who called me 'Liberian Queen' with that curl of the lip which signified the ultimate insult, started moving together and talking about 'race pride' and 'unity'.

Much of that pride and sense of unity remains with me. What this means for me now is that a sense of being Black has instilled a certain confidence in me – a sense of certainty about who and what I am. It has nothing to do with hating white people – it's just that I happen to love Black people. The word that most clearly defines my sense of blackness is 'rootedness'. By that I mean to say that I have and I rely on a sense of tradition that has been fashioned and grounded in the Caribbean, and tested by racism here, but which has deeper roots in Africa. When I talk about Africa, it's not in a sentimental way. I can't honestly see myself going to live there permanently, and I don't dream of returning to the ancestral home. Africa is a reference point to interpret my experience because it echoes it. We share the oppression in degree if not in kind. That's the negative side. On the positive side, we share the same spirit.

Because there is a tangible link, I would like to make a

237

contribution to Africa's overall growth, if I can. But if I can't do that directly, I still feel I can make my struggle where I am, because that sense of certainty overrides the lack of any direct physical ties. This is what I want to pass on to my children. We need to redress that balance somehow. Sometimes our own mothers didn't have time to revive all the songs, the stories, the things which would have helped us to overcome that shit we were going through here. But the little I was told, I keep. I put it with those grandmother tales and keep them like a tune playing in the background of my consciousness. I have to reaffirm those things which my mother couldn't – or didn't – have time to pass on to me. I do it for my children.

I'm aware all the time of what this society is trying to do to us. They need to steal those kinds of things from us. It happens almost without us knowing. So we have to start early with our kids before the weight of the experience of living in a racist country begins to crush them. We have to teach them how to know, examine, understand and embrace blackness.

It is by embracing our blackness and by reaching such firm conclusions about who we are that Black women have survived the many physical and psychological assaults on us, over the years. We have come to recognise that it is the bonds we have in common because of our history and our experience of racism and sexism which unite us; that whether raised in the security of our culture or in isolation from it, our unique experience as Black women and as Black people binds us closer together and gives us the strength to resist and overcome. By living, countering and shaping a way of life for ourselves which involves constantly reassessing those racist definitions and challenging the negative ways society has conditioned us to see ourselves, we are making a loud and positive affirmation about who we are. Through the choices we are making about our lives and the values which we are imparting to our children, we are making it clear that in whatever ways the society tries to constrain us, *we will break free.*

238

Even centuries of slavery, oppression and sexual abuse, of attacks on our culture and on our right to be, have not succeeded in breaking Black women's spirit of resistance. Instead of distancing us from the African heritage which has sustained us, the thousands of miles we have travelled and the oceans we have crossed have simply strengthened our collective sense of self-worth. It is this firm and durable tradition of drawing strength and purpose from the culture in which our experience is grounded that is Black women's most precious legacy to the next generation.

Note to 'Every Time Me 'memba'

Sixteen Black children died in a house fire in New Cross, London in January 1981; the Black community believes their deaths were the result of a racist arson attack.

Elaine Clair, a fifteen-year-old Black girl writer and poet, was found drowned under mysterious circumstances in four feet of water in July 1981. She had been on her way to school.

Colin Roach's body was found in January 1983 outside Stoke Newington police station with a bullet through his head. The police claimed suicide, but the Black community has consistently demanded an independent inquiry into the circumstances of his death.

Twenty-nine Black children were murdered between July 1979 and June '81 in Atlanta, Georgia. Although a Black man was later arrested and charged with the murders, the Black community insisted that the killings continued after his arrest and that their motive was racial.

In June 1976, several hundred schoolchildren were either killed or wounded by South African police during demonstrations against the compulsory teaching of Afrikaans in school.

Bibliography

Introduction

Alexander, Z. and A. Dewjee, eds., *Wonderful Adventures of Mary Seacole in Many Lands*, Falling Wall Press, 1984.

Augier, F.R. and S.C. Gordon, *Sources of West Indian History*, Longman, 1962.

Davidson, Basil, *Black Mother*, Penguin, 1968.

File, N. and C. Power eds., *Black Settlers in Britain 1555-1958*, Heinemann Educational Books, 1981.

Fryer, P., *Staying Power*, Pluto Press, 1984

Lambros, Comitos, and D. Lowenthal, *West Indian Perspectives: Work & Family Life*, Doubleday, 1973.

Lewis, G.K., *The Growth of the Modern West Indies*, Modern Reader, 1969.

Mathurin, Lucille, *The Rebel Woman*, Institute of Jamaica, 1975.

Patterson, Orlando, *The Sociology of Slavery*, Granada, 1967.

Rodney, Walter, *How Europe Underdeveloped Africa*, Bogle L'Ouverture, 1972.

Shyllon, F.O., *Black People in Britain 1555-1833*, Oxford University Press for Institute of Race Relations, 1977.

West Indian Royal Commission Report, HMSO, 1945.

Williams, E., *Capitalism & Slavery*, Deutsch, 1964.

Williams, E., *History of the People of Trinidad & Tobago*, Deutsch, 1963.

Williams, E., *From Columbus to Castro – The History of the Caribbean 1492-1969*, Deutsch, 1970.

Chapter 1

Black Health Workers & Patients Group, *Bulletin* No. 1, 1981.

Black Women's Group, Brixton, 'Black Women & Nursing: A job like any other', *Race Today* Vol. 6, No. 8, August 1974.

Davison, R.B., *West Indian Migrants*, Oxford University Press for Institute of Race Relations, 1962.

Foner, N., *Jamaica Farewell: Jamaican Migrants in London*, Routledge & Kegan Paul, 1979.

Jones, Claudia, 'The West Indian Community in Britain', *Freedom ways*, 1964.

Justus, J.B., 'Women's Role in West Indian Society' in Steady, F.E., ed., *The Black Woman Cross-Culturally*, Sahenkman Public Co., 1981.

Lewis, A., *Labour in the West Indies*, New Beacon Books, 1978.

Miles, R., *Racism & Migrant Labour*, Routledge & Kegan Paul, 1982.

Patterson, Sheila, *Dark Strangers*, Penguin, 1965.

Phixacklea, A., ed., *One Way Ticket: Migration & Female Labour*, Routledge & Kegan Paul, 1983.

Race Today Collective, 'Black People & Trade Unions', *Race Today*, Vol. 5, No. 8, August 1973.

Race Today Women, 'Caribbean Women & the Black Community', *Race Today*, Vol. 7, No. 5, May 1975.

West India Royal Commission Report, HMSO, 1945.

Chapter 2

Althusser, Louis, *Lenin a Philosophy*, NLB, 1971.

Amos, V. and P. Parmar, 'Resistances & Responses: the experiences of black girls in Britain' in McRobbie, A. and T. McCabe, eds., *Feminism for Girls*, Routledge & Kegan Paul, 1981.

Brixton Black Women's Group, 'Disruptive Units', *Speak Out*, 1980.

Coard, B., *How the West Indian Child is Made Educationally Sub-Normal by the British School System*, New Beacon Books, 1971.

Department of Education & Science, 'West Indian Children in Our Schools (Rampton Report) (Interim Report of the Committee of Inquiry into the Education of Children from Ethnic Minority Groups)', HMSO, 1981.

Dhondy, F., 'Teaching young Blacks', *Race Today*, Vol. 10, No. 4, June 1978.

Dodgson, Pauline, and D. Stewart, 'Multi-culturalism or Anti-Racist Teaching', National Association for Multi-cultural Education, 1980.

Driver, G., 'How West Indians do better at school (especially the girls)', *New Society*, January 1980.

Gibbes, N., *West Indian Teachers Speak Out*, Caribbean Teachers' Association & Lewisham Council for Community Relations, 1980.

Organisation of Women of Asian & African Descent (OWAAD), 'Black Women & Education'/OWAAD Conference Papers: *Black Women in Britain Speak Out*, Women in Print, 1979.

Race Today Collective, 'Who's Educating Who? The Black Education Movement & the Struggle for Power', *Race Today*, Vol. 7, No. 8, August 1975.

Race Today Special Report, 'Our ESN Children', *Race Today*, Vol. 5, No. 4, April 1973.

Stone, M., *The Education of the Black Child in Britain: the Myth of Multi-racial Education*, Fontana, 1981.

Tierney, J., ed., *Race, Migration & Schooling*, Holt, Rinehart & Winston, 1982.

Chapter 3

Black Health Workers & Patients Group, 'Psychiatry and the British State', *Race & Class*, Vol. 25, No. 2, 1983.

Black Women's Group, Brixton, 'Black Women & Nursing: a job like any other', *Race Today*, Vol. 6, No. 8, 1974.

Brent Area Health Authority, 'Black People and the Health Service', Amrit Wilson and Jeanette Mitchell, 1981.

Brixton Black Women's Group, 'Ban the Jab', *Speak Out*, 1980.

Counter Information Services, *Racism: Who Profits?*, 1978.

McNaught, Allan, *Race & Health Care in the United Kingdom*, Centre for Health Service Management Studies, 'Occasional papers in Health Service Administration', Polytechnic of South Bank, 1984.

OWAAD, 'Who Cares? Black Kids in Care', *FOWAAD* (Newsletter of the Organisation of Women of Asian & African Descent), No. 7, November 1980.

'Sickle Cell Anaemia and Sickle Cell Trait', OSCAR Publications, 1983.

Smith, D., *Racial Disadvantage in Britain*, Penguin, 1977.

Chapter 4

Bhavnani, K.K., 'Racist Acts', *Spare Rib* Magazine, Nos. 115, 116, 117, 1982.

Brixton Black Women's Group, 'Black Feminism', *Speak Out*, 1982.

Jones, Claudia, 'The West Indian Community in Britain', *Freedom ways*, 1964.

OWAAD, 'Black Women and the British Law', OWAAD Conference Papers: *Black Women in Britain Speak Out*, Women in Print, 1979.

Race Today Collective, 'Black People & the Police', *Race Today*, Vol. 5, No. 11, December 1973.

Rose, E.J.B., *et al.*, *Colour & Citizenship: A Report on British Race Relations*, Oxford University Press for Institute of Race Relations, 1969.

Runnymede Trust & Radical Statistics Race Group, *Britain's Black Population*, Heinemann Educational Books, 1980.

Sivanandan, A., *A Different Hunger: Writings on Black Resistance*, Pluto Press, 1982.

Chapter 5

Bailey, Beryl, *Jamaica Creole Syntax*, Cambridge University Press, 1966.

Barnett, Leonard, *The Sun and the Drum*, Songster, 1976.

Bell, R.P., Parker, B.J. and Guy Sheftall, eds., *Sturdy Black Bridges: Visions of Black Women in Literature*, Anchor Books, 1979.

Bennett, Louise, *Selected Poems*, Sangster Book Stores, 1982.

Black Scholar, Black Sexism Debate, Vol. 10, 1979.

Black Scholar, Vol. 12, 1981, and Vol. 13, 1982.

Black Women's Group, Brixton, 'Black Women & Feminism', *Speak Out*, 1983.

Braithewaite, E., *Folkculture of the Slaves in Jamaica*, New Beacon Books, 1971.

Cassidy, Frederic, *Jamaica Talk*, Macmillan, 1961.

Clarke, E., *My Mother Who Fathered Me*, Allen & Unwin, 1957.

Dalphinis, Morgan, 'Approaches to the study of Creole Languages: the case for West African languages', *The Black Liberator*, 1978.

Davis, A., *Women, Race & Class*, The Women's Press, 1981.

D'Costa, J., 'Language and dialect in Jamaica', *Caribbean language and dialect*, CCP, 1981.

Fanon, Franz, *Black Skin, White Masks*, 1970.

Hall-Alleyne, Beverley, 'Linguistic Notes', *Jamaica Journal*, No. 1945, 1981.

Hooks, B., *Ain't I a Woman: Black Women & Feminism*, Pluto, 1982.

Hull, G.T., Scott, P.B. and B. Smith, *But Some of Us are Brave: Black Women's Studies*, The Feminist Press, 1982.

Lewis, Maureen, 'The Nkuyu: Spirit Messengers of the Kumina', Savacou, 1977.

Noble, J., *Beautiful, Also, Are the Souls of My Black Sisters*, Prentice-Hall International, 1978.

Rawick, George, 'From Sun-down to Sun-up', Modern Reader, Greenwood, N.J., 1972.

Journals and Periodicals

Black Voice, 83 Astbury Rd, London SE15.

Dragon's Teeth, The National Commitee on Racism in Children's Books, Notting Hill Methodist Church, 7 Denbigh Road, London W11 25J.

Grassroots, 61 Golborne Rd, Ladbroke Grove, London W10.

Jamaica Journal, Institute of Jamaica, 12-16 East Street, Kingston, Jamaica.

Outwrite, Oxford House, Derbyshire Street, London E2.

Race & Class, 247 Pentonville Road, London N1.

Race Today, The Basement, 165 Railton Rd, London SE24 0LU.

Savacou, Journal of the Caribbean Arts Movement, PO Box 170, Mona, Kingston, Jamaica.

Spare Rib, 27 Clerkenwell Close, London EC1R 0AT

Speak Out, 45 Stockwell Green, London SW9.

The Black Liberator: publication suspended.

FOWAAD, Uhuru, and *Freedom News* are no longer in circulation.

Black Women's Groups

Abasindi Co-operative
Moss Side People's Centre, St Mary's Street, Manchester
061-226 6837

Battersea Black Women's Group
248 Lavender Hill, London SW11   01-733 6291
Access to library on Black experience

Birmingham Black Sisters
c/o Birmingham Trade Union Resource Centre, Victoria
Works, 7 Frederick Street, Birmingham B1 3HE
021-236 8323
Puts out a quarterly newsletter

Brixton Black Women's Centre and newsletter Speak Out
41a Stockwell Green, London SW9 9HZ   01-274 9220/7696
Meeting place for several Black women's groups. Has list of
many Black women's groups
in London and nationwide.

Camden–Islington Black Sisters
c/o Law Centre, 7b Ospringe Road, London NW5
01-485 6672
Claudia Jones Organisation Black Women's Centre
84 Dynevor Road, London N16   01-249 7612

Deptford Black Women's Group
c/o The Albany, Douglas Way, London SE8

East London Black Women's Organisation
747 Barking Road, London E13

Haringey Black Women's Centre
Somerset Lower School, Lordship Lane, London N17
01-808 7973

Leicester Black Women's Group
c/o 30 Westleigh Road, Leicester LE3 0HH   0533-55201

Liverpool Black Women's Group
Old Coach House, Back Sandon Street, off Falkner Square,
Liverpool 8   051-708 9698

North Paddington Black Women's Group
North Paddington Women's Centre, 115 Portnall Road,
London W9   01-960-7939

Nottingham Black Women's Group
c/o Ukaidi Centre, Nottingham   0602-583 173

Peckham Black Women's Centre
69 Bellenden Road, London SE15   01-701 2651

Sheffield Black Women's Group
39 Crescent Road, Nether Edge, Sheffield 7

Shepherds Bush Black Women's Group
c/o 139 Becklow Road, London W12

Southall Black Women's Centre
86 Northcote Avenue, Southall, Middx.   01-843 0578
Resource and drop-in centre, running many projects. Many
groups meet here, including Southall Black Sisters.

United Black Women's Action Group
c/o Black Women's Centre, Somerset Lower School,
Lordship Lane, London N17   01-808 7973

West Indian Women's Organisation
71 Pound Lane, London NW10   01-451 4827

Wolverhampton Black Women's Co-op Centre
c/o Wolverhampton CCR, 2 Clarence Street,
Wolverhampton WV1 4HZ   0902-773 391

Woolwich Black Women's Group
c/o Simba Project, 48-50 Artillery Place, London SE15
01-317 0451

Index

247

250